GHOST SIGNS
of Bath

GHOST SIGNS
of Bath

Andrew Swift & Kirsten Elliott

AKEMAN PRESS

Published by AKEMAN PRESS
www.akemanpress.com

© Andrew Swift & Kirsten Elliott 2016

ISBN 978-0-9933988-0-3

Cover: Cleveland Terrace, Bath by Nick Cudworth

Printed through SS Media Ltd, Rickmansworth

CONTENTS

FOREWORD

In my ten years of documenting and researching ghost signs, both in the UK and overseas, those of Bath have been a recurring theme. Their density, diversity of forms, and (oftentimes) age make this city's fading signs a valuable and unique collection. However, unlike many of their host buildings, these painted specimens of old aren't typically afforded any protection, either in law or from heritage organisations. Although the word 'ghost' belies their actual longevity, they remain as pieces of ephemera, often ignored, and prone to the whim of landlords. However, recognition does appear to be gathering momentum, with the city's first plaque for a ghost sign and a trompe d'oeil dedicated to another. And, of course, there is the volume that you are now holding.

This book serves as homage to the ghost signs of Bath, and presents them in the way that they are best viewed – on foot. Having researched my own ghost signs walking tours in North and South London I am well aware of the days and weeks that are required to uncover the stories that these fading apparitions can tell. It is therefore fitting that they should be catalogued and presented here by two exemplary historians who have (literally) gone the extra mile to detail more than 160 ghost signs in Bath and its surrounds.

In reading through the pages that follow, you will be taken on a journey back in time, in some cases more than 200 years. These signs speak of periods in history when 'polonies' were part of the common parlance, libraries were 'circulating', and bar customers were politely reminded to pay for their drinks when served. In addition to photographs of the signs themselves, and maps to find them, news clippings and other contemporary printed matter illuminate the fading paint that can now be seen on the walls. Archival photography also shows many of the signs as they once were, and a myriad that have since been lost.

Despite the threats to their existence, many of these ghost signs remain; enduring reminders of Bath's commercial and social history. Their bleached paintwork clings to the stones that characterise this city, while also adding to this very character. This book is a timely tribute to the contribution made by ghost signs of Bath – long may they remain!

Sam Roberts
London, July 2016

INTRODUCTION

Like many others, we have long been intrigued by Bath's ghost signs. These faded advertisements for long-forgotten businesses are a continual source of fascination for residents and visitors alike. Yet, while the most celebrated are regularly snapped by camera-toting tourists, scant mention of them is made in guides to – or indeed histories of – the city.

With the advent of the internet, interest in these signs has gone global, so that many who have never visited Bath are familiar with the reminders of a dimly-descried past that adorn its walls. And, as the world-wide community of ghost-sign aficionados has grown, so has the recognition that nowhere are ghost signs found in greater abundance or greater variety than in Bath.[1]

We first came up with the idea of a book on Bath's ghost signs over ten years ago, so this is a project that has had a long gestation period. And, while the ever-increasing availability of images on the internet has obviated the need for a straightforward photographic survey, there has never been a greater appetite – or a greater need – for a look at the stories behind the signs.

Bath's ghost signs are doorways into the city's hidden past. The keys to unlocking those doors are not always easy to find, although once again the internet has facilitated the quest, providing search engines for local newspapers and census returns that formerly yielded their secrets only to painstaking and exhaustive research. Not that all our forays into the past were conducted through the medium of mouse and keyboard. Bath is fortunate in that street directories, providing detailed records of residents and businesses, were produced on a regular basis from the early nineteenth century onward. Only a handful of these directories are available online, but virtually complete runs of them can be consulted in Bath Record Office and Bath Reference Library, so that tracking the history of a particular building, while time-consuming, can be done in meticulous detail.

Unlocking the histories of Bath's ghost signs not only gives fascinating glimpses into unexpected and overlooked aspects of the city's past; it also enables the signs to be dated, sometimes almost precisely, thus providing a record of how signwriting styles developed.

Bath's oldest ghost sign dates from around 1780, making it one of the earliest to have survived anywhere. The city is also rich in signs from the golden age of signwriting in the first half of the nineteenth century, before standardisation and conformity began to stifle individual creativity. These are justly celebrated as some of the finest examples to have survived from this period. Later decades did, however, see some remarkable signs produced; even those promoting companies such as Nestlé's or Wills's can convey a powerful sense of a world long gone.

We have aimed to include all of Bath's ghost signs – or at least all that we have managed to find – along with those in the surrounding villages and the towns of Bradford on Avon and Corsham. This adds up to over 160 signs, in addition to which a final chapter looks at signs which have disappeared, some of which may one day be uncovered.

Such a comprehensive approach naturally means that, alongside superb examples of the signwriter's art, there is much that is run of the mill. Nevertheless, all the signs featured have a story to tell, even though it may not be one that is easy to discover.

The two main problems anyone researching ghost signs will come up against are making out what the signs originally read and finding out who commissioned them.

While some signs have survived in their entirety and are clearly legible, many are not. Sometimes several signs have been painted on top of each other, and, as successive layers have faded, they have re-emerged to create a jumble of lettering, known as a palimpsest. Some signs can only been seen at certain times, usually when the sun shines on them, although a few are seen at their best in the rain. This elusive, evanescent quality, while frustrating, is also one of the most alluring aspects of ghost signs. Walk along a street at a particular time on a particular day, and the light falling across a wall may fleetingly reveal a message from the past. Pass by an hour earlier or later, or on an overcast day, and all you will see is a blank wall.[2]

Finding out why a sign was painted can be just as challenging. Often, all there is to go on is a random word or two, or even just a few letters. In some cases, we have managed to piece together what seems like a reasonable hypothesis from the most meagre scraps of evidence; in others, we have drawn a complete blank, leaving it for others to take up the challenge of sorting out when and why a particular sign was painted. Where we have not been certain of something, we have said so, offering suggestions rather than statements of fact. And where we have been unable either to draw conclusions or make educated guesses, we have made the evidence, such as it is, available for others, if they should feel so inclined, to use as they see fit.

This guide to ghost signs in and around Bath is not – if you will pardon the pun – set in stone. Apart from the obvious fact that they will all eventually fade to nothing (unless judiciously or injudiciously touched up), some will be covered over or scrubbed off, or will disappear when the buildings they appear on are knocked down. But they can just as suddenly re-emerge into the sunlight when render that has been hiding them for decades is peeled away. And there are undoubtedly signs that we have missed, still waiting to be discovered.

Ghost signs not only give glimpses into the past; more crucially, they provide inspiration for the future. After having fallen out of favour for the best part of a century, painted signs are finally making a comeback, as a new generation of signwriters reinterprets and reinvents traditional techniques to promote businesses whose emphasis is on craft rather than convenience.

This vade mecum to Bath's hidden histories is not, therefore, a celebration merely of the fleeting and the fugitive, but also of a living tradition. The ghost signs of the past, washed by rain, scoured by wind, dissolved by pollution, and mined by frost, will ultimately fade to nothing, but their place will be taken by new signs, to delight generations yet unborn.

The chapters that follow, after a preliminary one setting Bath's ghost signs in context, deal with the city area by area. Each chapter is organised as a walk and is prefaced by an archive map, indicating the location of the ghost signs featured. The numbers on each map relate to the numbers highlighted in red in the text, so that the signs can either be visited in sequence or located individually.

Some of the later chapters, covering villages around Bath, are not prefaced by maps; but the location of the villages is indicated on the map accompanying chapter 12. Chapters 14 and 15, however, which deal with the ghost signs of Bradford on Avon and Corsham, are organised as walks and accompanied by archive maps. Details of the maps used can be found on page 284.

Andrew Swift & Kirsten Elliott
Bath, July 2016

WORDS ON WALLS
A Brief History of Signs & Signwriting in Bath & Beyond

Words have probably been written on walls for as long as there have been walls – or at least since there have words to write on them. The impetus for painting signs on walls, as far as Bath is concerned, however, came in 1766, when the corporation banned hanging signs in the city. In this they were following the lead of London, where steps to outlaw hanging signs had been taken four years earlier. Most of those who had hanging signs simply took them down and fixed them to the front wall of their premises. Some enterprising individuals, however, realising that Bath stone made an ideal surface to paint on, painted signs directly onto their walls. Although this was done elsewhere, with signs painted on brick, render and less tractable types of stone, the smooth surface of Bath stone, with only the thinnest beds of mortar between ashlar blocks, made it ideal for signwriting. Signwriters developed ever more elaborate and intricate lettering, and, as Bath's economy boomed and shopkeepers vied with each other to attract customers, the city's streets became a riot of ever more flamboyant and colourful signs.

To understand the development of these painted signs – some of whose ghosts still glimmer dimly today – we must first look at the long tradition of hanging signs, which came to such a sudden and untimely end. Not surprisingly, the earliest businesses known to have displayed hanging signs were inns and alehouses. This was often enforced by statute. The Ordinances of Worcester, drawn up in 1467, for example, stipulated 'that no person sille none ale out of his place, but he haue a signe at his dorre'.[1] Other businesses were quick to see the advantages of hanging signs, however. When Wynkyn de Worde published a new edition of John Alcock's *Mons Perfectionis* in 1501, for example, it was 'enprynted at London in fletestrete at the sygne of ye sonne'. Some early signs were not paintings on boards, but actual objects. This practice survives in the three spheres still sometimes displayed by pawnbrokers, and the bell recently installed outside the Bell Inn in Bath is a noble continuation of this tradition. Signs were also carved in wood, or made of pewter, copper or iron and hung from 'sign-irons' – better known today as sign brackets.

Originally, signs were linked with particular trades, often echoing their use in the coats of arms of trade guilds. For example, salamanders appeared on the arms of the ironmongers' guild, roebucks on the arms of the leathersellers' guild, and elephants – or later the elephant and castle – on the arms of the cutlers' guild. Signs featuring salamanders, roebucks or elephants thus indicated these trades. There were many more examples. The sign of the Wheatsheaf, for example, denoted a haberdasher or linen-draper, the Golden Fleece or Indian Queen a mercer, and the Lamb a hosier or milliner. Over time, these distinctions tended to become blurred, however, as businesses changed but signs did not, so premises displaying the sign of the Wheatsheaf, originally occupied by a haberdasher, could be taken over by a grocer or an apothecary, but retain the old sign.

One of the reasons signs were so important was that buildings were not numbered, while the use of images rather than words reflected low levels of literacy. Although most of the customers who patronised businesses in the more affluent parts of London and the larger provincial cities would have been able to read, many of their servants, whom they sent to collect the goods they had purchased, would not. In time, as signs grew ever more imposing, they became the main means of finding your way around town. John Gay, writing in 1716, offered the following advice:

> If drawn by business to a street unknown,
> Let the sworn porter point thee through the town;
> Be sure observe the signs, for signs remain,
> Like faithful landmarks to the walking train.[2]

There were drawbacks to this means of navigation, however, especially if sign painters were not that competent. When lettering formed part of the sign, poor spelling caused problems as well. In 1709, a correspondent in the *Tatler* bemoaned the fact that

> there should be so many gross errors ... in the inscriptions on sign-posts. I have cause to know this matter as well as any body; for I have, when I went to Merchant Taylor's school, suffered stripes for spelling after the signs I observed in my way ... Many a man has lost his way and his dinner by this general want of skill in orthography; for, considering that the painters are usually so very bad, that you cannot know the animal under whose sign you are to live that day, how must the stranger be misled if it be wrong spelled, as well as ill-painted?[3]

A few years later, a correspondent in one of America's earliest newspapers, the *New-England Courant*, founded by Benjamin Franklin's brother, James, in Boston, warmed to the same theme:

> The Inscriptions on Signs, and sign Posts ... are generally so miserably spelt, that a stranger to the Town of Boston and the Orthography of it's [sic] Signs, can scarce tell what to make of them ... I dare say there has [sic] been twenty Boys whipt at School for every Sign in Town, for no other Reason but their Spelling after them ... As to the Shapes of the several Animals hung up for Signs, I have little to say to them: But I remember I spent half a day at Ipswich in quest of the Black Horse, which I mistook for a Lamb, till I was better inform'd ... Were

GHOST SIGNS OF BATH

it in my Power to redress these Grievances, I would oblige every Sign Painter to serve seven Years at College, before he presum'd to handle Pencil or Paint-Box, that the Grammatical Part of his Work might be better perform'd.[4]

By now, sign boards were everywhere. When Celia Fiennes visited Bristol in 1698, she discovered that 'in many places there are signes to many houses that are not Public Houses, just as it is in London'.[5] As Bath embarked on its period of prodigious growth in the eighteenth century, sign boards proliferated there too. In the wake of Queen Anne's visits to the city in 1702 and 1703, a purpose-built row of luxury shops was erected on the south side of the Grove.[6] By the mid-1720s, more had sprung up nearby, and 'a long shop-lined promenade [extended] from Abbey Churchyard through Wade's Passage all the way to Terrace Walk'.[7] By the 1740s, bow windows had started appearing and shops had opened in John Wood's newly-built development south of Terrace Walk, on North Parade and in Pierrepont Street.[8] Few, if any, of these businesses, would have been without a hanging sign.

In 1744, we hear of 'FRANCIS BENNETT, At the STAR in the Church-Yard, BATH, [selling] all Sorts of Linnen-Drapery, Woollen-Drapery, and Haberdashery Goods; all Sorts of Blanketting, Flannels, Swan-skin, and Shags; all Sorts of Teas, Coffee, Chocolate, and Sugar; with all other Sorts of Grocery-Wares; all Sorts of fine Snuffs, and Cards ... N.B. He also furnishes Funerals with a new Pall and Cloaks; and with all other Necessaries, as decent and cheap as in London'.[9]

In Bath Reference Library, there is a printed invoice of 1748 from 'Betty Coward, at the two Lappetts & three Cards of Lace in Stall Street', which includes an engraving of the sign hanging outside her premises, on which the aforementioned items appear, together with the words 'COWARD'S LACE SHOP'.[10] The library also holds a tradecard printed five years later, for 'John Pyke, Toyman, at the Golden Flower d'Luce in the Grove, Bath'.[11]

In 1761, John Bryant, upholsterer, could be found 'at the Sign of the ROYAL-BED in the *Market-Place*'.[12] In 1762, Thomas Harding, a hat maker from London, could be found 'at the Sign of the HAT and BEAVER, the upper End of the MARKET-PLACE', while William Street, an apothecary and chemist, was 'at the PHOENIX, next Door to the THREE-CUPS, in NORTH-GATE STREET'.[13] In 1764, a tailor called Thomas Farr announced that he had moved 'from the Market-Place to the Sign of the ADAM and EVE at the BEAR CORNER; where he sells all sorts of HOSIERY GOODS, likewise Haberdashery of Small Wares, with all Sorts of Knitting and Working Worsteds, on the very lowest Terms'.[14]

With all these signs around, there must have been a good deal of work for sign painters, but the first reference we have found to one comes in

1767, when Charles Davis, 'COACH, HOUSE, SIGN and HERALD PAINTER, GILDER &c' placed a notice in the *Bath Chronicle* to inform 'his Friends and the Public, that he is *Removed* to a Shop opposite his late Dwelling-House, near St James's Church' which was known as the 'GOLDEN-BOY'.[15] This was the year after hanging signs had been taken down in Bath, so perhaps his move – and the advertisement – was because orders had dried up.

Be that as it may, shopkeepers continued to display signs to let customers know where they were. In 1768, 'at Mrs Dart's, known by the Name of the *Green Tree-House* in *Stall-Street*, a most curious and valuable Collection of fine FOREIGN and ENGLISH *Useful* and *Ornamental* CHINA, Old Japan, India Dressing-Boxes, Dressing-Glasses, &c' was offered for sale.[16] In 1774, John Kendall was running a china shop known as the Golden Canister in Pierrepont Street, while Roe Palmer, 'weaver and mercer' had a shop called the Peacock in Union Passage.[17]

One particularly unusual sign was a larger than lifesize statue of Queen Elizabeth, which stood above the entrance to a milliner's shop at 5 North Parade. On 27 April 1775, the *Bath Chronicle* carried an advertisement for Messrs 'GEORGE and WITTS (Successors to Mr Paulin) at the Statue of Queen Elizabeth on the North Parade' who had 'just brought down a complete assortment of the most fashionable MILLINERY Goods, &c, whch they are determined to sell on the most reasonable terms'.

In 1783, Joseph Dibbens, 'Cheese-Monger and Corn-Chandler', took over the Phoenix, next door to the Three Cups on Northgate Street, which 21 years earlier had been occupied by the apothecary and chemist, William Street.[18] As indicated earlier, it was not unusual for two such different businesses to use the same sign. Although many shopkeepers used signs relating to the goods they sold, the Phoenix is likely to have been a well-known landmark. Had Mr Dibbens changed the sign over his shop to something connected with cheese or corn, its location – in the absence of street-numbering – might not have been immediately apparent to anyone reading his advertisement.

In 1789, William Marriott, hosier, perfumer, and snuff-dealer could be found 'at the Plume of Feathers, on the Walks, and fronting the North-Parade.[19] In 1791, C Abbott was running a '*Lace, Haberdashery, Hosiery, Glove, and Fur Warehouse*' at the 'THREE-PIGEONS,

CHARLES DAVIS,
COACH, HOUSE, SIGN and HERALD PAINTER, GILDER, &c.
At the GOLDEN-BOY, in HORSE-STREET,
INFORMS his Friends and the Public, that he is *Removed* to a Shop opposite his late Dwelling-House, near St. James's Church, where the above Branches is carried on as usual, in the best and most reasonable Manner.
Likewise sells, Leaf-Gold, Colours, Oils, Brushes, and every Article in the Painting and Drawing way.
☞ An APPRENTICE is wanted; A sober, ingenious Lad will be taken with a small Premium.

North Parade, Bath c1800 by JC Nattes, showing the statue of Queen Elizabeth above George & Witts' milliner's at N° 5. To the left of it, at N° 6, is the shop of Messrs Tully & George, hatters, while to the right, at N° 4, is the print shop of Peter Salmoni, both with fascia boards attached to the wall.

MILSOM-STREET'.[20] Five years later, an advertisement appeared for a '*CHEAP MUSLIN, GLOVE, FUR, & HOSIERY WAREHOUSE* ... at the THREE PIGEONS and SCEPTRE, No 13, BATH-STREET, NEAR THE GREAT PUMP-ROOM'.[21] This was run by R Arnell – who may or may not have been connected with Mr Abbott – but the interesting thing here is that the shop not only had a sign but also a number. This was a transitional period, when signs were still displayed because people were accustomed to them, but part of their function was becoming irrelevant as buildings were numbered.

The first record of street numbering is in 1512, when 68 new houses on the Pont Nôtre-Dame in Paris were numbered.[22] The practice was introduced to London in the early eighteenth century, but the earliest instance we have come across in Bath is in 1774, when Benjamin Forde opened an 'NEW ICE CREAM SHOP [at] 'Nº 13, on the New Bridge, leading to Spring Gardens'.[23] This is now known as Pulteney Bridge, and it is curious that Bath should have followed Paris's lead by giving the first street numbers to buildings on a new bridge.

Even though numbering soon become the norm, signs took some time to disappear. In 1799, Warren & Rosser, perfumers of London, had a shop called the Golden Fleece at 8 George Street.[24] As late as 1812, C Lucas advertised his 'Old-established well-known CHEAP WAREHOUSE, the BEE-HIVE' at 11 Union Street, while a Mr Gould, 'DRUGGIST, OIL, and COLOUR MAN, &c' could be found at 'the PESTLE and MORTAR, 14, *WESTGATE-STREET, BATH*'.[25]

Although the criticism of standards of sign painting in the *Tatler* and the *New-England Courant* was no doubt justified, it generally applied to businesses at the lower end of the market, which could only afford to commission indifferent artists. Fashionable businesses could afford fashionable painters – indeed, they had to afford them if their signs were to outshine those of their rivals. According to one of his pupils, Hogarth described the work of the best sign painters as 'specimens of genius emanating from a school, which he used emphatically to observe, was truly English'.[26] Very few signs survive from this golden age in England, but in Paris, where hanging signs were also banned, an extraordinary collection, displaying superb artistry, can be seen in the Hall of Signs in the Musée Carnavalet.

Such was Hogarth's regard for sign painting that, in the spring of 1762, he was involved in a Grand Exhibition of the 'Society of Sign-Painters', staged by Bonnell Thornton at his Rooms in Bow Street. Eighty-four signs and twenty-five carved figures were displayed, some specially commissioned, others provided by local businesses.[27] Although one of the aims of the exhibition was to cock a snook at the Society of Artists (which both Hogarth and Thornton had fallen out with), it also sought to give due recognition to an art form which they considered to be unjustly overlooked. It was very much a swansong, however, for a few months later the first edict banning hanging signs in the city of London was issued.

An attempt to prohibit hanging signs had been made almost a hundred years earlier, in 1667, when the Act for Rebuilding the City of London after the Great Fire stipulated 'that in all the streets no sign-posts shall hang across, but the signs shall be fixed against the balconies or some other convenient part of the side of the house'. This was largely ignored, and in the ensuing century signs grew ever larger and more elaborate.[28] In 1719, a French visitor to London compared the signs he found there to those in Paris:

> By a decree of the police, the signs of Paris must be small, and not too far advanced from the houses. At London, they are commonly very large, and jut out so far, that in some narrow streets they touch one another; nay, and run across almost quite to the other side. They are generally adorned with carving and gilding; and there are several that, with the branches of iron which support them, cost above a hundred guineas.[29]

Although signs had, by law, to be at least nine feet off the ground, this still made them a hazard for horse riders and coachmen as they were extended further and further out into the street. In Bath, there was also the risk of some of the taller and more elaborate sedan chairs coming into contact with them. Another danger, as signs grew heavier and more elaborate, was the frequency with which they parted company with the wall, crashing down on unfortunate passers-by. In 1702, a sign attached to the house of Grinling Gibbons in Bow Street, fell down, pulling part of the wall with it and killing a young girl. Some years later a similar accident occurred in St Bride's Lane, Fleet Street, killing two young women, the king's jeweller and a cobbler.[30]

Despite legislation to curb the excesses which characterised London's hanging signs, it was in Paris that hanging signs were first banned, with a decree of 1761 that all 'signboards ... were to be fixed against the walls of the houses, and not to project more than four inches, including the border, frame, or other ornaments; – also, all the signposts and sign irons were to be removed from the streets and thoroughfares, and the passage cleared'.[31]

Hanging signs started to disappear from the streets of London the following year, when 'the signs in Duke's Court, St Martin's Lane, were all taken down and affixed to the front of the houses.'[32] Other parts of the capital followed Westminster's example, and by 1773 the last hanging signs had disappeared.[33] The change in the appearance of the city's streets would have been dramatic. In June 1766, as an act of parliament ordered them to be cleared from yet another area, the *Bath Chronicle* reported that, 'it has been computed that the first Cost of the Signs and Sign-Irons (which are to be taken down) between Temple-Bar, and Aldgate, did not amount to less than Thirty Thousand Pounds or upwards.'[34]

By this time, Bath had decided to follow London's example, and in July 1766, 'at a General Meeting of the Commissioners for Paving, Cleansing, Lighting, Watching, and Regulating of the Streets, Lanes, &c, within the City of Bath, and Liberties thereof, held at the Guildhall ... pursuant to an Act of Parliament,' it was announced that 'the Commissioners ... intend to proceed to the taking down and removing ... all Signs, Sign-Irons, Sign-Posts, &c, of which all Persons are hereby required to take Notice.' How unpopular this was is unknown, but the removal of the signs must have gone smoothly, for when a visitor to Bath returned to the city in

The three shopfronts nearest the camera on this early twentieth-century postcard of Queen Street are among the earliest in Bath. The lack of fascia boards indicates that, when installed, the businesses that occupied them would have used hanging signs to advertise their wares, and they are believed to date from around 1760. The shopfront at the far end is a later addition in a matching style and dates from around 1910.

April 1767, he wrote that, 'since last year all the signs in Bath are taken down, and affixed to the respective Houses.'[35]

Fascia boards – not hitherto a feature of shopfronts – quickly became standard, but signboards were not restricted to the space above shop windows. In 1782, a German visitor to London remarked that, 'especially in the Strand, where one shop jostles another and people of very different trades often live in the same house, it is surprising to see how from bottom to top the various houses often display large signboards with painted letters. Everyone who lives and works in the house sports his signboard over the door; indeed there is not a cobbler whose name and trade is not to be read in large golden characters.'[36] Another German visitor, writing 20 years later, recorded one of the first instances of a painted sign covering the entire façade of a building, which was to become such a feature of the urban scene in the nineteenth century:

GHOST SIGNS OF BATH

As it is one of the principal secrets of the trade to attract the attention of that tide of people, which is incessantly ebbing and flowing in the streets, it may easily be conceived that great pains are taken to give a striking form to the signs and devices hanging out before the shops. The whole front of a house is frequently employed for this purpose. Thus, in the vicinity of Ludgate-hill, the house of one S-----, who has amassed a fortune of forty thousand pounds by selling razors, is daubed with large capitals three feet high, acquainting the public, that 'the most excellent and superb patent razors are sold here'.[37]

The main difference between hanging signs and signs painted on walls was that, while the former had been largely – and sometimes exclusively – pictorial, the latter consisted almost entirely of lettering. This reflected not just the growing literacy of the urban population, but also a shift in retail culture, with a far greater variety of goods available in shops. Along with a greater discrimination among shoppers, and a greater sophistication among shopkeepers, came the first stirrings of what is known today as brand loyalty. But, with signs relying on lettering alone, that lettering had not only to be of a high standard but also to have a strong visual appeal and interest. And so the characteristic nineteenth-century sign was born, a medley of fonts, sizes and colours – the more diverse and mismatched the better. It was akin to a melodramatic actor going through the gamut of his vocal repertoire – out-hectoring Hector, dropping his voice to a wheedling whisper, then croaking with emotion, narrowing his eyes, twirling the tips of his wax moustache and grinning through Terry Thomas teeth.

Despite complaints about bad spelling, at the top end of the market the lettering on hanging signs would have matched the quality of the painting. Crude lettering under a well-executed picture would simply not have done. The first book instructing sign painters – and others – how to form characters was published by Joseph Moxon in 1676. Its full title was *Regulae Trium Ordinum Literarum Typographicarum, or, The Rules of the Three Orders of Print Letters: viz. the Roman, Italick, English, Capitals and Small: Shewing How They are Compounded of Geometrick Figures, and Mostly Made by Rule and Compass: Useful for Writing Masters, Painters, Carvers, Masons, and Others that are Lovers of Curiosity.* It was printed in London, on Ludgate Hill 'at the Sign of the Atlas'.

It was in the mid-eighteenth century, however, that the English lettering tradition really came into its own, with typographical innovations from the likes of William Caslon and John Baskerville, and the development of what became known as English lettering. Graham Finch describes this as 'a handsome form with strong verticals and very slender horizontals,' and adds that 'the original incised street names of

Georgian Bath are outstanding examples of this form.'[38] This meant that signwriters in Bath had examples of superbly crafted letters to study on street corners throughout the city, giving them something not only to aspire to but also for their work to be to be judged against.

More details of what characterised English lettering come from Alan Bartram:

> The English form of seriffed, varied-weight (stressed) letter, the norm to which the vernacular form gravitates unless there is good reason for it to resist, has a rich full shape, a vertical stress, and fairly sharp gradation from thick to thin strokes ... The difference of weight between strokes thick and thin is often quite marked; the latter are often virtually hairlines. Rich bracketed serifs terminate sharply, if not always actually to a point. The tails of the Q and R usually have great verve, the tail of the latter being bowed, not straight. Proportions tend to be squarer and more regular than those of Roman forms.[39]

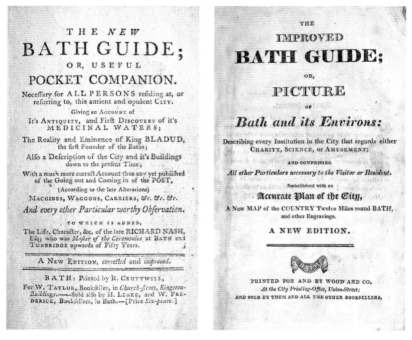

Developments in signwriting kept pace with those in typography, as signwriters picked up ideas from printers and vice versa. Because printed material has not only survived in far greater quantity than painted signs, but is usually dated, it can be used to chart stylistic developments relatively easily. Comparing the title page from a 1771 Bath Guide (above left) with one from 1813 (above right) demonstrates how much changed in just over 40 years. A similar contrast can be seen if the late eighteenth-century sign on Miles's Buildings (p. 89) is compared with the sign from about 1819 in Burton Street (p. 45).

Around 1800, however, things started changing very rapidly in the fields of both signwriting and printing. Strokes both thick and thin began to get thicker, modestly at first, before billowing out exponentially to become the uncorseted hybrid known as Fat Face. In this, they paralleled the growth of the Prince Regent's waistline, which saw him transformed from svelte dandy to corpulent gormandizer.

Other developments soon followed. The alternation of thick and thin strokes was abandoned in favour of strokes of uniform width – a bluff, no nonsense style which became known as Egyptian or – because serifs carried the same weight as the rest of the lettering – slab-serif. From here, it was a short step to abandoning serifs altogether, creating a plainer style known as Grotesque. This no-frills style, with all strokes of equal weight and all unnecessary adornment stripped away, represented a radical departure from previous models. When the first sans-serif type – Caslon Egyptian – was introduced in 1816, nothing like it had been seen before.[40]

Italic, bold and shadowed forms of all these styles were used, along with upper and lower case, giving signwriters and printers a wide range of options to choose from. Blackletter or Gothic script also saw a revival, along with a vogue for all things medieval, while freeform Copperplate, elaborated with decorative flourishes, offered opportunities for individual flights of creative fancy.

By the 1820s, the development of the craft of signwriting in Bath was effectively complete. Some of the signs that survive from the first half of the nineteenth century achieved a level of artistic excellence that was rarely, if ever, matched later. It is fortuitous that some of the paints used

An invoice from Thomas Henley for painting a signboard at Bath cattle market in 1836.

An elaborate billhead from 1838 for C Smith Jr, for whom signwriting clearly played second fiddle to fitting blinds 'as used in London'.

at this time have stood the test of time far better than those used in later periods. Some early nineteenth-century signs are still clearly legible, while some painted in the twentieth century have virtually faded away.

Signwriters remained in demand throughout the nineteenth century and for the first few decades of the twentieth. Some taught themselves, using signwriting manuals or adapting fonts used by printers. Others learnt as apprentices or by joining the family business. Many craftsmen combined signwriting with other trades, such as plumbing, glazing or decorating. Even gasfitters and general engineers, like the Bowler family of Bath, took up signwriting as a sideline. The Bowlers were typical in that skills were handed down, and someone with a special talent could use it to the firm's advantage. And the best way to let the public know how good you were was by painting a sign on the wall of your business.

Such a demonstration of the signwriter's art can be seen at 27a/b Belvedere, where Robert Bosley displayed his craftmanship in a plethora of styles. Boseley was active in the 1820s, so the famous circulating library sign in Milsom Street may have been by him. Typically, he had other skills – he was a slater and plasterer as well as a house, sign and decorative painter.

Despite their skill, signwriters were generally paid similar wages to others in the building trade. However, some skilled tradesmen, especially those running their own businesses, earned good money, which they sometimes invested in property development. William Cowell Hayes, for instance, was a signwriter who was involved in the development

GHOST SIGNS OF BATH

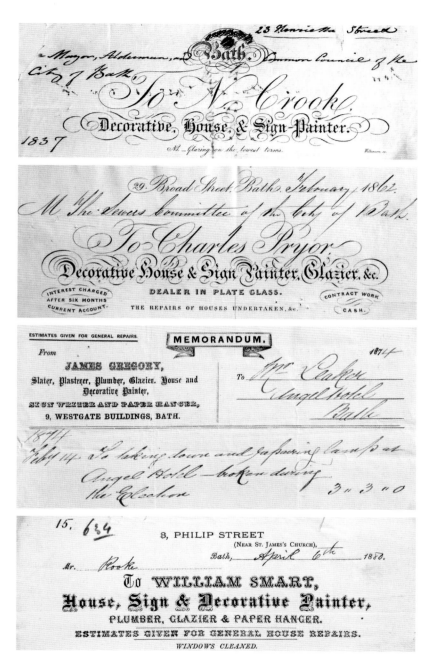

More billheads printed for Bath signwriters, dating from 1837, 1862, 1874 and 1880. Note that James Gregory's invoice was not for painting a sign but for 'repairing [a] lamp at the Angel Hotel broken during the Election'.

of the Sion Hill area. Unlike his business partner, the surveyor and architect Thomas Chantry, he survived the bank collapses of the 1790s and went on to help build Sion Hill Place.

Eventually, big business saw the advantages of large painted signs. However, companies such as Player's or Nestlé's demanded consistency of design. This was achieved through the use of painters' guides. These were issued centrally, either by the marketing department or an advertising agency, and then scaled to the appropriate size before the preparation of paper or fabric to set the design onto the wall. Such companies may also have hired a travelling team to produce signs, producing a consistent result, but eliminating any artistic input from the signwriter.

Local businesses did not share this desire for a corporate image. For them, the more elaborate and eye-catching a design, the better. Given a free hand, the signwriter, assisted by his apprentice, would employ ornate lettering, adding scrolls and lines, and using mortar lines in the stonework to ensure consistency of scale. For companies who wanted to spread their fame, householders and landlords were happy to hire out their walls to advertisers and those near the new-fangled railway commanded high sums.

In the mid-Victorian period, hanging signs, of more modest dimensions than those that had prompted their proscription a century earlier, started to reappear, and today are virtually ubiquitous – along with a hazard unforeseen in the eighteenth century, the dreaded A board, which manages to combine ugliness and inconvenience in an unprecedented way. Another regrettable feature of today's streetscapes is the absence of any form of numbering on most retail premises. Given that numbering was introduced to help people find their way around after hanging signs were banned, the extent to which it has fallen into disuse is tiresome, to say the least. Anyone who has struggled to find a particular address in a street where numbers are the exception rather than the rule will doubtless know the feeling of baffled frustration that something so inconspicuous – yet so useful – should be so anathema to present-day shop-front designers.

Another regrettable feature of today's streetscapes is the lack of painted signs. With a few exceptions, pubs are the only businesses still sporting words on walls. In Bath, the Star on the Vineyards has long been famed for its splendid painted signs. More recently, the Royal Oak in Widcombe has received an ultra-modern makeover featuring a diverse display of lettering along with a stylised oak tree, while the Locksbrook Inn (formerly the Dolphin), the Salamander on John Street and the White Hart in Widcombe have acquired some more traditional-looking signs. Apart from the pubs, though, just about all we have to remind us of a glorious tradition are the fading ghost signs of businesses long gone.

Signwriting did not simply fall out of fashion, however. In Bath at least, it seems, it was killed off. In 1926, Bath Corporation published a *Schedule of the Ancient Property belonging to the Mayor, Aldermen and Citizens of Bath administered by the Corporate Property Committee and let for various terms.* Hardly the snappiest of titles and not, it has to be admitted, the most gripping of reads. For the student of ghost signs, though, it is of great interest, for it listed all the historic buildings owned by the corporation, and laid down the conditions under which they were leased. Two conditions recur time and again: the leaseholder must either not paint the front wall, or not paint the front wall above the level of the shopfront; and no sign or advertisement is to be affixed to or painted on the building.

The corporation did not own all the buildings in the city, although it was, and still is, the biggest landowner. It was also responsible for enacting by-laws and enforcing planning regulations, so, by opposing painted signs in this way, it set a precedent others ignored at their peril.

We do not know when these clauses began to be added to the corporation leases – but, given the number of signs painted in the years leading up to the First World War, and the general disregard of the finer points of Georgian architecture until the early years of the twentieth century, it is unlikely that they had been in force for long.

What this edict had the effect of doing, however, was not only to prevent new signs being painted over earlier ones, but, where the stonework was not cleaned or not cleaned well, to preserve what was already there. The legacy is the rich variety of ghost signs we see today.

Yet, despite restrictions on painted signs, and the advent of billboards, plastic and vinyl lettering, illuminated signs and other soulless manifestations of homogenised retail culture, the skilled signwriters never really went away. As controls on listed buildings tighten and our interest in historic crafts grows, so their craft – inspired by the examples of the past – is starting to flourish once again.

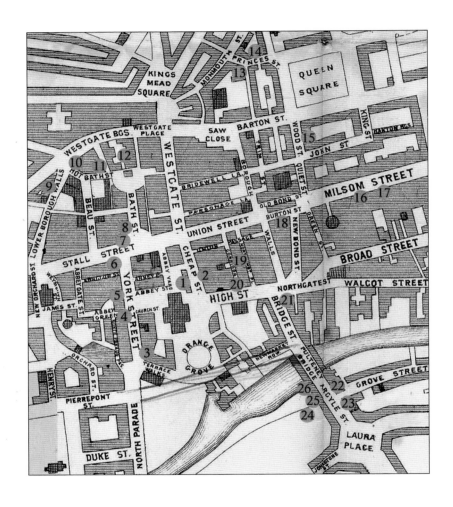

1
CITY CENTRE

We start with a demonstration of how quickly things can change in the evanescent world of ghost signs. On the north side of Abbey Church Yard, at Nº 15, is a sign which, until recently, no one knew existed (1). It had lain hidden under successive layers of paint and plaster for well over a century. Today it not only stands revealed – at least partially – in all its glory; it is also accompanied by a plaque outlining its history. This is the first time such a plaque has been devoted to a ghost sign in Bath – proof of the enormous growth of interest in these fascinating echoes from the past in recent years.

The business it advertises – Rodway's Wholesale & Retail Straw & Millinery Rooms – has a fascinating history. Sarah Rodway came to Bath from Nailsworth in Gloucestershire, and by 1829 had set herself up as a 'straw bonnet maker' at 6 Church Street. By 1833, she had moved her business to 4 St James's Parade. She was still there in 1837, but, by the time of the 1841 census, she and her husband, William, were living in Abbey Church Yard with their four children. Sarah was described as a bonnet maker, and there were three other people living in the house – a 'work woman' aged 20, a 15-year-old apprentice, and another 15-year-old whose status is not clear.

By 1846, according to that year's *Directory*, the Rodways were back at 4 St James's Parade, where William was running a lodging house. Sarah, however, was also listed as a 'straw bonnet manufacturer' at 6 Abbey Church Yard. This is the only reference to Nº 6, which is at the west end of Abbey Church Yard. Frustratingly, the 1841 census does not include street numbers, so there is no way of telling which building in Abbey Church Yard the Rodways had occupied then. It also seems strange that they moved from 4 St James's Parade sometime between 1837 and 1841, but had moved back by 1846. The lack of any reference to William Rodway in the *Directories* for 1829, 1833 and 1837 means that we know neither where he was living nor what he was doing.

By the time of the 1851 census, however, Sarah's business was definitely at N° 15 – either it had moved or, if the 1846 *Directory* had printed the address wrongly, it had been there all the time. As today, the shop extended through to Cheap Street, so it had two addresses – 15 Abbey Church Yard and 14 Cheap Street. There is no mention of William Rodway in the 1851 census; Sarah Rodway, living above the shop in Abbey Church Yard with four daughters, two employees and a servant, has 'W' alongside her name, indicating that she was by now a widow.

In 1852, Sarah Rodway's daughter, Ellen, married Henry Roberts, a silk mercer and undertaker in business at 1 Gay Street. Like Sarah Rodway, he came from Nailsworth, and may have been a relative. By April 1854, when the *Bath Chronicle* carried an advertisement for Sarah Rodway's business, it had been renamed Rodway & Co – suggesting that Henry Roberts had joined forces with her – and a major expansion was under way:

> WANTED IMMEDIATELY, at Messrs RODWAY & CO'S Wholesale and Retail STRAW and MILLINERY ESTABLISH-MENT, 14 CHEAP STREET and 15 ABBEY CHURCH YARD, TWENTY Good STRAW BONNET HANDS, & SIX Competent MILLINERS; also an Opening for FOUR APPRENTICES.[1]

The following year, another advertisement announced that 'velvet and cloth mantles' had been added to the range of items available.[2]

WHOLESALE AND RETAIL STRAW BONNET AND MILLINERY ESTABLISHMENT,
15, *ABBEY CHURCH YARD*, and 14, *CHEAP STREET*, *Bath*.
RODWAY & COMPy.
RESPECTFULLY acquaint their Friends and the Public generally, that, in addition to their usual
LARGE STOCK OF
MILLINERY, COLOURED STRAW, TISSUE, AND OTHER BONNETS,
They will be Prepared, on MONDAY NEXT, the 29th Inst., to Show an ENTIRELY NEW ASSORTMENT of
VELVET AND CLOTH MANTLES,
The WHOLE of which is NOW READY for INSPECTION.
BONNETS DYED, CLEANED, and ALTERED to the NEWEST STYLE and SHAPE.

From the *Bath Chronicle*, 25 October 1855

The business continued to prosper. By 1861, Sarah Rodway was living with her son-in-law and his family at 4 Sydney Buildings. Ten years later, they had moved to Bathwick House, and, when Sarah Rodway died in 1880, the real-estate portfolio she had built up – Bathwick House, 1 Rochfort Place, 6 Seymour Street, 8 St James's Place and Winifred's

Well Cottage – demonstrated how far a canny entrepreneur could go in nineteenth-century Bath.

Rodway & Co survived for a few more years, but by the time of the 1892 *Directory*, the premises in Abbey Church Yard had been taken over by FW Palmer, Tailor & Hatter.

Head through the archway into Cheap Street to see, above N°s 7 and 8, one of Bath's most celebrated ghost signs – DILL'S FAMOUS BATH POLONIES (2).There appear to be at least two layers of lettering here, but the only one legible looks to date from no earlier than the late nineteenth century. That said, it commemorates a business whose roots go back to the late eighteenth century.

Polonies were – and still are – sausages made from finely ground meat, sliced and eaten cold. The word is believed to be a corruption of Bologna – famous for its sausages – and polonies have been popular in England since the mid-seventeenth century.

The first butchers recorded at 8 Cheap Street were Messrs Shums, described in the 1792 *Directory* as 'German Pork Butchers'. Their memory lingers on in the name of Shum's Court, reached by an alleyway at the side of the shop. The first we hear of John George Dill, who took over from them, is as a pork butcher at 47 Walcot Street in 1800. By 1819, however, he was listed as a 'pork and bacon factor' at 8 Cheap Street. Like the Shums, Dill came from Germany and became a British subject.[3] After he died, aged 79, in 1855, the business was carried on by his family, before being taken over by Thomas Whatley, a close relative who was also a Bath alderman.[4] It later became Whatley & Sons, before

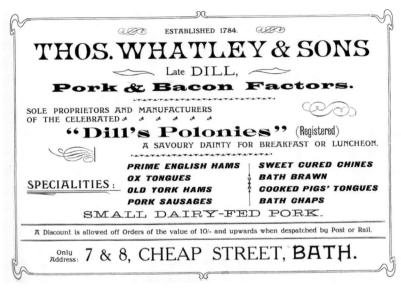

An advertisement from 1909

amalgamating with Shipp, Teagle Ltd in the 1930s to become Shipp, Teagle & Whatley's, but Dill's Polonies, prepared to the original recipe, remained the flagship brand of the company until the Second World War. On 25 July 1942, however, the *Bath Chronicle* carried a report which would have been greeted with dismay by polony lovers:

> Like several other special dishes one either likes polonies intensely or not at all – there is no half-way in one's attitude to a length of polony. Those who are fond of them are agreed that Dill's polonies far exceed in quality and choiceness any other, and for that reason they have for many years enjoyed a national sale like that other fine edible Bath product, the Oliver biscuit. The announcement by the makers, Shipp, Teagle and Whatley Ltd of Cheap Street, that the meat content of polonies must be cut and the famous recipe no longer be implemented will be received with real regret, though naturally not surprise, in view of the food situation generally. The decree of the Ministry of Food is absolute.[5]

Shipp, Teagle & Whatley's was taken over by Dewhurst's in 1950, but continued to trade under the old name until the 1960s, and, although Dill's Famous Bath Polonies were presumably made once more to the original recipe when rationing ended, all we have today to remind us of one of Bath's lost culinary delights is a fading sign.

Head east along Cheap Street, continue past the abbey and along the south side of Orange Grove, turning right along Terrace Walk and right into York Street to see a ghost sign for the REGENCY RESTAURANT above Nº 17 (3).

In the early twentieth century, Nº 17 was the Egremont Hotel. This closed in the early 1940s, and by 1947 a café had opened here, which by 1955 was known as the Regency Restaurant. By 1957, however, its place had been taken by an upholstery store called the Little Dutch Shop, while Regency Snacks – later renamed the Regency Cafe – had opened next door at Nº 16. Today Nº 17 is home to the Real Italian Ice Cream Co, while the Real Italian Pizza Co is at Nº 16. The sign for the Regency Restaurant has been all but painted out, but, if the light is right, you can still just about decipher it.

Carry on along York Street to the corner of Church Street to see another sign which has been largely painted out, on the side wall of 4 Church Street (4). This one, for some reason, caused us no end of trouble. Having

been told, years ago, that the sign on the wall of the shop occupied by the House of Tupra was for the Old Red House Bakery, we assumed that it was – until we checked it out. Despite the similarity of the lettering to that on the OLD RED HOUSE sign in Rivers Street (see pp. 75-76), it soon became apparent that this was a sign for something else.

The only three letters visible – USE – came at the end of a word – quite possibly HOUSE – but there was no way that the letter at the beginning of the next word – partly painted over – was a B. And there was no room for the words OLD and RED before HOUSE. Moreover, a quick trawl through the directories revealed that there had never been a branch of the Old Red House Bakery in Church Street.

Eventually, we decided that the second line read WATCHMAKERS JEWELLERS, which sent us back to the directories in search of a watchmaker and jeweller called Parkhouse, Hobhouse or something else that would fit the lettering on the top line. The obvious solution, that it read HOUSE OF TUPRA, did not occur to us, until, while conducting a guided tour, one of the party suggested that it might read HOUSE OF something.

Not only was the solution blindingly obvious; when you know what it says you can start to make some of the letters out. The reason it did not occur to us earlier is that we never suspected a business which had been trading here since the mid-1960s would have painted – or partly painted – over their name. And that gives rise to the question of whether – although this looks like a *bona fide* ghost sign – it can really be considered one at all.

A little further along York Street are signs for Hand's Dairy, claiming that it was established in 1850 (5). When we turned to the 1851 census, however, we discovered that Charles Hand, who founded the company, was at that time working as a servant for John Carey at Holloway Farm (for which see pp. 188-92), while 9 York Street was occupied by John Batt, an upholsterer and paperhanger. Charles Batt was still listed as living at 9 York Street in the 1852 *Directory*, but, by the time of the 1861 census, Charles Hand had indeed established a dairy here.

Initially, he leased the building from the Manvers Estate for £20 a year, but, when it was put up for sale in 1874, he bought it for £315. His wife died in 1886, and two years later he married Annie Hall from Camely. In the mid-1890s, he retired to live at 10 Cynthia Road, leaving his son, Charles Jr, who had previously worked as a draper's clerk, in charge of the business. This was a critical time for the business, as the disruption caused

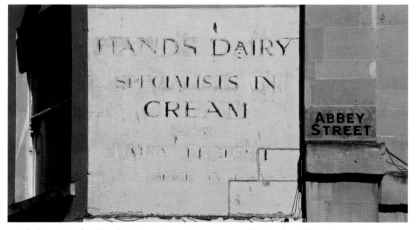

A fading sign for Hand's Dairy, alongside a sans-serif sign for Abbey Street, beneath which traces of a far more elegant street sign can just be seen.

GHOST SIGNS OF BATH

by the council's excavation of the Roman Baths was placing its very future in jeopardy. On 12 November 1896, the *Bath Chronicle* published a letter sent by Charles Hand Jr to the council's Baths Committee, outlining how disruptive the work had been and claiming compensation for loss of trade:

I have been most unwilling to interfere in any way with what is thought to be for the city's welfare, but the serious falling-off of my business for the last year or two, and especially for the summer just ended, compels me to bring before you the following facts:

1 The great loss of the over-counter trade owing to the closing of the thoroughfare leading from my shop to and from the Abbey Churchyard for such a very long period, the closing of the thoroughfare having entirely diverted the traffic into other directions.

2 That the building operations have also to a very great extent affected the traffic through York-street, passengers being unwilling to face the various nuisances.

3 That my business has been affected more or less for many years by the operations of your Committee.

4 That the nature of the work for some considerable time has caused a large amount of extra work in my business owing to the effect of the dust and dirt.

5 That the work done twelve months ago at the Roman duct (of which I said nothing at the time) seriously affected the health of the whole of my family, the stench of itself being bad enough, but the loss of rest was almost worse, owing to the fact of the hauling and excavating being done at nights within a few feet of my bedroom.

Lastly, I would intimate as to the legality or not of the entire closing of a thoroughfare extensively used and exactly opposite a business so dependent on its publicity.

I wish to approach your Committee on the grounds of fairness and equity apart from whatever my legal position may be, and I trust that my claim will receive at your hands the justice it deserves.[6]

The *Chronicle* added that, when the letter was read out to the committee, Alderman Commans agreed that he had 'been put to great inconvenience'.

The matter was referred to the General Purposes Committee, which determined that compensation was not appropriate, and the town clerk was instructed to 'inform Mr Hand that the Committee had only carried on necessary alterations in as short a time as possible, and that when the new building is completed the surrounding property will be greatly improved, and that there is every probability that Mr Hand will profit in his business by the improved locality'.[7] At this, Charles Hand instructed his solicitor to appeal against the decision, but the council refused to budge.[8] Once the work was completed, however, business soon bounced back.

Charles Hand Sr died, aged 84, in 1912, at 10 Cynthia Road. After Charles Hand Jr died, also at the age of 84, in 1936, the business passed to his son, Matthew. Matthew's death eight years later was, according to the *Bath Chronicle*,

> a great blow to the world of dairymen, for he gave much of his time and energy to help his business associates. He was a past president of the Bath Dairymen's Association. He leaves a widow and an only son, Mr Maurice Hand, who hopes to carry on his father's business, but is at present engaged on essential work.[9]

After the war, the dairy continued to prosper, and to move with the times – in the 1952 *Directory* it was listed as Hand's Dairy Milk Bar – and, although it eventually succumbed, like Bath's other dairies, to competition from supermarkets, it is not just its signs that survive to remind us of a business that lasted for well over a century: next door, at 1 Abbey Street, Hand's Georgian Tearooms also perpetuates its memory.

Carry on to the end of York Street for a ghost sign that you will be lucky to see at all (6). On the side wall of Nº 5 Stall Street – facing into York Street – is one of the most elusive ghost signs of all, only really visible when the sun shines on it shortly after dawn for a month or so either side of midsummer day, and we are grateful to Paul De'Ath not only for alerting us to it but also for providing the photograph below. Deciphering its first two lines – GROCERY and PROVISION STORE – was relatively

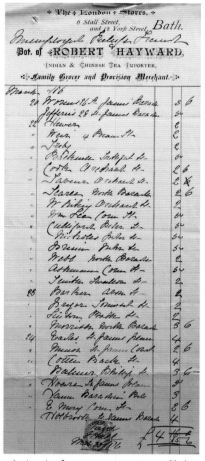

An invoice for payments – or more likely for goods supplied – by Robert Hayward on behalf of the Unemployed Relief Fund in 1886. It also reveals that his business was known as 'The London Stores' and that he was an 'Indian & Chinese Tea Importer'. Two years later, after his business was effectively placed under siege, he was declared bankrupt.

easy. It was with the next line that the fun started; only the first three letters survived, the others having disappeared when the street name was painted over the top of them. The letters were R, followed, after a gap, by HA, and looked as though they formed part of the name of the proprietor. To try to discover what this was meant a comprehensive trawl through the Bath directories, which would have proved fruitless had not we discovered, at an early stage, that Nº 5 had been Nº 6 before renumbering in the early twentieth century. Armed with this information, we eventually established that, of all the people who had occupied this building, the only one whose name tallied with the letters on the sign was a grocer called R Hayward.

Robert Hayward came from Maisey Hampton in Gloucestershire and took the lease of Nº 6 (as it was then) around 1879, when he was 29. This must have seemed like a prime site, and, full of confidence in the future, he had an eye-catching sign painted on the side wall. Whether he was made aware of it or not when he signed the lease, however, within a few years his shop would effectively be in the middle of a building site, as work got under way to excavate the Roman Baths.

Charles Hand's problems, serious though they undoubtedly were, were nothing compared to Robert Hayward's. The building behind him was demolished, York Street was dug up and a large hoarding was erected, making it difficult, and at times impossible, for people to get past. His premises were flooded, looters gained entry through the back of the property, much of his stock was ruined by dust and his customers forsook him to shop in more salubrious surroundings. The council, responsible for this state of affairs, expressed sympathy for his plight and offered to recompense him for loss of trade, damage to stock and theft caused by the contractor's negligence – to the tune of £50. He claimed his losses were more in the region of £700, but they were not persuaded, and in 1888 he went bankrupt. He moved to 30 Cornwell Buildings (now part of Walcot Street) and in the 1891 census was recorded as a grocer's assistant. Ten years later, by now a widower and described as a 'licensed valuer', he was living as a lodger at 10 The Vineyards. His hopes of commercial success at the heart of the city had come to nothing; it could all have been so different if his business had not effectively been placed under siege.

If you look across to the other side of Stall Street, you will see a colonnade. For the next ghost sign, cross over, walk along to where it curves into Bath Street and take a close look at the third column along (7). The lettering here seems to have been revealed when the paint which had covered these columns for well over a century was removed. It now seems to be fading fast, which, although inevitable, is a great shame, for not only does it appear to date from the early days of Bath Street, but attempts to decipher it have so far proved unsuccessful. There have been suggestions that it may be of more recent vintage, having been applied to give some period flavour to one of the numerous costume dramas that have been filmed in Bath, but, while this cannot be discounted, it does not seem likely.

At least three rows of lettering have survived, with several letters clearly visible, but the curved surface on which they are painted and the deep

Lettering on a column outside what was once N° 1 Bath Street. On the left, 'N° 1' is clearly visible. On the right are the enigmatic lines of lettering that follow it.

          GHOST SIGNS OF BATH

shadow over the back of the column makes interpretation of them very difficult. The three rows of lettering are preceded by 'Nº 1' – the shop behind was originally Nº 1 Bath Street, although it has now, somewhat confusingly, been renumbered as 36 Stall Street. On the top row, four letters – SHOP – are clearly visible. These are preceded by what appear to be two more letters, the first of which may be a D. On the middle row, the letters DORE are clearly visible. Again, these seem to be preceded by two letters, which may be MY. On the bottom row, only two letters – possibly RR – can be made out.

Unfortunately, none of this ties in with what we know of the early history of Nº 1 Bath Street. The original leaseholder was Mary Lamb or Lambe (the spelling varied), who had previously held the lease of the building on this site that was demolished when Bath Street was built around 1791.[10] Before the rebuilding took place, she had been a grocer, but, when she moved into the new property, she called it India House, advertising it as the 'first-established tea warehouse in Bath', and stocking a range of top quality candles. Nº 1 was later taken over by a haberdasher called Mary Smith, who in 1797 accused Jane Austen's aunt, Mrs Leigh-Perrott, of stealing lace from her. By 1819, it was occupied by a linen draper called WH Lawrence; it was still a linen draper's in 1826, although by then Edmund Bilson had taken over.

If you walk to the end of the quadrant and look at the second pillar along, you will see more traces of black paint (8). When first uncovered, the word LONDON could be clearly seen. Less than three years later, it has

On the left, the column bearing the word LONDON photographed in October 2013; on the right, the same column in June 2016

all but disappeared. It looks as though it has been deliberately obliterated, but this may just reflect the speed with which Bath stone can succumb to air pollution. From the style of the lettering, this also appears to date from the early days of Bath Street, but what sort of business it advertised is anyone's guess.

 Head south along Stall Street and turn right into Beau Street, where you  will see two glazed and gilded numbers – 4 and 5 – above a shop on the left. Although, at first glance, these look as though they have been here for a long time, they cannot have been. This shop was originally Nº 4 Beau Street; its division into Nᵒˢ 4 and 5 only happened in the latter half of the twentieth century.

Carry on along Beau Street, turn left into Bilbury Lane and right along Lower Borough Walls to see, above Nº 13, the surviving two sections of what appears to have been an elaborate glazed and gilded triptych (9).

 Directories show that this shop was unoccupied in 1916, but that WD Lane established a dairy here a year later. He may have commissioned the sign straight away, but, due to the exigencies of the war years, it is possible that he waited until after the armistice to have it painted.

The business prospered and, when Mr Lane died in 1947, the obituary in the *Bath Chronicle* included a detailed account of his career:

> The death of Mr William Daniel Lane, at his home, Beulah, Upper Wellsway, Bath, at the age of 64, is the cause of deep regret among a wide circle of friends and acquaintances in the city.
>
> With a dairy at 22 Westgate Buildings and only a hand can for delivering milk, Mr Lane set up in business as a dairyman 47 years ago, when he was only 17. Later he transferred to 36 St James's Parade, still carried on as the Abbey Dairy, with a second dairy at 13 Lower Borough Walls. Keen and hardworking, from these small beginnings he built up a considerable business. He saw many developments in milk retailing, and often contrasted present-day methods with the way

in which, as a young man, he sold milk from a can at a farthing a time
to attendants at all the bathing establishments. He was one of the
prime movers in the re-starting of the Bath Dairymen's Association,
25 years ago.

Owing to ill-health, Mr Lane retired 23 years ago, but, recovering
somewhat, he often assisted his daughter and, until his death, her first
husband, Mr WL Cleaver, nephew of the late Councillor H Cleaver,
at their dairy, the Alexandra Park Dairy, on the Bear Flat.[11]

The dairy on Lower Borough Walls closed in the early 1970s, but most
of its sign survived its demise and, almost a century on, despite all the
tarnishing, is still a superb example of the signwriter's art.

Carry on to the end of Lower Borough Walls, and ahead, on the corner
of Hot Bath Street, you will see one of Bath's most intriguing signs – a
palimpsest whose two layers are both clearly visible (10). The earlier
sign reads:

ALWAYS USE
Milkmaid
Milk
LARGEST SALE
LARGE'S GROCER[Y STORE]S

The later one reads:

NESTLÉ'S
[Trade Mark]
MILK
RICHEST IN CREAM

Finally, HOT BATH STREET appears in the bottom right-hand
corner.

To try to date these advertisements, we will take the brand names first. Milkmaid Milk was produced by the Anglo-Swiss Condensed Milk Company, which established its first UK base at Chippenham in 1873. In 1905 It merged with its rival, Nestlé's, to form the Nestlé & Anglo-Swiss Condensed Milk Company. In practice, the name of the company was generally shortened to Nestlé's, but it adopted a trademark – the one seen on the later Hot Bath Street sign – of a white oval containing a red flag with a white cross, on which appeared the word SWISS. If you look carefully at what looks like a white rugby ball on the later sign, you will see the outline of the flag and of the cross – which now appears black rather than white – with SWISS faintly visible.

Turning now to the commercial history of the building, the Misses M & K Large opened a grocer's and confectioner's at 1 Hot Bath Street around 1892. It survived until after the First World War, latterly run just by Miss M Large, but was last listed in the 1919 *Directory*.

Turn into Hot Bath Street, following it as it curves left to the old Hetling Pump Room, with its slab-serif sign still bright over 140 years after its waters ceased to flow **(11)**. Its name commemorates a remarkable

family. Ernst von Hetling came to England to serve as a doctor at the Hanoverian court and was appointed 'Page of the Back Stairs to Her Royal Highness the Princess Amelia'. He changed his name to Ernest Hetling and took a lease of the building which lies behind the old pump room and is still called Hetling House today. Also known as Abbey Church House, and now part of the Gainsborough Hotel complex, this was built on the site of an earlier building in the sixteenth century. In the seventeenth century it was acquired by the Hungerfords of Farleigh Hungerford and was known as Hungerford House. Later, when Lord Lexington married into the Hungerford family, the lease was transferred to him and it became known as Lexington House. By 1694, however, after Lord Lexington had assigned it to a Mrs Savil in lieu of a legacy, it had become 'Mrs Savil's Lodgings Nere the hot Bath'.[12] In 1697, Mrs Savil married an apothecary called Mr Skrine and its name was changed to 'Skrine's Lower House'.[13]

According to John Wood, it was at this time 'the second best House within the Walls'.[14] Wood also tells us that it was 'not only made the Habitation of her Royal Highness the Princess Caroline, in the Spring Season of the Year 1746; but of the same Princess, and her Sister, the Princess of *Hesse*, in the Autumn Season of the same Year.'[15] It was around this time that the lease was taken by Ernest Hetling and its name was changed again, to Hetling House. He died in 1753, leaving it to his wife, who ran it as a lodging house until 1775, when the *Bath Chronicle* announced the sale of 'all the neat and genuine

HOUSEHOLD FURNITURE, belonging to Mrs Hetling, in her large Lodging-house near the Cross-Bath'.[16]

The Hetling family retained the lease, however, and five years later Ernest Hetling's son placed an advertisement in the *Bath Chronicle*:

> WILLIAM HETLING, WINE and BRANDY-MERCHANT, Hetling-Court, Westgate-Buildings, Bath, begs leave to inform his friends and the public, their orders shall be supplied with any quantity of the best goods imported.[17]

According to one of his descendants, William Hetling was something of a character, who 'pursued his adventurous and ruinous career of Surgeon, Distiller of Spirits, absconder to Gretna Green with an heiress for his wife, finishing up with a seizure of the Distillery by the Excise and Company of Light Infantry, a bankruptcy, a flight to Paris, and most probably a bloody end during the orgies of the Revolution, for when that was over Mr William Hetling appeared to be over too, for nothing more was heard of him'.[18] The heiress in question was a Miss Rishton, descended from the Hungerfords who had once owned Hetling House. Her guardian intended her for his son, but 'she fell in love with Mr H, who was a dashing, handsome man. They agreed that he should wait at a famous pye-shop in Broad Street; and here, having joined him, he popped her into a post-chaise and rattled off to Gretna Green'.[19] On their return to Bath, a further wedding was held in the Abbey on 1 June 1767.

As for William Hetling's bankruptcy, this occurred shortly after he had placed the advertisement quoted above. On 26 October 1780, the *Bath Chronicle* announced that

> the Partnership of William Hetling, of the city of Bath, distiller, Thomas Cave, of the city of Bristol, distiller, and Samuel Atlee, of the parish of Walcot, distiller, in the trade or business of Distillers and Makers of Spirits, carried on at Walcot ... in the Firm of *William Hetling and Company*, is this day mutually dissolved so far as respects the share and interest of the said Thomas Cave therein, who is hereby declared to be no further concerned in the partnership with the said Wm Hetling and Samuel Atlee. All persons to whom the said partnership are indebted, are requested to apply at the *[illegible]* house in Walcot for payment.[20]

Three months later, Hetling House was advertised 'to be let, and entered upon immediately'. It was described as

> that Large and Commodious DWELLING-HOUSE, situate in Hetling-Court, adjoining to the Hot-Bath Pump-Room, lately put in excellent repair, and ... now fit for the immediate reception of a Nobleman's or Gentleman's Family; or it also may be converted into a Lodging-House, or for the carrying on of any extensive business, being suited with every conveniency requisite for the above purposes.[21]

GHOST SIGNS OF BATH

The partnership of Hetling and Atlee – who was also a wine and spirit merchant in Stall Street – stumbled on for a little while longer, until, on 5 September 1782, the *Bath Chronicle* announced that 'the Creditors of Messrs HETLING and ATLEE, of Walcot, Distillers, are particularly requested to meet at the White-Lyon in the Market-Place, on Monday next ... to take into consideration some propositions that will be then made, and to consult on several special affairs relative to the estate of the said Hetling and Atlee'.[22]

Less than a year later, another advertisement appeared:

DISTILLERY
TO be LETT for an absolute Term of 11 years, or SOLD immediately, by Private Contract, That capital STILL-HOUSE, late in the occupation of Messrs HETLING and ATLEE, Bankrupts; together with the spacious Brew-House, Rectifying-House, Slaughter-House, Salting-House, Drying-House, with all the extensive appurtenances, Still-Worms, Coppers, Coolers, Engines, Backs, &c &c, all in perfect good condition, and fit for immediate working; also the Dwelling-Houses, Compting-House, Stables, &c, having plenty of water, and every requisite to render it completely eligible for the trade.[23]

Although that is the last we hear of William Hetling, his son, also called William, not only stayed behind when his father left for France but had an eminently respectable career. He was indentured to Joseph Metford, a surgeon at Bristol Royal Infirmary, for which his father paid three hundred guineas, and, after studying at Guy's and St Thomas's Hospitals, he returned to practice as a surgeon at Bristol Royal Infirmary until his death in 1837.

So much for the Hetlings. What of the Pump Room that bears their name? In 1772, St John's Hospital, who owned the site, leased it to the corporation, which wanted to open a new pump room to ease overcrowding at the pump room in Abbey Church Yard.[24] Although it was officially known as the Hot Bath Pump Room (to differentiate it from the 'Grand Pump Room' in Abbey  Church Yard), its address was Hetling Court, and it soon came to be referred to as the Hetling Pump Room. In 1799, for example, Jane Austen wrote to her sister Cassandra that her brother Edward had taken the waters 'at the Hetling Pump.'[25]

The corporation acquired the freehold in 1805, when the building was either refurbished or rebuilt. The extent of the makeover is unclear, although a guidebook of 1815 tells us that the building was erected under the direction of John Palmer.[26] It continued to be known – officially at least – as the Hot Bath Pump Room until 1840, when the corporation renamed it the Hetling Pump Room, and promoted it as a cheaper alternative to the Grand Pump Room, with a glass of water costing threepence rather than fourpence.[27]

In the latter half of the nineteenth century, the number of people coming to Bath to take the waters fell dramatically, and in 1871 the *Bath Chronicle* reported that the Baths & Pump Room Committee had recommended that, 'inasmuch as the Hetling Pump Room was kept open at annual loss to the borough, it should be closed'.[28] As a result of numerous objections, a compromise was reached, and, when the Hetling Pump Room closed in 1875, the spring was redirected to the Hot Bath opposite.[29] Four years later the building was converted to a hostel for nurses. Today, it houses the spa visitor centre.

Carry on along the back of the Cross Bath, turn left through an archway into St John's Hospital and look to the right to see what is perhaps Bath's most baffling sign on the wall of 3 Chapel Court (12). On the platband above the ground-floor windows is some faded and fragmentary lettering, probably dating from the early nineteenth century, which once spelt out CHAPEL-COURT HOUSE. So far, so straightforward. It is what comes next, after a long gap, that poses the puzzle – the letters ORA H. A postcard published in the early twentieth-century, when the lettering was already incomplete, shows that that there was an L in front of ORA, and it has been suggested in a recent history of St John's Hospital that it originally read LORA HOUSE.[30] As indeed it might, but all attempts to find a reference to a Lora House or indeed to a Lora associated with

Opposite: Fragmentary lettering spelling out 'CHAPEL-C...' and 'HOU...', with the mysterious sequence 'ORAH' at the bottom.

Above: A postcard published in the early twentieth-century, when 'HOU' read 'HOUSE' and there was an 'L' before 'ORAH' – not that that solves the mystery.

Chapel Court have so far proved fruitless. It may be that there were other letters in front of LORA; it may be that the H is not the first letter of 'house'; given the way the letters are spaced, there may not even be a break between the A and the H. The possibilities, if not endless, are certainly, numerous, but, whichever way we have looked at the problem, we have failed to come up with any meaningful suggestions as to what the letters originally spelled out – or why.

Carry on through Chapel Court to emerge onto Westgate Buildings. Bear right and continue on up through the Sawclose. Carry straight on past the Theatre Royal, turn left into Beauford Square and, after turning right into Princes Street, look back to see a sign above 11 Beauford Square (13). However wide your definition of ghost signs is, it is unlikely to be wide enough to include the superb ironwork advertising J ELLETT, SMITH & PLUMBER. Yet, as a fascinating

reminder of a long vanished world and an entrée to the history of another remarkable family, it amply merits inclusion here.

The story starts in Chardstock – then in Dorset, but now in Devon – in 1841. This is a glorious part of the world, but in the 1840s – since dubbed 'the Hungry Forties' – life for many would have been desperate. The 1841 census lists John Ellett, aged 35, as a farmer in the hamlet of Alson, married with three sons and five daughters. Ten years later, after a run of bad harvests and deepening agricultural depression, the 1851 census finds him living in a cottage in the same hamlet, working as a blacksmith, with his two eldest sons, Thomas and Henry, helping him.

At some stage during the next decade, he decided that he needed to move away from Chardstock to seek work elsewhere. Unfortunately, this meant that his family had to split up, at least temporarily. By the time of the 1861 census, he was living with his eldest son, Thomas, in the hamlet of Howley near Whitestaunton (six miles north of Chardstock), where he was working as a blacksmith and his son was a carpenter. His wife and the rest of his children, meanwhile, were living in a tenement at Nº 2 Trim Street in Bath.

His sacrifice paid off, and by 1871 the family, now reunited, was living at 16a Monmouth Place. John, now 67, was still working as a smith, as were two of his sons – Azariah, aged 24, and John, aged 20 – while Thomas, the eldest, had become a wheelwright. Henry, who had also worked alongside his father, had married and moved to 15 Beauford Square, where he was working as a blacksmith.

John Ellett Sr died three years later, soon followed by two of his sons – Thomas, aged 46, in 1877, and Henry, aged 45, in 1880. The 1881 census finds Henry's widow, Ann, 'carrying on business as a general smith', assisted by the eldest of her three sons, at 15 Beauford Square, and the business was henceforth known as A Ellett & Sons. Azariah, meanwhile, was working as a whitesmith and living at Bellott's Hospital, having married its matron. As for John Ellett Jr, he had set up in business at 11 Beauford Square, and erected a sign on the roof as a demonstration of his handiwork.

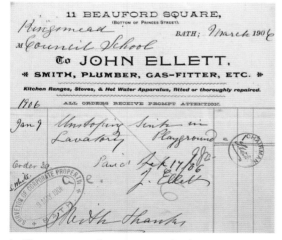

Invoices from A Ellett & Sons and John Ellett from 1905 and 1906

So by 1881 – and for a good time afterwards – there were three firms by the name of Ellett in Bath. The 1901 *Directory* lists George Ellett, trading as 'Ellett & Sons, gasfitters, bellhangers, &c' at 15 Beauford Square; Azariah Ellett, 'smith and hot water fitter' at Bellott's Hospital; and John Ellett, 'smith, gasfitter and plumber' at 11 Beauford Square.

John Ellett retired just before the First World War, but, on the outbreak of hostilities, went back to work, eventually retiring for the second time in 1919, when he handed the business over to his son. He moved to 22 Crescent Gardens, where he spent much of his time gardening. The spirit of showmanship that had led him to erect the sign and weathervane on

11 Beauford Square did not desert him, however, and he became a skilled topiarist, trimming various shrubs in his front garden in the shape of birds, and attracting a good deal of attention from passers-by. Reporting his sudden death in 1930 at the age of 79, the *Bath Chronicle* included the information that 'he formerly served in the Queen's Westminsters, and when he came to Bath he joined the old 1st Somerset Volunteers ... He was a keen rifle shot and a member of the Battalion shooting team. He won many cups and trophies'.[31]

Azariah died at Bellott's Hospital a few months later, severing the last link with the village of Chardstock. By now there was only one firm by the name of Ellett in Bath – Ellett & Sons of 11 Beauford Square, which after the Second World War expanded to take over a yard in Tennyson Road, before finally closing in the 1960s.

A little further along Princes Street, on the left at Nº 6, is one of Bath's most artistic signs, for SHEPHERDS HALL **(14)**. In the days before the welfare state and the National Health Service, friendly societies played a vital role, collecting weekly subs from their members and helping them out at times of sickness or misfortune. The Loyal Order of Ancient Shepherds, originally known as the Ashton Unity Society, was founded in Ashton under Lyne in Lancashire in 1826. Its aims were 'to relieve the sick, bury the dead, and assist each other in all cases of unavoidable distress, so far as our power lies, and for the promotion of peace and goodwill towards the human race'. It soon became a nationwide

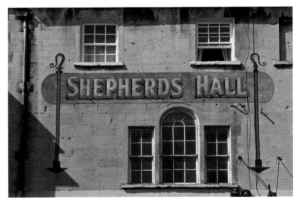

organisation, with branches – or lodges – in scores of towns and cities. By 1914, it had 143,000 members, and Bath had three lodges, meeting at the Foresters' Hall in Bath Street, St Paul's Parish Hall in St John's Place (now the Egg Theatre) and the Baptist Church Hall in Oldfield Park. In the late 1920s, the society acquired a permanent home at Nº 6 Princes Street, painted a superb sign on the wall to celebrate, and continued to meet there until comparatively recently. Now renamed Shepherds Friendly, the society still survives as a mutual organisation offering a range of savings, insurance and protection plans to its members.

At the end of Princes Street, turn right along the south side of Queen Square, carry on into Wood Street and look up to the left to see a ghost sign above Nº 4 **(15)**. In contrast to the ghost signs that only reveal themselves when the sun shines on them, this is one that is seen at its best – albeit a very poor best – in the rain. Unfortunately, even after tracing the history of this building, the lettering is so fugitive and fragmentary that we have failed to decipher what it once spelled out.

But, in the hope that someone else will have more luck, here is a potted history of Nº 4 over the last two centuries. In 1800, it was occupied by a carver and gilder called John Self. Two years later, William Smith took over the business. He was still there in 1819, but had left by 1823, when J & T Howell placed an advertisement in the *Bath Chronicle* for their auction warerooms at 4 Wood Street.[32] By 1826, J & H Barker, drapers and tailors, had taken over, but in 1834 the *Bath Chronicle* carried an advertisement for 'J Harrison's Carving, Gilding, Looking-Glass and Picture-Frame Manufactory'.[33] Two years later, Mr Harrison left for London and put his stock up for sale.[34] Nº 4 was taken over by William Lewis, a cabinet maker, upholsterer and auctioneer, but by 1842 was back in the hands of a carver and gilder, called Mr Hill. Before long, it had become Hill & Son, and in 1848 it was announced that a 'Gallery will be Open for Public Inspection ... commencing on Monday, May 15'.[35]

In 1868, JM Hill announced that he was 'retiring from the Business of GILDER and PICTURE RESTORER', and that his son, EL Hill, was taking over.[36] Between 1871 and 1874, Nº 4, along with the rest of the buildings on the north side of Wood Street, had a single-storey extension, with new shopfronts, added. By 1886, Nº 4 was home to the 'Bath Fine Art Galleries'. Ten years later, in 1896, EL Hill transferred the business to Messrs FJ Freeth Smith & Ernest Collins Chard.[37] Just over two years later, the building was gutted by fire.[38] Despite their loss, Messrs Freeth Smith & Chard reopened the galleries the following year, and remained there until the early 1920s, when Bentley-Hunt & Vanstone, Electrical & Radio Engineers, took over.

The words on 4 Wood Street almost certainly relate to one of the businesses listed above; the question is which one?

Around the corner from Wood Street is Quiet Street, where you will find not only find Mr B's Emporium of Reading Delights but also the Salamander pub, with newly-painted signs by the Bristol-based signwriter and illustrator Hannah Sunny Whaler.

Carry on along Wood Street and Quiet Street before turning left into Milsom Street. A little way along on the right, at Nº 43, we come to a sign for a CIRCULATING LIBRARY & READING ROOM, BOOKSELLER, BINDER & STATIONER, NATIONAL LOTTERY OFFICE (16). This sign can be dated almost precisely to 1823. It was on 9 May 1822 that Francis Joseph, previously employed at Barratt & Sons' Bookshop at 17 Old Bond Street, placed an advertisement in the *Bath Chronicle*:

> **FRANCIS JOSEPH**
> (Many years Assistant at Mr. BARRATT's Library)
> MOST respectfully informs his Friends, the Inhabitants and Visitors of Bath, that he has opened a
> *Circulating Library and Reading-Room,*
> No. 43, MILSOM-STREET,
> (THREE DOORS ABOVE THE OCTAGON CHAPEL);
> And trusts he will, by assiduity and attention, obtain their support and patronage.
> **THE READING-ROOM**
> Will be regularly supplied with the
> *London, Irish, Edinburgh, and most of the Provincial*
> NEWSPAPERS, REVIEWS, MAGAZINES, &c.
> **THE LIBRARY**
> Will have every NEW WORK of merit put into circulation as soon as published:—and
> **THE SHOP**
> Is stocked with the choicest Assortment of STATIONARY, which will be rendered on the most reasonable terms.
> *All orders for Standard or Periodical Works executed with promptitude.*
> BOOKBINDING in all its branches, in the neatest and most expeditious manner.
> *Card Plates engraved and printed.*
> LODGINGS to be LET, newly and Elegantly Furnished. *(One Concern.)*

Less than a year later, on 3 April 1823, he announced that his bookshop had become a State Lottery Office:

His timing could not have been worse. State lotteries had been running for over 250 years, but in 1823 the government announced that they would be phased out. Although a useful way of raising revenue, corruption and mismanagement by private contractors had made their demise all but inevitable, and the last one was held in 1826. It seems that Francis Joseph did not even last long enough to participate in that final flutter, for, by the time of the 1826 *Directory*, Ferguson, Todd & Co, linen drapers, were at 43 Milsom Street. Whether it was the lottery that brought him down or whether he simply overreached himself, we will probably never know, but, short though his tenure was, he at least created one of the finest ghost signs to be seen anywhere.

Milsom Street in the early twentieth century, with the sign on N° 43 on the right. Despite its superb draughtsmanship, this celebrated sign includes a calligraphic irregularity – the Y at the end of LIBRARY has a thick stroke on the wrong arm. The Y at the end of LOTTERY, however, is formed correctly.

A few doors along, at N° 35, we come to a sign for a BRUSH MANUFACTORY (17). These days, 'manufactory' has been shortened to 'factory', and it may seem strange that an area as fashionable as Milsom Street was once home to something as downmarket as a place making brushes. These brushes, though, were not the sort used to sweep spit and sawdust off bar room floors or dislodge soot from chimneys. The brushes made here graced the boudoirs and dressing tables of the gentry and the business was as upmarket as any in the street.

It was owned by John Strawbridge, who was born in Frome around 1815 and opened a brush manufactory at 11 New Bond Street some time before 1841. In November 1846, he placed an advertisement in the *Bath Chronicle*:

FANCY & HOUSEHOLD BRUSH MANUFACTORY
35 MILSOM STREET, BATH
REMOVED FROM NEW BOND STREET

J STRAWBRIDGE, in returning his sincere thanks to his Friends and Patrons for the liberal support he has received during a Residence of many years in New Bond Street, begs to acquaint them he has taken a lease of the Premises, late in the occupation of Mr FASANA, as above; the eligibility of which, for manufacturing, will enable him to supply goods of the first quality and workmanship, and as cheap as any house in the trade. By the strictest personal attention to the demands of his customers, he trusts he shall not only retain their confidence, but secure an increased amount of public patronage and support.[39]

J. STRAWBRIDGE,

FANCY AND GENERAL

BRUSH MANUFACTURER,

35, MILSOM STREET, BATH,

In returning his grateful acknowledgments for the liberal patronage he has received since his removal from New Bond Street, respectfully solicits a continuance of the same, assuring those who may honor him with their commands, it shall be his constant endeavour to supply them with Goods of the best quality and workmanship, at the very lowest prices.

EVERY DESCRIPTION OF

BRUSHES IN GREAT VARIETY.

A LARGE ASSORTMENT OF

COMBS, IN IVORY, HORN, & TORTOISESHELL,

Rope, Cocoa, and Bordered Mats.

WOOL RUGS, IN VARIOUS COLOURS,

For Doors and Carriages.

A CHOICE ASSORTMENT OF

FRENCH & BERLIN FANCY BASKETS,

Sieves, Mops, Chamois Leathers, Sponges, Whisks, Rope, Twine, Bowls and Wooden Ware, &c., at very Low Prices.

Brushes, &c. made to Order on the Shortest Notice.

A LIBERAL ALLOWANCE TO THE TRADE.

Less than six years later, in April 1852, another advertisement appeared:

SELLING OFF
AT STRAWBRIDGE'S BRUSH MANUFACTORY
35 MILSOM STREET
The whole of the excellent STOCK of Household and fancy BRUSHES, COMBS, Foreign BASKETS, MATS, SPONGES, &c, at such REDUCTION IN PRICES as must ensure an Early Clearance.[40]

And with that, John Strawbridge, with his wife Ann and eight-year-old son John, seems to have shaken the dust of Bath, and of England, from his feet and sailed for Australia, where he settled in Magill, a suburb of Adelaide. In the *South Australian Directory* for 1884, John Strawbridge Sr is listed as a 'district clerk', while John Strawbridge Jr, having followed in his father's footsteps, is listed as a brushmaker. John Strawbridge Sr died the following year at the age of 70.

The BRUSH MANUFACTORY sign in 1981 before the missing lower part of the first letter was reinstated.

After John Strawbridge left Bath, Nº 35 Milsom Street became an 'American Portrait Gallery', where daguerreotypes as well as paintings were available, and his brief tenure was forgotten – apart from the enigmatic sign which continues to intrigue visitors and Bathonians alike. You will notice, however, that the first letter of the sign looks somewhat peculiar, due to the stones on which the original letter was painted having been replaced, and an attempt made to replicate it.

Retrace your steps along Milsom Street, head to the left of the building with a cherub in a niche at the end, and, between the first and second floor windows of Nº 1 Burton Street, you will see a ghost sign for NIBLOCK & CO, CLOTH FACTORS & COMMISSION AGENTS (18). James Niblock is an intriguing character. Although we know when he was in Bath, we do not know for certain where he came from, although, given that his was an uncommon name, it is possible to piece together a probable

scenario. The first time Bathonians would have come across it was in the *Chronicle* in 1791, when a list of bankrupts transcribed from the *London Gazette* included 'James Niblock and William Hunter, of Liverpool, linen-drapers'.[41] Eight years later, they would come across it again, when the *Chronicle* published a list of bankrupts which included 'Jas. Niblock and Geo. Burgess, of Bristol, linen-drapers'.[42]

Move forward eleven years, to 1812, when the following advertisement appeared in the *Bath Chronicle*:

TO BE SOLD BY AUCTION
By Mr. NIBLOCK

At Nº 4 UNION-STREET, this present Thursday, April 2nd, and following days, commencing each morning at 11 o'clock, and will continue till 4 in the afternoon, and from 7 till 10 in the evening,
A MOST Excellent and Valuable Assortment of LINEN and WOOLLEN DRAPERY, Hosiery, Haberdashery,
and various other Fancy Goods
All of which must positively be sold
without the least reserve whatever, in suitable lots.
Suffice to say, delicacy towards the proprietors, whose connections are truly respectable, prevents any further publicity, than to assure the lovers of good Bargains, that they will be highly gratified in the attendance at the sale.[43]

Mr Niblock held several more sales of bankrupt stock at various addresses in the city over the next few years. By the time of the 1819 *Directory*, however, 'Niblock & Co, cloth-factors and commissioned agents' are listed as being in Burton Street. This is the only reference to their being at this address – and, as with the earlier advertisements in the *Chronicle*, Mr Niblock's first name is not given. For that, we have to wait until 1823, when the *Chronicle's* list of bankrupts includes 'Jas. Niblock and Richard Stanley Latham, of Bath, woollen-drapers'.[44]

Once again, James Niblock bounced back, and on 18 January 1827 the *Chronicle* carried an advertisement for 'JAS. NIBLOCK & Co' at Northumberland Place.[45] A further advertisement appeared a few months later:

> J NIBLOCK most respectfully announces to the Public generally,
> that he has this day received on Commission
> AN EXCELLENT ASSORTMENT OF
> SUPERFINE CLOTHS and KERSEYMERES,
> Embracing almost every Colour and Quality, particularly extra Saxon
> Blues and Blacks, all of which will be sold remarkable cheap. Also
> about 150 REMNANTS, including from one to six yards lengths,
> of the best Superflues, which will be remarkable cheap.
> *Woollen Hall, Northumberland-Place.*[46]

The following year, 'a daring attempt was made upon the premises of Mr Niblock, proprietor of the Woollen Hall, Northumberland-place. The thieves sought to effect an entrance by endeavouring to remove one of the shutters; but it is supposed they were disturbed by the person who sleeps in the shop'.[47] The Woollen Hall was to carry on for several more years, under new ownership, but that is the last we hear of James Niblock in connection with it. Two years later, the *Chronicle* reported that 'James Niblock, formerly of this city, woollen-draper', had died in Bristol at the age of 66, leaving only the lettering in Burton Street, now almost two centuries old, to remind us of his colourful career.[48]

At the end of Burton Street, turn left along Upper Borough Walls, then right down the steps into Union Passage, and second left along the Corridor. Look out for the brass sill plate on Nº 18, bearing the name of Edward Bussey, who opened a stationer's here sometime between 1864 and 1876 **(19)**.[49] There are several other sill plates with the names of

defunct businesses in Bath, but, like entrance mosaics, they are not true ghost signs, and including them would have made the book untenably long. Mr Bussey's sill plate, however, is such a work of art that we could not pass it by without comment.

At the end of the Corridor, look above the shopfront on the left to see a sign which has only recently been uncovered, but is one of the most intriguing in the city **(20)**. All that can be seen are the letters OWN and, below them, a word ending ER. Not much to go on, you might think,

but these letters tally with only one of the businesses that have occupied this shop.

The building dates from 1825, when Henry Edmund Goodridge built the Corridor, along with the two shops – Nᵒˢ 18 and 19 – flanking the entrance to it on the High Street, or the Market Place as it was then known. The 1826 *Directory* lists George Brown as a haberdasher in the Market Place, and, although it does not give a street number, we know he was at Nᵒ 19, because in 1831 he got together with the proprietor of the shop on the other side of the Corridor to create a display for the coronation of William IV and Queen Adelaide. According to the *Bath Chronicle*, 'Mr Bennett, tea-dealer, and Mr Brown, haberdasher [erected] a splendid Crown in the centre of the east-end of the Corridor, with the letters WR over the former, and AR over the latter'.[50]

George Brown was still at Nᵒ 19 in 1841, but, sometime between then and 1846, he handed the business over to his two sons, Thomas and Joseph. By 1854, Thomas was the sole proprietor, and by 1862 was listed not as a haberdasher but as a hosier. Two years later he had gone, and Nᵒ 19 had been taken over by a Mr W Cutter who was exhibiting a 'fine collection of shells, fossils, insects, etc'.[51] Against all the odds, the sign, despite being covered up, survived the rebuilding of the Corridor in 1870 and the installation of a glazed canopy over the entrance in 1927, to re-emerge into the light of day over a century and a half later. Even though the canopy has unfortunately encroached onto part of the sign, it is still a remarkable survival.

Not only that – if you look above the shop on the other side of the Corridor, it is just about possible to make out the remnants of a sign, painted in a similar style, with what appears to be a T at the end. That gives very little to go on, but it may be what remains of the sign for Samuel Bennett, the tea dealer.

Corroborative evidence for all of this comes in the form of an engraving, which we discovered by chance after researching the surviving lettering. and is reproduced overleaf. Dating from shortly after the Corridor was built, it shows the shops on either side, with BENNETT'S TEA ESTABLISHMENT at Nᵒ 18 and BROWN HABERDASHER at Nᵒ 19.

Above: Nᵒˢ 18 & 19 High Street in the 1830s, with signs for Bennett's Tea Establishment and Brown, Haberdasher.

Below: Nᵒˢ 18 & 19 in June 2016, with the newly-revealed sign for Brown's Haberdasher's on the right.

Standing outside the entrance to the Corridor, look north to the building on the corner of Bridge Street, now occupied by Mallory's, where you may be able to make out a ghost sign on the roof (21). Thanks for nailing this extremely fugitive sign must go to one of the party on a guided tour of shopfronts and ghost signs during the 2015 Bath Literature Festival, who, when invited to admire the elaborate shopfront on the corner of Bridge Street, asked 'what about the ghost sign?', and proceeded to point it out. At the time, it seemed incredible that, after diligently hunting out the city's ghost signs, we had overlooked one so obvious. On returning a couple of days later, however, the reason for this oversight was clear – unlike the ghost sign, which had all but disappeared. When the guided tour had come by, the sun was shining from just the right angle, and the sign appeared in all its faded glory. When the sun shines from almost any other direction, however, or on an overcast day, it is much more difficult to spot.

Above: Faded signs on the slates on the corner of Bridge Street.

Below: An advertisement from 1909, showing that the painted signs were just part of an eye-blitzing display of advertising.

Above: Wright's tobacconist's around 1910, a riot of gilded lettering, with painted signs on the slates at the top. The densely-packed telegraph poles in the background mark the site of Bath's telephone exchange from 1893 to 1929.

Right: An advertisement from 1937.

GHOST SIGNS OF BATH

And, in all fairness, the slates above the parapet are not the most obvious place for a ghost sign, but the words CIGAR STORES, on either side of the garret windows, are among the city's most tangible links with the golden age of smoking. Although there are several other tobacco and cigarette-related signs around the city, they are all on small shops, whereas this was a veritable temple to the tawny weed. N° 17 Northgate Street was a tobacconist's at least as far back as 1878, when a Mr Packer held the lease. Back then, however, the building, along with those adjoining it to the north, extended much further forward. The council wanted to widen the street and soon afterwards they served compulsory purchase orders on the properties and rebuilt them, taking the opportunity to give N° 17 a curved frontage so that vehicles could turn the corner more easily.

In December 1887, with the work completed, the *Bath Chronicle* advertised 'the very valuable freehold house and premises, situate and being N° 17 Northgate Street' for sale. 'The house,' it added, 'has recently been entirely Rebuilt and is fitted with Plate-glass Windows, and is now let on a lease of 7, 14, or 21 years to Mr Boulger, Tobacconist (for which Business the Situation is almost better adapted than any other house in the City) at the very moderate Rent of £75 per annum.'[52]

In 1911, the lease was transferred to Frederick Wright, who also had a tobacconist's at 8A Westgate Street, as well in Cheltenham and Gloucester, as signs mounted on the building proclaimed. It remained Wright's tobacconist's for almost 60 years, last being listed in the 1969 *Directory*, but by the time of the 1970 *Directory* an even older company, Mallory's, who already occupied N°s 1-4 Bridge Street, took it over and converted the entrance to a window.

Turn right down Bridge Street, cross Pulteney Bridge, continue along Argyle Street, and, on the corner of Grove Street look up to see Bath's most photographed false window, painted trompe d'oeil-style and showing a bearded gent perusing a tome selected from the well-stocked shelves in the background (22). Tour guides have allegedly been known to claim this is Charles Dickens, a frequent visitor to Bath, leafing through one of his novels. It isn't. Charles Dickens' beard looked nothing like that, and as for the book – well, more of that later.

The reason this particular window was painted in this particular style – we haven't been able to ascertain exactly when, but sometime in the 1970s or 1980s – was because of the ghost sign

above it, which is considerably older. It is, if you like, an *homage* to the ghost sign, the only one – so far – in Bath, but a trend that certainly needs encouraging.

The sign may seem rather dull by comparison with the brightly-coloured painting, but the business it advertises not only dates back over 150 years but is still very much active today. It began not with George Gregory, but with his father, William Gregory, who was born in 1816.

William Gregory's father, a saddler and harness maker in Southgate Street, apprenticed him to Thomas Raines, a bookbinder at 7 Kingston Buildings. After finishing his apprenticeship, William worked in Cheltenham, London and elsewhere, before marrying a girl from Cardigan and returning to Bath, where he set up in business as a bookbinder at 14 York Street. His first son, William, became a linen draper's assistant, but his second son, George, followed him into the business, which soon expanded to include bookselling, and moved to larger premises at 9 Bath Street.

In the mid-1870s, the business was renamed William Gregory & Son, and, while bookbinding and second-hand bookselling continued at 9 Bath Street, a circulating library was opened at 1 Wood Street. In 1885, after his father's retirement, George Gregory changed the name of the business to George E Gregory and moved it to 5 Argyle Street, in premises recently vacated by Alfred Wills (for whom see pp. 56-60). Bookbinding had by now taken a back seat to second-hand books, and by 1894 George Gregory was describing himself as an 'English, Foreign, Colonial and General Book Merchant, Library Buyer and Exporter', issuing monthly catalogues and with 'upwards of 100,000 volumes always on sale'. In 1898 he expanded into 5a Argyle Street, adding 27 Grove Street and Argyle Yard two years later. In 1901 he was appointed Bookseller in Ordinary to Her Majesty Queen Alexandra, and from 1915 to 1918 was president of the International Association of Antiquarian Booksellers. He also built up a large stock of prints, engravings and illuminated manuscripts, and published many local books, the most celebrated of which, Mowbray Green's *Eighteenth Century Architecture of Bath*, is the one being read by the man in the window. George Gregory retired following major surgery in 1922 and the business was taken over by George Bayntun, who had established a

GEORGE .. GREGORY, ..

5, ARGYLE STREET, BATH [ENG.]

THE IMPERIAL BOOK STORE
And TEMPLE OF LITERATURE AND ART

Contains one of the largest and finest stocks of Second-hand Books in the World; it comprises upwards of a quarter of a million volumes, carefully arranged on the alphabetical principle, and classified under subjects and languages and displayed in THIRTY-ONE CONVENIENT ROOMS. Three houses are here devoted to the display of the Works of the greatest writers, thinkers, and men of action of all Ages and Nations. It is one of the most interesting attractions of the West Country. Many of my American and Foreign customers, when visiting Bath, assure me they know of no other Bookstore to equal " THE IMPERIAL " in point of magnitude and comfortable arrangement. This is frequently the deciding factor to visitors, both British and Foreign, when contemplating a place of sojourn or recuperation. There is no need to ask " What shall we do ? " or " Where shall we go to-day ? " while " THE TEMPLE OF LITERATURE " is open.

300,000 VOLUMES IN STOCK.

LIBRARIES BOUGHT; DISTANCE IMMATERIAL.

LICENSED VALUER for PROBATE or DIVISION.

Rare Mezzotint and other Old Engravings.

RARE AND VALUABLE EDITIONS IN SUPERB BINDINGS.
CATALOGUES MAILED FREE.

Mowbray Green's Great Work on Bath,
XVIII Century Architecture of Bath, 4to., gilt cloth, 28/-, pub. 42/- net.

GEORGE GREGORY, Sole Proprietor.

Telephone 555.
Telegrams and Cables, "GREGORY, BOOKSELLER, BATH."

An advertisement from 1914

bookbinding business at 9 New Bond Street in 1894, before moving to larger premises at 18 Walcot Street around 1900.[53]

George Gregory's success was tempered by personal tragedy, however. His only son, who joined the merchant navy, died at the age of 21 in 1900 when a three-master called the Yarana, in which he was sailing from Santa Rosalia to Iquique in South America, disappeared without trace.[54] And in 1930, when George Gregory was being treated in the Forbes Fraser Hospital at Combe Park (later part of the Royal United Hospital), his wife was killed by a tram on the way home from visiting him.[55] He died a few weeks later.

When George Bayntun took over the business in 1922, he moved it out of Argyle Street and opened the 'George Gregory Bookstore' at 1 Broad Street, with additional premises at 7 & 8 Green Street. He also had a sign painted on the wall of the old premises, directing customers to the shop in Broad Street. George Bayntun built on George Gregory's success as a bookseller, and in 1950 was appointed Bookseller to Her Majesty Queen Mary, echoing the accolade of almost half a century earlier. He also built up an international reputation as a bookbinder, and in 1939 moved his bookbinding business to the former Royal Mail sorting office in Manvers Street. The George Gregory Book Store remained at 8 Green Street, however, until 1983. George Bayntun's Booksellers and Bookbinders, now owned and managed by George Bayntun's great-grandson, Edward Bayntun-Coward, is still in Manvers Street, where George Gregory's name is commemorated in the name of the antique print gallery on the ground floor.

On the opposite corner, above the convenience store at 6 Argyle Street, is a far less straightforward ghost sign, which appears to consist of at least two sets of lettering (23). One of them reveals only a couple of fragmentary letters, but the other seems to read NUREMBURG HOUSE – an unusual designation, to say the least, and one for which we have found no record. However, between around 1858 and 1864 – a period which accords with the style of lettering – this building was known as the GERMAN HOUSE. The business was the brainchild of Simeon C Silverstone, identified in the 1861 census as of Prussian origin, although his wife came from Middlesex. Everything German was madly fashionable at the time, largely thanks to Prince Albert, who died in 1861, and Silverstone capitalised on this by offering a range of goods imported from Germany: ladies' and gentlemen's dressing cases, reticules, writing cases, bows and arrows, backgammon boards, toys, conjuring tricks, self-speaking and composition dolls, blotting books, jewellery, and, somewhat incongruously, 'every article in connection with [the] Manly and truly English game' of cricket. It lasted only a few years, and in 1866, Simeon Silverstone's household furniture and

PARLOUR CROQUET.

EXTRAORDINARY OPPORTUNITY.

ECONOMY in CHRISTMAS PRESENTS, NEW YEAR'S GIFTS, &c., &c.

S. C. SILVERSTONE,

GERMAN HOUSE, 6, ARGYLE STREET,

BEGS to announce that he has had consigned to him from Neurenberg, *for bona fide sale,* an Immense STOCK of the Newest and Choicest TOYS, CONJURING TRICKS, &c. Also, all the NEW GERMAN GAMES, with full instructions in English.—S. C. S. respectfully invites an Inspection of the above, being the best and largest Assortment in Bath, the whole of which is bound to be Sold, consequently NO REASONABLE OFFER WILL BE REFUSED.

In ENGLISH GOODS, GAMES, &c., &c., the Public will find a most Extensive Assortment, at a wonderful Reduction in Price.—Games of Every Description Lent on Hire, Illustrated Catalogues of which can be had Post-free.

OBSERVE!—GERMAN HOUSE, 6, ARGYLE STREET, Bath.

Top: The faded sign on N° 6 Argyle Street.

Above: An advertisement from 7 January 1864.

Left: Although we have found no images of N° 6 Argyle Street during Simeon Silverstone's tenancy, this photograph of the building in the late 1890s gives an idea what it would have looked like. Only the skeleton of this ornate early-nineteenth century shopfront survives today, with the central columns moved closer together to create a central lobby.

remaining stock in trade was sold at auction.[56] The question remains why, if in advertisement after advertisement in the *Bath Chronicle* – and he was an indefatigable publicist – he described his business as the German House, it should have had a sign proclaiming it to be the Nuremburg House? We do not know. All we can say is that, in an advertisement in 1864, he drew especial attention to a consignment of toys and conjuring tricks from 'Neurenberg' – a name the *Bath Chronicle* compositor was clearly unfamiliar with.[57]

Head down Grove Street before turning left to double back along a road leading to a tunnel under Argyle Street. Before going through the

tunnel, however, look to your right, to see a faded and fragmentary sign above the t r a d e s m e n ' s entrance to the Rajpoot restaurant. This was to direct potential customers to A Wills & Sons' builder's yard on the other side of the tunnel.

Carry on through the tunnel to Spring Gardens Road, turn right along a narrow walkway and look up to your right to see signs for A WILLS & SONS LTD (24). This collection of signs, dating from the mid-twentieth century, lies at the back of 15 Argyle Street, and recalls a

remarkable dynasty. Alfred Wills Sr was born in 1851 at 2 St Michael's Place (where the Little Theatre now stands). He was the fourth son of a plumber from Ilminster called William Wills. By the time he was ten, the family had moved to 18 Grove Street. In 1871, when he was 20, he married Elizabeth Dark from Twerton, moved to 2 Roebuck Place on the Lower Bristol Road and set up in business as a plumber on his own. Ten years later, by which time he had three sons and a daughter, the family were living at 5 Argyle Street.

The sign for A Wills & Sons can be seen on the right in this view from around 1950 of anglers on the old weir below Pulteney Bridge, with the remains of Bathwick Mill in the background

On 15 January 1885, his 'STOCK-IN-TRADE, FIXTURES and EFFECTS, comprising Pumps, cisterns, buoys, cyphons [sic], lead piping, wc basins, water cocks, a large assortment of brass taps, gas chandeliers, brackets, piping, globes, burners, &c, gas and oil stoves, paint, ochre, and oils, a general assortment of ironmongery, plated goods, &c, excellent mahogany counter, glass case, shelves, drawers, &c, suitable for drapers', was put up for auction. Whatever was the reason for this setback, it was only temporary. Less than a year later, the *Bath Chronicle* reported that he had been awarded the prestigious contract for 'plumbers' and zinc-workers' work' for 'the enlargement of the King's and Queen's Bath', amounting to £1,760.[58] The following year, he undertook the remodelling of the spa at Woodhall Spa in Lincolnshire under the direction of Major Davis, the Bath City Architect.

Spring Gardens Road around 1905, with the entrance to Wills & Sons' yard on the right.

GHOST SIGNS OF BATH

Alfred Wills was now based at 3 Argyle Place (where the United Reformed Church Halls now stand), but by 1892 had moved to 5a Argyle Street (now 2 Grove Street). By 1897 his business had expanded to take over the yard at Spring Gardens, south of Pulteney Bridge, and he was living in Spring Gardens House. All three of his sons joined the business, which was now styled 'Alfred Wills & Sons, Contractors & Plumbers', and in 1901 he was elected president of the Bath Master Builders Association. He died in 1904, after a short illness, at the age of 53, the mantle passing to his eldest son, also called Alfred.

By any reckoning, Alfred Wills Jr, who left school at the age of twelve to work alongside his father, was a remarkable man. It was his association with another remarkable Bathonian, however, that elevated his career from the mundane to the near legendary. Born at 32 Daniel Street in 1874 – two years after Alfred Wills – and with a name that all but ensured his life would be anything but ordinary, Melmoth Leicester Swale Gataker was the son of a Captain in the Bengal Staff Corps. By the time Alfred Wills met him, Gataker was living in Weston Super Mare and had a growing reputation as a water diviner. Gataker was called in to locate the springs feeding a troublesome well on Little Solsbury that Alfred Wills had contracted to improve. The two men hit it off instantly: Gataker realised that Wills could build the necessary infrastructure to extract any water he discovered; Wills realised that teaming up with someone in demand worldwide would be an astute business move. That was not all: Wills already seems to have acquired a

A view of the recreation ground around 1905 with Wills & Sons' yard on the left

reputation for clairvoyance. Now he discovered that he had the gift of dowsing, and before long Gataker was describing him as his assistant.

As an article published in 1918 indicates, it really was a case of 'today Grove Street, tomorrow the world':

> Mr Wills was invited by the Egyptian Government to go out with Mr Gataker ... to give advice on the water supplies of various areas. Mr Wills then met the now deposed Khedive, for whom actually he was working, and spent some time with him. He was driven across the desert in the Royal coach with an escort of native guards. This tour occupied about four months, and Mr Wills personally supervised native workmen. Two years later he went to Tunis, indirectly for the French Government, and was engaged at Nedjez-el-Bab, which is some distance inland, in connection with the water supply. In this case the firm sent out their own men from Bath to carry out or supervise the operations. Since that time Mr Wills has twice been to Portugal for British firms, and has travelled over a large portion of the continent, having visited Italy, Switzerland, Germany, Belgium, France and Spain. During the last few years the firm's contracts have extended from John o'Groat's to Land's End and from Derry to Cork.[59]

The profile was published not on account of the success of the firm of A Wills & Sons, but because Alfred Wills had just become mayor. He had been elected a Liberal councillor for Walcot in 1908 and was appointed chairman of the Surveying Committee in 1915. In 1917, as food shortages escalated, he was appointed chairman of a newly-formed Food Control Committee and introduced a local rationing scheme that was later adopted nationwide. After the war, he continued to serve as chairman of the Surveying Committee, overseeing the discussions that led to the 1925 Bath Corporation Act and playing a crucial role in the redevelopment of the city until he eventually stepped down in 1945. He died in 1949 at his home, Highbury,

Alfred Wills as mayor in 1918

on Sham Castle Lane, and his funeral service was held in the Argyle Congregational Church, which he had been born next door to and whose history he later wrote. His son, Norman, had taken over the running of the business some years earlier. It continued to operate out of the Argyle Street premises until 1968, when it moved to Cheltenham Street, and was last listed in the 1971 *Directory*.

To the left you will see a sign for NORTON DAIRIES RESTAURANT (25). Norton Dairies – which we will be coming across again later – has not had a restaurant here for well over 65 years. For many years there was a shop selling office equipment here, but now it is a Thai restaurant. Old photographs (such as that on page 57) show that the words NORTON DAIRIES RESTAURANT or NORTON DAIRIES CAFÉ were painted on the wall, although they looked very different to the sign here today, which has nothing ghostly or faded about it. It does, however, provide a sense of continuity with Bath's past.

Finally, if you carry on up the steps and round the corner, you will come to a patio area with Pulteney Bridge ahead and a couple of windows protected by bars on the right. There was once a public house called the Argyle Tap here. It opened in 1791, and was linked to the Argyle Coffee House and Tavern, which occupied the floors above. It was licensed and operated separately, however, and survived the closure of the coffee house and tavern in 1816, eventually closing some time in the early 1830s.[60] Inside the former Argyle Tap is a sign requesting customers to pay for their drinks when served, which probably dates from when the tap opened in 1791 (26). Although this is the only interior ghost sign we know of in Bath, there may well be others hidden from public view in dusty cellars or storerooms, and we would very much like to receive news of any such survivals. Sadly, just before publication, we learned that the Argyle Tap sign has been covered up by a false wall and is no longer visible. Until such time as it is revealed again, the rather murky photograph below will have to suffice as a reminder of this remarkable legacy of Bath's Georgian drinking culture.

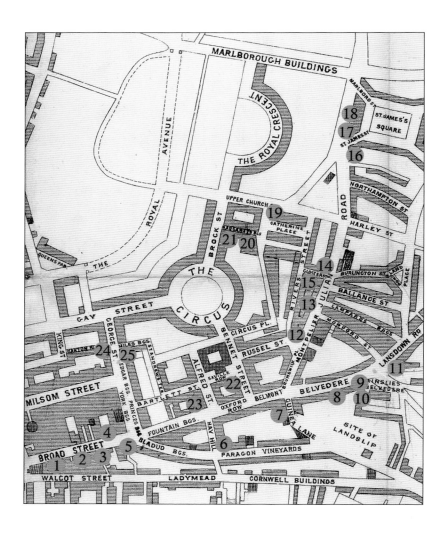

2

UPPER TOWN

Walk up the left-hand side of Broad Street, and, four doors up from the Saracen's Head, look across at N° 37 to see a sign for SYDENHAM BROS: REGD. PLUMBERS & SANITARY ENGINEERS (1). Although not especially old, this sign introduces us to another notable Bath dynasty.

James Sydenham, born in Wiveliscombe in 1832, was the son of an agricultural labourer. He moved to Bath as a teenager, and by the time of the 1851 census was living with a family in St James Street South. Ten years later, he had married and was living in Philip Street with his wife and a one-year-old son called Sydney. Both St James Street South and Philip Street are long gone, but 13 Broad Street, which he moved to around 1872, not only survives but still bears the name of the business he established here. By then, he had three sons – another would follow four years later – and a daughter. His two eldest sons, Sydney and Hector, followed him into the business, and carried it on after his death in 1889. Sydney, the eldest, never enjoyed robust health, and died, after a long illness, at the age of only 52. Despite this, and despite leaving school at an early age to join his father in the business, he not only served with distinction as a councillor but also made a major contribution to local historical research, as revealed in his obituary:

The death of Mr Sydney Sydenham removes a citizen who was passionately fond and proud of his native place. He took an intense pleasure in researches connected with the ancient history of Bath, and possessed a wonderful fund of local lore as regards buildings, personages, and other interesting details. [He] was an enthusiastic collector of Bath antiquities, and possessed an extremely interesting display of curios. His collection of Bath tokens is absolutely unique, while of prints, books, and other treasures he owned a rare assortment.[1]

What the obituary fails to mention is that he also wrote books on Bath trade tokens and a monograph on tokens issued by the city's pleasure gardens, and was an historical adviser to the 1909 Bath Pageant. He also contributed a chapter on 'Bath Buildings as Illustrated by Tokens of the Eighteenth Century' to Mowbray Green's *Eighteenth Century Architecture of Bath*.

He left six children, his eldest son, Henry, carrying on the business with Sydney's brother, Hector. Hector died in 1943, the business closed at around the same time, and the building was taken over by Coward & Gerrish, a printing firm from Kingsmead Street, who presumably moved here because their premises had been destroyed by bombing in 1942.

Carry on up Broad Street, and, four doors up from the corner of Saracen Street, look up to see a ghost sign, faded almost to nothing, high on the side wall of Nº 25 (2). Although better in some lights than others, it is impossible to decipher more than the odd few words of what, to the casual observer, is nothing more than a wall painted blue. It is, almost certainly, an advertisement for Nestlé's – the most faded of three such signs in the city – all of which are painted on blue backgrounds. One word that stands out is RICHEST – Nestlé's used the slogan 'RICHEST IN CREAM' – and the letter M, at the start of the word MILK, can be made out above it. At the bottom, sloping upwards to follow the roofline of the adjoining building, the word 'Grocery' can also be seen. Traces of other words are visible but only as faint, tantalising fragments.

As far as dating the sign goes, the earliest advertisement for Nestlé's found in the *Bath Chronicle* dates from 1885. However, 25 Broad Street only became a grocer's around 1890. Before that, it was home to a variety of businesses, including a hosier, an optician and a shoemaker. It continued to be a grocer's until after the Second World War, when it became a tailor's, before becoming a second-hand bookshop in the 1960s.

Next door but one to Nº 25 is the entrance to Broad Street Place. Over the centuries, many of Bath's street names have been painted onto the walls of buildings, and the practice still continues today. In most cases, the names have either been repainted or covered with modern street signs. There are, however, many instances of street names which have fallen into disuse. Generally, these were names of terraces lining roads such as Wellsway and the Upper and Lower Bristol Roads, which, as time went on, fell out of use, with the houses being renumbered as part of the main road. So it is that, all over the city, there are reminders of these old names in lettering growing fainter by the year.

We decided, at an early stage, that, whether or not these qualified as ghost signs, including them would not only be wandering perilously

close to train-spotter territory, but would make the book unfeasibly long. We have made a couple of exceptions, however. and one of them can be found on the right-hand side of the entrance to Broad Street Place, which, as you can see, was once called Gracious Court (3). It was originally known as Gracious – or Gratious – Street, and featured as such in John Wood's *Description of Bath*:

> GRATIOUS STREET is no more than a little Alley lying between *Waldcot [sic] Street* and *Broad Street*; it is about seven Feet, eight Inches broad, contains fifteen Houses, and had its Name from the Builder, Mr *Gratious Stride*, a Carpenter of the City.[2]

It was renamed Gracious Court in 1773, but, while its name may have fooled the unwary into imagining it a haven of elegance, a visit would soon have dispelled their illusions. John Wood also described the buildings in the Walcot Street area as 'for the most part ... Hovels for the Refuse of the People', and these certainly fitted that description.[3] They were so shoddily built that, on 8 November 1827, the *Bath Chronicle* reported that on 'Thursday the back and part of the interior of three houses in Gracious-court, Broad-street, fell with a tremendous crash; but the inhabitants (having been forewarned by a cracking noise) fortunately escaped without injury'.[4] And it was appallingly crowded. At the time of the 1851 census, when the number of houses lining this narrow alley had risen to 19 – four of which were uninhabited – exactly 100 people were recorded as living here. Not surprisingly, it had an unenviable reputation, so much so that in 1865, 'at the request of the inhabitants, the name of Gracious court, Broad-street, was changed to Broad-street place'.[5]

This means that the name painted on the wall must be well over 150 years old. But, if the inhabitants thought that a change of name would solve their problems, they were mistaken. This report from 1927 – when the number of houses seems to have risen again, to at least 22 – recalls an aspect of Bath's past often overlooked:

> Mr Albert Edward Baker, a jobbing gardener and his wife have resided at 22, Broad Street Place for 12 years, and they have a family of six children, the eldest being 17 and the youngest an infant of 15 months. Some time ago the house was certified as unfit for habitation, and a week last Monday the Bath Municipal authorities served a statutory notice on the owner of the property 'to take down, secure or repair the said dangerous building, within a space of three days after this notice, and complete the work as quickly as the nature of the case will admit'.
>
> The work was put in hand at once, but the occupants were faced by the fact that they could not find another habitation. As the work of the builders proceeded, the family were driven downstairs. At present they occupy the kitchen and one bedroom on the floor above only. A substitute for a roof has been made by the kindly builders, who have provided a canvas covering, but, in spite of this, the discomfort and inconvenience – not to say danger – experienced by the occupants are great.
>
> The case throws a lurid light on the problems presented by the shortage of suitable houses at cheap rents. Mrs Baker stated that she and her husband have made every possible endeavour to secure another place of abode, but their search has been fruitless. The first question she is asked, she says, is 'How many children have you got?' and on being given the answer, has received the reply: 'I am sorry, but you have got too many' ...
>
> The builders are now starting to rebuild the chimney and replace the roof. Afterwards they will deal with the front of the house, in which there is a pronounced bulge. Mrs Baker is now wondering how the family will be able to get into the two rooms when this operation is commenced.[6]

The buildings in Broad Street Place were demolished in the 1960s, and today it is an oasis of calm at the heart of the city, with little save the ghostly traces of its former name to remind us of what once stood here.

Further up Broad Street, on the left-hand side is a large archway. Once the entrance to York House Mews, it now leads to a municipal car park. There appears to have been writing on both sides of the archway: to the left the letter R can be made out with an A above it; on the right is another R (4). If you walk through the archway, you will see, on the left at the end, a small rectangle, painted dark red. In it, if the light is right, you may be able to make out the start of the word OFFICE. It used to be much clearer, and a manicule

could be seen as well, but it has now faded almost away.

Faded lettering on the left and right-hand sides of the archway

York House Mews was for many years home to one of the city's top livery stables. In 1872, James Stuckey from Clevedon took over the business from a Mr Ashplant, and in a subsequent advertisement described it as a 'Job, Posting and Funeral Establishment'. By 1890, the vehicles offered for hire included 'Landaus, Victorias, Phaetons, Dog Carts, &c, Large and Small Breaks [sic] and Waggonettes, Wedding Carriages of the Best Description'.[7] James Stuckey died in 1906 and the Bath Carriage Company, which he had helped establish, took over the business.

By now, motor vehicles were starting to replace horse-drawn carriages, and in 1916 the business was taken over by Ernest Ames, who already owned livery stables and a garage in Circus Mews. In 1920, he advertised 'pleasure brakes for picnic parties', as well as 'motor hearses and motor landaulettes' for hire.[8] Horses still had a part to play, however, for he also advertised 'funeral hearses and carriages for hire with black or bay horses'.[9] By 1922, however, he had moved out of York House Mews to concentrate on building up his business in Circus Mews. No one took over from him at York House Mews, and the next we hear of the premises is in 1932, when the council decided to demolish the stables, coach houses and garages which covered much of the site and turn the area into a municipal car park.

As for the ghost signs, the lettering on either side of the archway looks as though it once read GARAGE, while the small sign through the archway pointed to the office of the livery stables or garage.

Cross at the traffic lights at the top of Broad Street, where you will see, to the left of the newsagents, a gilded number 17, somewhat distressed but still eye-catching, and raising the question of what else might lie waiting to be discovered under the paint of the fascia board (5).

Carry on past Topping & Company, Booksellers, at 3 Bladud Buildings, and, at the lights, cross the main road and turn right to the bottom of Hay Hill, where you will see a sign for Hay Hill Dairy (6).

Hay Hill Dairy had a comparatively short life. First listed in the 1868 *Directory*, it was established by Alfred Taylor, born the son of a brushmaker at Coburg Square in Melksham in 1841. The 1868 *Directory* lists him as a dairyman, but in the 1871 census he is recorded as a 'butter factor', while the 1881 census has him as a 'milk and provision merchant'. By the time of 1884 *Directory*, he had become a 'farmer and butter merchant' and, as well as having the dairy on Hay Hill, was 'also at Bridge Farm, Bathford'.

Although the business had clearly done well, that is the last we hear of it, as Alfred Taylor had decided on a change of career. In the 1886 *Directory* he is listed as a baker and confectioner at 8 New Bond Street, and shortly afterwards a Deaf & Dumb Home was established in the old Hay Hill Dairy.

We will be coming across Alfred Taylor again later, but for now walk up Hay Hill, turn right up Belmont and then right down Guinea Lane to see a ghost sign for William Cottell, furniture remover, on Nº 17 (7).

William Cottell was born around 1860, the son of a haulier and coal merchant who lived on Margaret's Hill, behind Walcot Parade. He set up in business on his own as a haulier and furniture remover, a trade which must have come in handy given the number of times he moved house. In 1891 he was at 6 St Swithin's Place; ten years later he was at 2 Brunswick Street. By 1904, he had moved to 26 Brunswick Street, in 1906 he was at 1a Walcot Parade, but by 1908 he was at 17 Guinea Lane, where his sign still survives. He was here for less than five years, however, for in 1913 he was at 114 Walcot Street.

Head back up to Lansdown Road and continue on up Belvedere. After passing Belvedere Villas on your right, look up ahead to the side wall of Nº 30 to see a sign advertising LONG & SON ... DECORATORS, GENERAL CON-TRACTORS (8). The stonework of this building was patched and repointed in 2015, but, although the sign is now less clear, it has survived virtually intact.

George Long was born in Bath around 1823. In the 1861 census, he was described as a 'master painter' and was living at 3 Camden Row with his wife, Harriet, and four children. Ten years later, he had moved to 30 Belvedere and was working as a 'painter and glazier'. By 1881, now nearing 60, he was still at 30 Belvedere and working as a 'house decorator'. His eldest son, Arthur, had married and moved a little way up the hill to Ainslie's Cottage, where he too was working as a painter. His second son, Ernest, aged 22, meanwhile, was living at home and working as a 'painter, [sign]writer and grainer'.

Sometime after this, Arthur moved to 35 Belvedere, five doors up from his father, and went into partnership with his brother Ernest. We only know about this because, in February 1890, the *Bath Chronicle* carried a notice to the effect

> that the Partnership heretofore subsisting between ... ARTHUR WILLIAM LONG and ERNEST LONG carrying on business at 35 Belvedere and the Rear of Belvedere in the City of Bath as Decorators under the style or firm of Long Brothers has been Dissolved by Mutual Consent as from this date all debts due and owing to or by the late firm will be received and paid by the said Arthur William Long.[10]

By the time of the 1891 census, George Long had moved out of 30 Belvedere, and Ernest, now described as a 'house decorator', was living there with his wife Sarah, whom he had married in 1887, and a one-year-old son. Arthur, still at Nº 35, was now described as a contractor.

The following decade saw tragedy overtake the family. Arthur died in 1898, at the age of 47; Ernest died a year later, aged only 39. He had been cleaning the top-floor windows at the back of Nº 30 one Saturday afternoon, when he lost his footing, falling about 30 feet, crashing through the roof of a greenhouse and landing in the yard. He was rushed to the Royal United Hospital, but never regained consciousness, dying of his injuries four days later.[11]

In the 1901 *Directory* the two brothers' widows are listed as running lodging houses at 30 and 35 Belvedere. As for George Long, having retired to 12 Berkeley Place on Snow Hill, he outlived both his sons, dying in 1921 at the age of 98.

Carry on up Belvedere to Nº 27a/b (on the corner of Caroline Place) to see a sign for 'Bosley, Slater. Plasterer, House Sign and Decorative Painter, Glazier, &c' (**9**). Robert Bosley came to Bath from Lydeard St Lawrence in west Somerset, where he was born around 1788. He is first recorded as a slater and plasterer on Lansdown Road in the 1826 *Directory*. In 1838, his wife, Elizabeth, died at the age of 43,

'leaving eight children to lament the loss of an affectionate and tender mother'.[12] The following year, he married Jane Hutton, over 20 years his junior, from Farmborough, and proceeded to father a further two children.

In December 1850, when he was in his early sixties,

> Mr Bosley, slater and plasterer, of Ainslie's Belvedere, was engaged in repairing the roof of N° 6, Richmond Place, Beacon Hill. Having occasion to go to the roof of some premises adjoining, he placed a ladder from one roof to the other, and was proceeding across it with a large stone in his hand, when, owing to the tiles being slippery, the ladder gave way, and the unfortunate man was precipitated to the ground, a distance of between 30 and 40 feet, alighting in his descent on top of an outbuilding. He was taken up insensible, and removed to his residence, where medical aid was promptly in attendance. On examination, it was found that Mr Bosley had broken three of his ribs, fractured his elbow, and injured his spine, besides having sustained several severe bruises. His recovery is almost hopeless.[13]

Robert Bosley was made of tougher stuff than his premature obituarist gave him credit for. He not only survived, but returned to work in partnership with his son William, who lived at 3 Hay Hill. Not until 1869 was 'the PARTNERSHIP ... in the trade of Slaters and Plasterers ... carried on at N° 1a, Ainslie's Belvedere, in the city of Bath, under the Name or Style of "BOSLEY and SON" ... dissolved by mutual consent'.[14] Robert Bosley died two years later at the age of 83. The odd thing is that none of the references to him in newspapers or censuses mention him being a signwriter, although, on the evidence of the sign he left behind him, he was a very good one.

Step round the corner and look up, as we move from what is possibly Bath's most exquisite and artistically assured ghost sign to what would have been, when new, its biggest, boldest and brashest (10). Today it has faded almost to nothing, but its scale is still apparent; it would look more at home in the downtown of an American city than in a quiet backwater of Georgian Bath.

Although a few words at the top are easy enough to make out, much of the sign is indecipherable. The first four lines read

FOR

SAFE MILK

THE BATH & SOMERSETSHIRE

DAIRY CO LTD

After that there are just scraps of lettering – the letters REA probably forming part of the word CREAM or CREAMERY, and what look like the words TRY COWS, but everything else has just about vanished.

Another odd thing about this sign is that there does not seem to have been a dairy here – bootmakers, confectioners and bakers all operated in this building at various times, but no dairy. Although there are instances of ghost signs on buildings that have no connection with what they are advertising – in much the same way that billboards operate today – in Bath they are the exception rather than the rule. All of which makes this very much the odd one out among Bath's ghost signs.

The Bath & Somersetshire Dairy Company originated in 1806 and became a limited company in 1882. Its head office and 'working dairy' was at 3 Bladud Buildings, and by the early twentieth century it had ten branches around the city – but not on Belvedere.[15] It was taken over by Norton Dairies around 1920.

Above: The logo of the Bath & Somersetshire Dairy Co in 1893.

Right: The 'working dairy' at 3 Bladud Buildngs – now Topping & Company, Booksellers – decorated for Queen Victoria's Diamond Jubilee in 1897.

Below: An advertisement from 1909.

BATH·IS·RENOWNED FOR·ITS·HEALING·SPRINGS

AND

THE BATH & SOMERSETSHIRE DAIRY C.º L.TD

FOR ITS

SAFE-GUARDED

MILK SUPPLY.

"The Times"
AFTER EXAMINATION WROTE
"THE LARGE POPULATION OF BATH IS NOW IN THE ENJOYMENT OF A REGULAR SUPPLY OF MILK OF FAULTLESS CHARACTER."

THE WORKING DAIRY (BY G.P.O.)
IS DAILY OPEN TO PUBLIC INSPECTION

ELEVEN HIGH-CLASS DAIRIES IN BATH.

Cross the main road at the traffic island, walk up to the corner of Morford Street and look across to Ye Old Farm House **(11)**. In 2003, when we published *Bath Pubs*, two pubs – the Belvedere Wine Vaults and Ye Old Farm House – faced each other across the road here.[16] Today, the Belvedere is a guest house, while Ye Old Farm House offers osteopathy and acupuncture. Memories of the Belvedere will, in all probability, soon fade, but the loss of the Farm House is likely to be rued for many years to come. Of all the signs featured in this book, this is the one we wish we did not have to include. Central Bath is not over-endowed with pubs built during that brief golden age at the end of the nineteenth century, when the wealth of breweries anxious to expand their trade coincided with

one of the high points of building design, and the monumental opulence of the Victorians was tempered by the expansive affability of the Arts and Crafts movement.[17] Ye Old Farm House not only looked – and looks – fantastic from the outside; it worked supremely well as a pub, and, in its heyday, was one of the best – and best designed – music venues in the city. More on Ye Old Farm House can be found on pages 274-76.

Heading down Morford Street, go through an archway on the left just past a small parking area. This leads into a courtyard in front of the Museum of Bath at Work, housed in an eighteenth-century real tennis court and an essential stop for anyone interested in ghost signs or the commercial, industrial and social history of the city. Turn right down the steps to Julian Road, and look to the right to see a sign for the Old Red House Bakery on the wall of 31 Rivers Street (12). We last

encountered Alfred Taylor at Hay Hill Dairy, which he left between 1884 and 1886 to take over the Old Red House Bakery, previously run by William Amery, at 8 New Bond Street. Mr Amery had been there since at least 1844, but Alfred Taylor claimed that the business was established in 1798, and, while he undoubtedly had good reason for this, no reference to it has been found before 1844, and, if it was founded in 1798, it was not founded in New Bond Street, work on which did not start until 1805.

To say that Alfred Taylor made a success of his new venture is something of an understatement. In 1893, less than a decade after he switched careers, he was elected president of the Master Bakers' Association of Great Britain and appointed a director of the annual exhibition organised by the baking and allied trades in London. He also opened a restaurant in the New Bond Street premises and became a wine and spirit merchant. His eldest son, Arthur, and his third son, Edward, followed him into

the baking business, but his second son, Alfred, became an architect, who in 1903 designed a new bakery for him on Walcot Street.

As well as building up a national reputation as a baker and confectioner, Alfred Taylor also found time to stand for the council. In 1880, while still at Hay Hill Dairy, he became a Liberal councillor for Walcot. He went on to served on several committees and eventually became an alderman.

The Old Red House in New Bond Street

After his death in 1909 at the age of 68, his eldest son continued to expand the business, opening branches at 17 Newbridge Road and 31 Rivers Street, and engaging his brother Alfred to redesign the New Bond Street premises. Alfred J Taylor not only became one of Bath's top architects; his daughter, Molly, who later took over his practice, went on to achieve even greater success, designing Bath's fire station and the city's greatest modernist building, Kilowatt House on Bathwick Hill. The Old Red House Bakery closed in 1978, and, although its name has long disappeared from its New Bond Street premises, in Rivers Street at least Alfred Taylor's legacy lingers on.

Turning right along Julian Road, the building on your right with a large Venetian window originally formed part of an eighteenth-century riding school, the rest of which was demolished in 1973 to build Jaguar House next door. A little further along, look across to 3 Rivers Street Place (three doors before the zebra crossing). Until 2015, this was a branch of McColl's. When it closed, the sign was removed to reveal an older one underneath, with the name KERR flanked by the words Newsagent & Tobacconist **(13)**. Frederick Cane opened a newsagent's and tobacconist's here in the

1940s, and the sign looks to date from this time. In the 1960s, the business was taken over by GM Kerr, who painted his name over Mr Cane's, but left the rest of the sign as it was. By the time you read this, the sign may well have been covered up again. It is included, however, to indicate the sort of thing that can suddenly appear in the most unlikely places.

Cross the zebra crossing and carry on to Gloucester Street, where the white rectangle on the curved corner of N° 2 indicates that a sign lies underneath (14). Indeed, the outlines of a letter or two can, if the light is right, still be made out. As early as 1800, Charles Skrine had a grocer's here, and a grocer's it remained, with numerous changes of ownership, until it became a greengrocer's shortly before the Second World War. Which of its many proprietors was responsible for the sign, however, must remain a mystery, at least until some of the paint which covers it is removed.

For now, though, turn down Gloucester Street to look at one of Bath's finest and most intriguing ghost signs on the bottom left-hand corner (15). The ghost sign on this building – 16 Rivers Street – is a palimpsest, with at least three different signs visible. As each was painted, the one underneath would have been covered up, but over time they have resurfaced, like forgotten voices from the past. What is astonishing is how clear much of the lettering is, and how straightforward it is, based on a knowledge of how signwriting styles evolved, to make an informed guess as to the sequence in which they were painted. First would have come the large black lettering, all of which, except for the top line, is italicised. The larger – and clearer – white lettering came next, followed by the smaller white lettering. (It is worth mentioning that, while the letters look black and white today, they may have been entirely different colours when first painted.)

Trying to make out what the signs said is complicated by the presence of the false window, on which the lettering is much less clear. The oldest set of lettering – curiously, the easiest to read – can be deciphered as M(-)LES / GROCER / AND TEA DEALER. It probably dates from the early 1830s, when Thomas Miles – first recorded in the 1833 *Directory* – opened a grocery shop here. In 1841, or thereabouts, the business was taken over by John Carter, who was here until 1875. Next came John Presley, who stayed until the early twentieth century, when Goodway & Cox took over. During all this time, it remained a grocer's. Such continuity is not only remarkable; it also gives us the probable names of those responsible for having the two later signs painted. Unfortunately, although plenty of words relating to the grocery business can be made out, we have not been able to detect anything that looks like CARTER or PRESLEY. Perhaps someone else will have more luck.

The sign at the back of N° 1 St James's Street

Turn right along Rivers Street, left at the end and right along Crescent Lane. Cross Julian Road at the zebra crossing, and turn left to look at the back of the building on the east corner of St James's Street (16).

This is the first of a set of three ghost signs which, although not that old – probably dating from the 1920s or 1930s – are among the most enigmatic in the city. They have not worn well and only a tentative stab can be made at deciphering them. On this one, scraps of four lines can be made out:

... OICE [or OFFICE?]

... CABS [or ... SABS?]

... CARS [or ... GARS?]

TE...ARS

GHOST SIGNS OF BATH

Turning to the twentieth-century history of this building (1 St James's Street): in 1901 it was occupied by James Scott, a bootmaker, by 1914 it was empty, but by 1920 it had been taken over by the Bristol Tramways & Carriage Co Ltd. A year later, Albert Davis, a taxi proprietor, had moved in. He was still here in 1930, but had become a tobacconist. He carried on as a tobacconist until after the Second World War, and by 1952 the business had become AG Davis & Sons. The chances are, then, that the sign was the work of Albert Davis. CABS and CARS suggest that it dates from when he was a cab proprietor. If, however, it is not CARS we are looking at, but GARS, this could be part of CIGARS, which would date from after he had switched to being a tobacconist.

For the second of the signs, carry on for a few metres and look across at a faded sign above the entrance to N° 11, on the west corner of St James's Street (17). This sign is even more frustrating. It consists of only five words, of which the first two and the last can be read easily: 'Get Your .... Here'. The other two words are bigger, but written in a curious font that has so far defied interpretation.

The sign above the entrance to N° 11 St James's Street.

Carry on to look at the back wall of N° 11, and another baffling sign (18). Above the word JAGUAR, in large white letters, is the original trademark of the company which later became Jaguar Cars. Founded in 1922 as the Swallow Sidecar Company, it later moved on from making sidecars for motorcycles to building bodies for cars. Although the cars were sold under the name 'Jaguar', the company was known as 'SS Cars'. The letters 'SS' appeared on the head of a stylised eagle and can just be made out on this ghost sign. Not surprisingly, given the notoriety attached to these initials after their use by another organisation during the Second World War, the name of the company was changed to Jaguar in 1945.

So far so good, but if you scroll down, past fragments of paint which, if they ever made up words, have long ceased to do so, you should be able

to make out fragments of some more words, with the roofline of a former lean-to running through them. There are two lines. Part of the first one appears to read CORNER HOUSE, while the second contains the letters ARETTES which can only be part of the word CIGARETTES.

As for the twentieth-century history of the building: in 1901 it was a dairy, but after the First World War it was taken over by Arthur John Burcombe, who established a taxi and car hire business here. By 1930, it had become 'Burcombe Bros', described in the 1934 *Directory* as 'taxi-cab proprietors, engineers and petrol-service station and chimney sweeps'. Quite how sweeping chimneys fitted in with the rest of their operations is unclear, but their cars and taxis were garaged on Crescent Lane, and their own brand of petrol – Burcombe's Special Mixture – was available from the petrol station at the top of Marlborough Lane. Curiously, though, one thing lacking from any of their numerous advertisements in the *Bath Chronicle* is any mention of Jaguar cars.

Jaguar cars were, however, a mainstay of another company based nearby, in part of the old riding school you saw earlier. This was Brown's Garages, an agent for Jaguar in the 1930s. When the agency was renewed in 1945, they renamed the building Jaguar House, a name still carried by the flats that now occupy the site. This suggests that the Jaguar sign on 11 St James's Street advertised Brown's rather than Burcombe's, but whether there was any connection between the two businesses or Brown's simply paid to have a sign painted in a prominent position is unclear.[18] As for the words CORNER HOUSE and CIGARETTES, these probably date from around 1950, when a Mrs Lodder was a 'shopkeeper' here.

Retrace your steps to Rivers Street and take the first right into Catharine Place to find a ghost sign on Nº 15 at the end **(19)**. The MEDICAL AND SURGICAL HOME was a private nursing home which operated from the late nineteenth century to the late 1940s, and which, according to the directories, occupied 8 Upper Church Street and 16 Catharine Place. As these are opposite Nº 15, on the south side of the street, it is unclear why the sign was painted here.

Turn left and then right

into Margaret's Buildings to look up to the left above Nº 9 (**20**). Although only the central section of this ghost sign is legible, enough survives to deduce that it once read

FRAMPTON

CARPENTER & JOINER

John Shellard Frampton was born in Hanham around 1837, and grew up in Weston village. His father was a jobbing carpenter, who taught him his trade. He married in 1862 and by 1871 was a master carpenter, living at 7 Circus Mews. Shortly afterwards, he moved to 9 Margaret's Buildings, and by 1881 both his eldest son and his father were working for him as carpenters. A detailed account of the business, published in 1893, described it as consisting of a warehouse at the front and workshops at the back:

> The warehouse is replete with general ironmongery, brushes, china and earthenware, table and ornamental glass, wood and galvanised pails, saucepans, kettles, and all kinds of culinary and kitchen requisites, chamois leathers, housemaids' gloves, sponges, &c. The proprietor also undertakes every branch of carpentry, cabinetmaking, building, and general house repairs, for which estimates are supplied, and, in addition, conducts funeral furnishing on the most moderate scale of charges. The business in each department is of the most substantial order.[19]

On 18 March 1893, however, disaster struck, when

> an alarm of fire at Catherine Mews, at the rear of Brock-street, was given, and the Fire Brigade and Police were soon in attendance. The outbreak occurred in the carpenter's shop of Mr Frampton, who has a hardware and brush shop in Margaret's-buildings, close by, but the flames spread so quickly that the stables and coach-houses of Mr Goldsworthy and Mr James, immediately adjoining, were soon affected. The huntsman of the Bath Harriers, a man named Barnfather, was the first to give the alarm, and happily there was time to remove a number of valuable horses before they were suffocated, though the task was by no means an easy one, the animals being greatly frightened by the glare and smoke. Several broughams belonging to medical men and other residents in the neighbourhood also were speedily taken to places of safety, but some of the vehicles were badly damaged. The

firemen – both brigade and police – worked with a will, but owing to the inflammable nature of the contents of the building in which the fire originated, more than an hour elapsed before the conflagration was fully got under [sic] and all danger of the flames spreading removed. Mr Frampton, whose workshop was gutted, is insured (though only partially), and so are the owners and tenants whose property suffered. Being in the midst of a residential neighbourhood the outbreak created much alarm.[20]

John Frampton's business survived this setback, and he remained at 9 Margaret's Buildings until his death in 1910, aged 73.

Head along Margaret's Buildings to look above the door of N° 2 on the left (**21**). Although purists may argue that this is not a ghost sign, it has most assuredly been painted over, and Bass's famous red triangle now appears, like Tom Pearce's grey mare, ghastly white. Bass first labelled its bottles

of India Pale Ale with a red triangle in 1855, and was constantly resorting to legal action to stop competitors using misleadingly similar logos and unscrupulous tradesmen filling its empty bottles with inferior brews and selling them as the real thing. When the government passed a Trade Mark Registration Act in 1875, Bass ensured that one of its employees was at the head of the queue when the registrar's office opened for the first time, thus making the red triangle Britain's oldest registered trademark. It was also one of best known, featuring in Manet's painting, *A Bar at the Folies-Bergère*, as well as on many of Picasso's canvases. It also made an honourable appearance in that paean to the noble art of drinking (among much else), James Joyce's *Ulysses*:

> During the past four minutes or thereabouts [Bloom] had been staring hard at a certain amount of number one Bass bottled by Messrs Bass and Co at Burton-on-Trent which happened to be situated amongst a lot of others right opposite to where he was and which was certainly calculated to attract anyone's remark on account of its scarlet appearance. He was simply and solely, as it subsequently transpired for reasons best known to himself, which put quite an altogether different complexion on the proceedings, after the moment before's observations about boyhood days and the turf, recollecting two or three private transactions of his own which the other two were as mutually innocent of as the babe unborn. Eventually, however, both their eyes met and as soon as it began to dawn on him that the other was endeavouring to help himself to the thing, he involuntarily determined to help him himself and so he

accordingly took hold of the neck of the medium-sized glass recipient which contained the fluid sought after and made a capacious hole in it by pouring a lot of it out with, also at the same time however, a considerable degree of attentiveness in order not to upset any of the beer that was in it about the place.[21]

N°s 1 and 2 Margaret's Buildings were, from the 1870s to the 1970s, part of a grocery store, which also included 24 Brock Street. It started out as Ransom & Sons, then became Kempster's, Shirley & Ridge's, and finally Norris's West End Stores. At times it was also a wine merchant's, but seems to have sold bottled beer from the start, and the famous red triangle was well placed to catch shoppers' eyes as they entered the store.

A dray delivering Mackeson to Norris's West End Stores

Turn left along Brock Street, cross the Circus and head along Bennett Street, past the Assembly Rooms, to the corner of Saville Row. The ghost sign here is easy to miss and, even when the late afternoon sun shines on it between May and September, it is difficult to decipher very much (22). On the bottom line the word GROCER is fairly clear; then, after a gap, comes DEALER, with the ghost of an A in front, suggesting that the sign originally read GROCER & TEA DEALER. On the top line all that can be made out is CORN, which initially we thought may have been followed by MERCHANT, even though this would have been an unusual trade to combine with that of grocer and tea dealer, especially in such a genteel part of the city.

This building – its address variously given as 6 Bennett Street or 8 Saville Row – has been a shop for a very long time, and, while the style of lettering indicated that the sign probably dated from the early nineteenth century, we thought the chances of ascribing it to a particular occupant were pretty remote. Then we looked in the 1800 *Directory*, to find, listed at 8 Saville Row, James Cornwell, Grocer & Dealer. Despite going back to look at the sign and searching in vain for the letters that would have followed CORN, it seemed likely that this was our man. He was still there in 1819, but by 1826 another grocer, called John Elliott, had taken over. To see if we could track him back any earlier than 1800, we looked

Above: The sign on the corner of Bennett Street and Saville Row.

Below: A detail of the sign showing 'CORN' and 'GROCER'.

Bottom: Another detail showing '...A DEALER'.

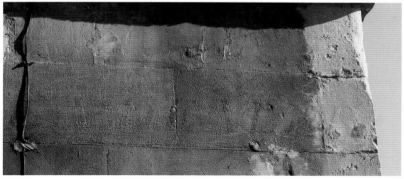

at the 1792 *Directory*, to find James Cornwell listed as a haberdasher in Bennett Street, although with no number given. There are three possible explanations for this curious anomaly: perhaps the editor of the 1792 *Directory* got it wrong, entering 'haberdasher' instead of 'grocer'; or maybe this was another James Cornwell – possibly the father of the one who became a grocer; it could also be that it was the same James Cornwell, who decided on a change of career. The lack of any other information makes it impossible to say which was the case; what we can say is that this rather insignificant sign probably dates from before 1800 and cannot be any later than the early 1820s.

Walk down Saville Row, cross and turn left along Alfred Street, turn right at the end, and, wedged between the back of N° 1 Alfred Street and Mandalyns pub, you will see a wall with blocked-up windows and a door with a combination lock **(23)**. This was N° 12 Fountain Buildings, built in the late eighteenth century and occupied until the 1950s. Now just the façade remains, and the door leads into the garden of N° 1 Alfred Street. But the façade has a ghost sign – a very shadowy ghost sign, it is true – but a ghost sign nonetheless.[22] It also has a special claim to fame, for this is a ghost sign on a ghost building.

If you look to the left of the blocked-up first-floor windows you will see some lettering that appears to date from the early nineteenth century. At the top is a word starting with the letters 'HOL'. Then, after what seems to be another word, 'and' appears in lower case. Below it is another word beginning with what appears to be an 'L' or an 'E'. The rest of the letters in the word are very indistinct, although the third letter seems to have a thick diagonal stroke which may have been part of a 'Z'.

The earliest reference to N° 12 Fountain Buildings comes in the 1826 *Directory* when James Davidge, a shoemaker, was living here. It subsequently had a high turnover of tenants. These included Robert Nash, chairman (1846-50); Solomon Price, livery-stable proprietor (1852); William Blandford, fly proprietor, and Mrs Blandford, greengrocer (1860-64); the Misses Francis and Dayer, dressmakers, Fred Byrt, painter, and Mrs and Miss Byrt, dressmakers (1868-70); Mrs Elizabeth Gibbon (1876); Charles Castle, mason (1878); Joseph Newton, upholsterer (1880); and James Stone, groom (1884). None of these names or trades has any obvious connection with what remains of the sign, which, judging by the style of writing, may well date from before 1826 anyway.

So a mystery it must remain for the time being. One possibility is that the first word may be HOLLAND – possibly someone's surname or more likely part of the phrase HOLLAND CLOTH. As for the building, it was still occupied – by a Mr Arthur Raleigh Jones – in 1957, but he died the following year, and, as N° 12 is omitted from subsequent *Directories*, it seems that his demise was followed by its reduction to a mere façade.

The sign on N° 12 Fountain Buidings

Carry on down Fountain Buildings and turn right along George Street. Two doors along from where the broad pavement narrows, stop outside Nº 16 and look across to the chimneystack above Nº 6 – now Instant Vintage – where you will see the words FRUIT and FLOWERS (24).

These date from the first decade of the twentieth century when Arthur Vaughan opened a fruiterer's and florist's here.

Arthur Edwin Vaughan was born in 1871, the son of Edwin Vaughan, landlord of the Garrick Hotel on Park Row in Bristol. Three years later, his father went bankrupt and by the time of the 1881 census had moved to Ealing, where he was running a pub on Kew Bridge Road. By 1891, Edwin had died, and his widow, who was originally from Bath, was living with her five children in the red-brick cottage near the Bladud's Head in Larkhall and working in the laundry, owned by the Royal United Hospital, attached to it. Arthur, her eldest son, was working as a wine-merchant's assistant.

By 1901, Arthur was married with two children, running a fruiterer's and florist's at 6 George Street, and living above the shop. The business prospered. Around 1909 he moved his family across the street to Nº 16 and commissioned Spackman & Sons to design an art-nouveau style shopfront for Nº 6, with full-height curved-glass windows flanking the entrance, where brass letters, spelling out Vaughan's name, were set in marble. The sign on the chimneystack also dates from this time, as does the art-nouveau style sign bracket still in use today.

In 1913, he decided to build on his success by taking a 5/16 stake in the Vaudeville Picture House in Westgate Street, which stood on the east corner of the entrance to St Michael's Place. For a time all went well, but in 1922, as a result of increased competition and a fall in revenue, the partnership was dissolved and he became sole proprietor of the cinema, assuming liabilities of £1,791. He gave up the shop in George Street and, after being declared bankrupt, moved to Cheltenham and took a job in the commercial department of a newspaper. He died in 1936 at the age of 66.

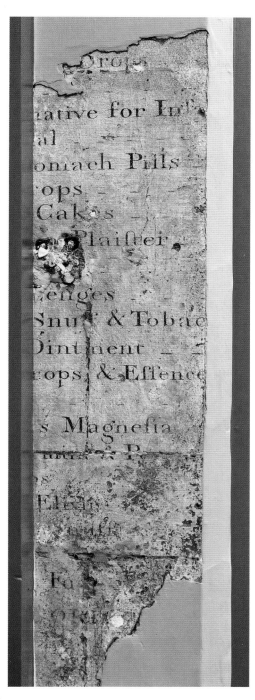

Two doors along from Nº 16, on the corner of Miles's Buildings, we come to the earliest ghost sign in Bath and one of the earliest anywhere **(25)**.

When the Porter pub was being refurbished in 2013, some of the render which covered the Bath stone was removed, revealing some mysterious lettering. For fear of damaging what remained, work stopped on this portion of wall, leaving a scattering of words exposed. These include 'Stomach Pills, ...rops [probably sirops, the eighteenth-century spelling of syrups], Cakes, Plaister, Snuff and Tobacco, Ointment, ...rops and Essence, Magnesia, ... and Perfume'. Further down, the word 'Elixir' is visible. Just as curious as this inventory of archaic items is the style in which it is written. 'Essence' and 'Magnesia' feature the 'long s' – the letter that looks like an f but with only half a cross bar. This was only used within words; a normal 's' was used at the beginning and end of words, and we can see that here too. We can also see that all the nouns have capital letters. The 'long s' had virtually disappeared by the end of the eighteenth century – so much so that antiquarians use its presence or absence to date undated books. Beginning all nouns with capital letters became fashionable in the early eighteenth century, was ubiquitous by 1750, but then abruptly went out of fashion so that it too had vanished by 1800.[23]

While the indications are that this sign dates from before 1800, discovering who commissioned it is more problematic. The items advertised are an eclectic mix, but all of them were routinely sold by hairdressers and perfumers at this time, and late eighteenth-century advertisements in the *Bath Chronicle* suggest several possible candidates.

At first sight, the most likely are Richard Warren or R Carpenter. Warren was a highly respected and well-known perfumer, based in the City of London, with a branch in Tunbridge Wells, and shops licensed to sell his wares in Margate, Deal, Dover, Rochester, and Brighthelmstone (Brighton). In 1772, he supplied Mr Banks – later Sir Joseph Banks – with some of the provisions for his second voyage with Captain Cook.

Warren also set up a business in Bath. In 1771, he was described as 'late of N. Parade, Bath, now of London' but he had returned by 1774, when his shop in Bath is described as being on 'St Andrew's Terras [sic] leading from Miles's Court [now Miles's Buildings] to the New Assembly Rooms'.[24] However, he moved shortly afterwards into a shop 'in Bennett Street fronting the Assembly Rooms'.[25] What was meant by fronting? If it meant 'opposite to', it would have been in Bennett Street or possibly in Saville Row; if it meant 'on the front of', it would have been in the colonnade on the north side of the Assembly Rooms. Originally intended as a storage place for sedan chairs, this colonnade was soon converted to shops to earn more money for the proprietors. Another perfumer, Nathaniel Jones, had a shop in the colonnade in the 1780s. This may have been the shop previously occupied by Warren, who in 1778 placed a notice in the *Bath Chronicle* announcing his removal from Bennett Street 'to Mrs Carpenter's, milliner and haberdasher, in George Street, fronting Miles's Court, Bath.'[26]

In 1780, an advertisement appeared in which Mrs Carpenter assured the 'publick' that she had a fresh assortment of millinery and haberdashery. The advertisement also included the following announcement:

> R. Carpenter, Perfumer, at the Golden Sheaf, in George Street, leading from the upper end of Milsom Street to Gay Street, truly sensible of the many favours received from his friends and the publick, most respectfully informs them he continues selling Mr RICHARD WARREN's Perfumery as usual, and has this day received a fresh assortment for the present season. – In order to give his friends and the publick general satisfaction, he has also laid in a stock of every other noted man's perfumery in the kingdom, which he is determined to sell on the very lowest terms.[27]

Although this is clearly the shop to which Warren had moved two years earlier, it is possible that, by now, Mr Carpenter, far from acting as his agent, was operating in competition. Warren now had his own shop in Alfred Street, and in 1782 took steps to warn the public that 'a base mendicant composition', purporting to be Warren's Milk of Roses, was being offered for sale, and advising them that the genuine article was only available from selected outlets.[28] The Golden Sheaf in George Street was not one of the outlets listed. Mr Carpenter later turned his skills to running an academy in George Street, and offering an accountancy service.[29]

Confusing though all this is, it seems to suggest that either Warren or Carpenter may have had the sign on the Porter painted around 1780. However, there is (appropriately, given the items listed) a fly or two in the ointment. First, none of the advertisements placed in the *Bath Chronicle* by Warren or Carpenter mention snuff – and it appears twice on the ghost sign. Second, we are once again presented with the word 'fronting'. Street numbering in early directories is often absent or inconsistent, but the 1800 *Directory* lists R Carpenter at 5 George Street, which is opposite the Porter. So once again – does fronting mean opposite?

This brings us to the other possible candidate – William Woollard, who started out as a peripatetic hairdresser, working first with someone called Davis and then on his own.[30] In the winter, when Bath was full of fashionable visitors, he plied his trade at a grocer's shop in Bond Street, but, when the visitors left, so did he, moving first between towns where race meetings were being held, such as Exeter, Bridgwater, Blandford and Sherborne, before spending the summer in Weymouth. However, by 1777, although still travelling to race meetings, he had settled in Miles's Court.[31] In 1778, he described himself as a hairdresser and perfumer, selling 'Cephalick Essence for Nervous Headaches' and a 'great choice of Snuffs from Harham, Arnold, &c. &c.'[32] So successful was he, that four years later he moved to larger premises in Fountain Buildings.[33]

Woollard's 'great choice of Snuffs', along with an address in 'Miles's Court', does seem to clinch the matter, although, with so little to go on, it is impossible to be certain. Whoever commissioned the sign, however, all the indications are that it dates from around 1780, which makes it a very early ghost sign indeed – certainly the earliest we have found in Bath. Unfortunately, parts of it have been lost, due to the corner of the building having been chamfered and a new shopfront inserted, but more of its secrets – possibly including the elusive name of the shopkeeper – may still lie hidden beneath the render.

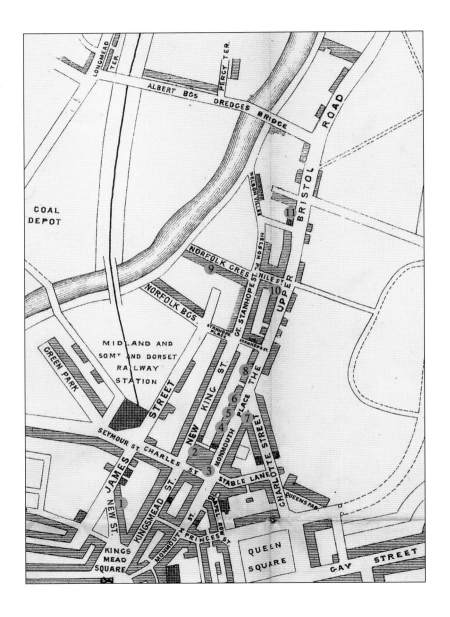

3

UPPER BRISTOL ROAD

This walk starts in New Street, at the south-west corner of Kingsmead Square, outside the furniture store of SILCOX, SON & WICKS (1). Here, as with the House of Tupra, we come to the thorny question of

whether you can have a ghost sign for a business that is still trading. This is one of Bath's oldest and best-known businesses, whose sales regularly attract hordes of people, some of whom are prepared to sleep outside overnight to be first in line to snap up the bargains. Francis Silcox established himself as a cabinet maker around 1900 at 2 Sydenham Buildings, opening a shop on New Street shortly before the First World War. Originally in N° 5, it later expanded into 6 and 7, as more family members joined the business, and now occupies 14 rooms on seven levels. It also has the rare distinction of having its own ghost sign.

At the end of New Street, turn right along James Street West and right at the lights along Charles Street. At the pedestrian lights, cross and walk along New King Street for a few metres to see a ghost sign on the side wall of the Christadelphian Hall (2).

Like many of Bath's best ghost signs, this one advertised a very short-lived business. The Marvel Cycle Company, first listed at this address in the 1898 *Directory*, had gone by 1902. The company, which was based in Birmingham, had a slightly longer run, but still seems to have lasted less than a decade, with no reference found to it before 1896 or after 1905. Surprisingly, given its obvious willingness to attract customers, it placed no advertisements in the *Bath Chronicle*, nor did the *Chronicle* see fit to report on any of its activities. The only newspaper that seems to have referred to the company's operations in Bath was the *Bristol Mercury*, which on 9 February 1898, as part of a review of *The Gay Parisienne*, a musical comedy at Bath's Theatre Royal, mentioned that

MARVEL
CYCLE CO.
MAKERS OF
the 'MARVEL' &
NORTHAMPTON

FOR HIRE
LADIES, GENTS & LADIES
REPAIRS

STRUCTE
ST STYLE
DING

'the bicycles used by the ladies in Act I are supplied by the Marvel Cycle Manufacturing Company, New King Street, Bath'.[1]

The Marvel Cycle Company was one of many such companies that sprang up – and, more often than not, sprang back down again – in the golden age of cycling before the First World War. After the shop here closed, the building was taken over by a Christian sect called the Campbellites, or Disciples of Christ, and today is a Christadelphian Hall.[2] Curiously, although it bears a datestone of 1880, N° 56 does not appear in a *Directory* until 1898, when the Marvel company took it over. Although its original function is unclear, there was a Dr Barnardo's Home next door, at N° 55, and N° 56 may have been built as a hall or chapel, before being disposed of to the Marvel company.

Head back to Charles Street, turn left uphill and left again into the Upper Bristol Road, where you will see a white painted panel on the shop on the corner (3). Painted panels like this often indicate that an old sign lurks beneath. Despite having been photographed under a variety of lighting conditions, however, it

has resolutely clung on to whatever secrets its holds, with only the merest hint of ghostly lettering glimmering through. Although that could, of course, be wishful thinking.

As you carry on along Monmouth Place, look up ahead to see a ghost sign for Spratt's (4). This company was founded in the United States in the 1870s and began operations in Britain soon afterwards. It was the first to make dog biscuits on an industrial scale, and, in the early twentieth century, claimed that its

dog biscuit factory in Poplar, East London, was the largest in the world. Spratt's was also one of the most heavily marketed brands, and its logo, introduced in 1936, of a Scottie with a waggly tail, was a work of genius, using the name of the brand to create an image of what its products would achieve – a happy dog.[3] The building it adorns was originally a mineral water factory, but by the 1930s had been taken over by Pointing & Sons, corn merchants, who also dealt in 'animal feeding stuffs, bird and dog food, and garden seeds and fertilisers'. The Spratt's logo was almost certainly suggested by a representative of the firm, and executed at their expense, as part of a campaign to encourage dog owners to buy their products. Another Spratt's Scottie was painted on the west side wall of the building, but, while you can see the white background as you carry on past it, the logo itself has all but disappeared.

We now come to Bath's most recent ghost sign (5). In 2015, the King's Arms, which had been refurbished as recently as November 2013, was refurbished again and re-named The Thief. As part of the 2013 refurbishment a large sign had been painted between the windows on the second floor for 'THE KINGS ARMS Ale House & Kitchen'. As

Above: The new sign being painted in November 2013.

Below: The same sign in July 2015.

part of the 2015 refurbishment, the sign was painted out, creating a blank rectangle, through the words are now starting to re-emerge.

Next door to the former King's Arms, on the west-facing side wall of the Chinese takeaway at 2 Monmouth Place, is a ghost sign for TEAS, CAFE, SNACKS, dating from when this was the Crescent Cafe, which opened after the Second World War (6).

Carry on and, just before joining the main road, look across to see a sign for the Commercial Garage on the corner (7). This was established in 1934 by a trio of motor engineers – FC Adlam, RF Brice and CE Reakes – and was in Palace Yard, at the back of the houses on the west side of Queen Square. Access to it was via Palace Mews, which ran between Monmouth Place and Charlotte Street – hence the choice of routes to get to it. It survived until the 1970s, latterly trading under the name of Jolly & Son. Cleveland Petrols will be a name familiar to anyone who was driving in the 1960s. Founded in the north east of England in the 1930s, it was gradually bought up by Esso, who phased out the use of the name by the early 1970s.

A few doors further along, look out for the old signboard of the Royal Oak on the left (8). This building, dating from the seventeenth century, became a beerhouse in the 1840s. It had only one bar, but a parlour at the back, used by the family, was open to selected guests. When an inventory was drawn up in 1886, the bar had a four-motion beer engine, a two-light gasolier and smoke consumers, two drinking tables on iron stands, fixed seating round the wall and nine spittoons. Among the furnishings in the parlour were a mahogany drinking table, two Windsor chairs, a box of dominoes and a copper beer warmer. In 1903, when few pubs served food, the Royal Oak sold bread and cheese to its customers. A licence to serve wine was granted in 1927, which means that the sign – which includes the word WINES – can be no earlier than that. The Royal Oak was never granted a spirit licence, however, and closed in 1961. Over half a century later, its weathered signboard still recalls one of Bath's more intimate hostelries.

A little further on, turn left into Little Stanhope Street, right along Great Stanhope Street, and left into Norfolk Crescent, stopping outside Nº 13 (9). For the story behind this sign, we can do no better than quote a report from the *Bath Chronicle* of 28 July 1928:

GHOST SIGNS OF BATH

The Bath Tenement Venture Trust made another forward step in their praiseworthy work on Monday afternoon when, on their behalf, the Mayoress of Bath (Madame Sarah Grand) formally opened Moody House (No 13, Norfolk Crescent), which has been converted into five flats, at rentals ranging from 7s 6d to 12s 6d a week.

It is just five years since the Trust opened its first tenements at Chandos House. That venture was an immediate success and so, too, was the one at Abbeygate House, which followed some time later. These two houses accommodate 14 families, but as there are many other prospective tenants on a waiting list, Moody House (named after Miss Moody, to whose idea the Trust owes its existence) will only partially meet the demand. It is, therefore, pleasing to know that there is a prospect of still further development of the work by the adaptation of other houses before very long.[4]

Three years later, Nº 12, next door, was acquired by the trust. It was named Stirling House in honour of Miss Marion Stirling, another of the trust's founding members.

Retrace your steps along Norfolk Crescent and continue along Nile Street to the Upper Bristol Road, where, on the right-hand corner, at 17 Monmouth Place, you will see a ghost sign that appears to have been painted over (10). It also looks to be a palimpsest with several layers of lettering, very little of which makes any sense. What appears to be the latest sign consists of the words '& PROVISIONS' at the bottom and the proprietor's name in copperplate script written diagonally upwards from the left. Whatever is above it – possibly GROCER – is not clear. Apart from that, there are only tantalising clumps of the odd letter or two, such as the enigmatic combination of N and O at the top.

Regarding the building's commercial history, in 1876 it was a lodging house run by Mrs Sarah Burge, but by 1888 a photographer called Frederick Mills had moved in. By 1896, it had become a grocer's run by Charles Sealy. He left before the First World War, transferring the business to Alfred Hill. It remained a grocer's, with HW Nicholas taking over by 1952, and AW Perkins by 1961. The only one of these names which seems to tally with the name on the sign is HW Nicholas: the first initial looks like an H and the name looks to contain the right number of letters, but for the moment this must remain very much a tentative identification.

Turn left along the Upper Bristol Road and, at the end of St George's Place, look for a sign consisting of one word – ENTRANCE (11). To the right of it you will see a modern sign for ALBION PLACE attached to the wall, with the first two letters of the old painted sign above. Albion Place, which predated St George's Place, consisted of two short terraces – Nᵒˢ 1 to 7, and then, after a gap giving access to buildings at the rear, Nᵒˢ 8 to 11. Only Nᵒˢ 8 and 9 survive today, and can be seen a little further along.

Beyond them, Nᵒˢ 10 and 11 were so badly damaged by bombing in 1942 that they had to be demolished. Nᵒˢ 1 to 7, which adjoined St George's Place, survived the bombing but were demolished in the 1950s to make way for the garage that has itself recently been demolished to make way for student accommodation.

At Nᵒ 1 Albion Place was Bath's Western Dispensary. This, like the Eastern Dispensary on Cleveland Place East and the Southern Dispensary on Claverton Street, supplied 'medical and surgical relief to the sick poor'. In 1839, shortly after it opened, the *Bath Chronicle* directed the attention of its readers

> to the first report of the Western Dispensary, an institution lately established for the benefit of the western extremity of Walcot, and a portion of the adjoining parish of Weston. The want of an increased supply of medical relief has been long felt in the above populous district. We are confident that this Charity needs only to be known in order to meet with that support which its object deserves.[5]

It survived, supported by charitable donations, until the establishment of the National Health Service in 1948. Today, all that survives to remind us of the tens of thousands who sought treatment here is the sign that directed them to its entrance.

From here, you can either head back into town, or, if you are up for a 1000m walk (referring to the map opposite) to see a rather curious sign, cross the road, head up Marlborough Buildings and carry on up Cavendish Road. After passing Cavendish Crescent, look for a painted sign on the house on the right (12). It reads

POST OFFICE

CLOSED

1857

This building dates from around 1792, but the first reference to a post office here comes in 1853, when a tutor advertising for students asked them to contact him via the post office at Sion Hill.[6] In 1857, a cook seeking a position placed an advertisement in the *Bath Chronicle* advising prospective employers that she could be contacted at 'Mr Parsloe's, Post-office, Sion Hill, Bath'.[7] Two years later, when a house was advertised to let, interested parties were asked to apply at the same address.[8]

In 1860, however, when another house was advertised to let, particulars were to be obtained from 'Mr E Parsloe, Ivy House, Sion Hill'. The lack

of any reference to the post office suggests it had closed. This seems to be confirmed by an advertisement which appeared the following year, when Somerset House – which you can see towering above the telephone kiosk across the road – was advertised to let, and prospective tenants were asked to 'apply to Mr Parsloe, Family Grocer, opposite'.[9]

Edward Parsloe, aged 60, was still at Ivy House, and still working as a grocer, at the time of the 1891 census, and died eight years later, in 1899. Why a sign was felt necessary to record the building's brief spell as a post office is unknown, as is the date is was painted. One thing seems clear, however: the date of closure cannot have been 1857, as the post office was still operating in 1859.

This building has one more hidden secret. If you turn the corner, you will see a doorway flanked by two Doric columns. A ghost sign, revealed in the 1980s after lying hidden for decades, lies hidden once again beneath a coat of paint applied around ten years later. A photograph and further details about it appear on page 263, in the chapter on lost signs.

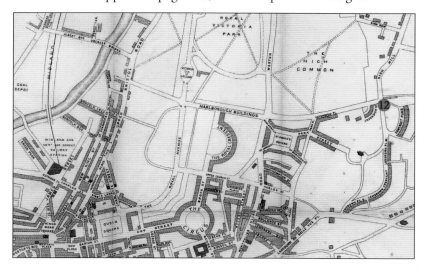

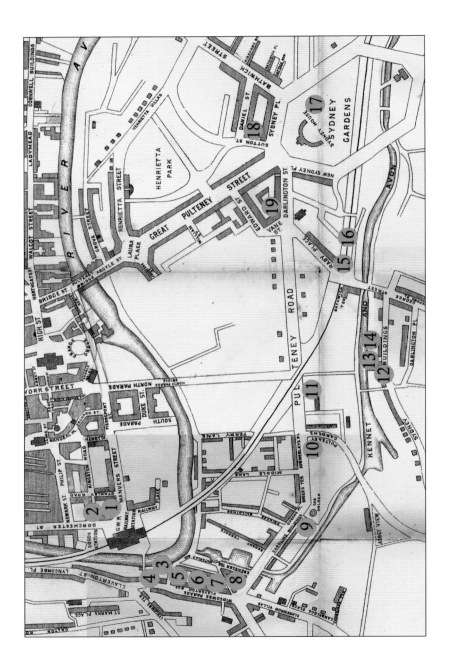

4

WIDCOMBE & BATHWICK

This walk heads across the river to take in the ghost signs of Widcombe and Bathwick. Even without the signs, this would be a splendid walk, taking in one of the most scenic canal towpaths in the country, a pleasure garden frequented by Jane Austen, magnificent Georgian terraces, and some close encounters with Brunel's Great Western Railway.

En route to Widcombe, stop outside the front of Bath Spa railway station and look across to the corner of Manvers Street, where, above a pair of Corinthian columns, you will see the words ARGYLL HOTEL. (1) Beneath them an earlier sign for FAMILY AND COMMERCIAL ROOMS can also be made out.

Like the Royal Hotel opposite, this building dates from the 1840s, shortly after the railway opened. Although the architect is not known, it was probably Henry Edmund Goodridge, who not only designed the markedly similar Cleveland Place East and West a few years earlier, but was also engaged by Brunel as surveyor to the Great Western Railway in Bath. It was not originally an hotel. When the freehold was advertised for sale in 1854, N°s 13, 14 and 15 Manvers Street were described as 'Three Substantially-built Shops and Dwelling-Houses, of uniform elevation ... the corner house being known as Marchant's Coffee-house'.[1]

By 1866, Marchant's Coffee House had become Marchant's Commercial Coffee Hotel, and was later renamed the Great Western

Temperance Hotel.[2] In 1896, however, its owners decided that it was time to start serving something stronger than coffee, and

> Mrs Julia Ryall, proprietress of the Great Western Temperance Hotel, Manvers-street, applied for a full Excise license. Mr Vachell appeared for the applicant, and said she had carried on the business for many years. He knew he was handicapped by the fact that the place had been called a 'temperance' hotel but it did not follow that the people who went to such hotels were abstainers; the contrary was the fact ... Unquestionably people went to a temperance hotel because the charges were less. His client's guests averaged 25 a week, and she repeatedly had to send out for intoxicants for them. The Royal Station Hotel, which nodded gracefully and laid by when the GWR Company applied for a license, opposed the application, but he would point out that this house catered for quite a different class of guests than the palatial Royal Station Hotel.[3]

The Royal Station Hotel (now the Royal Hotel) was not alone in opposing the application: the Railway Hotel in Railway Place and three pubs in Dorchester Street – the Full Moon, the South Pole and the Great Western – also spoke out against it. After the magistrates turned it down, Mrs Ryall sold the contents of the hotel and the building was advertised to let.[4] The following September, the building's owner, John Rubie, who already owned several licensed premises in the city, applied for a licence again, and was again refused.[5] It reopened the following year as the Argyll Hotel, a name it retained until it closed in the 1950s. Despite the sign proclaiming it to be the Argyll Hotel, however, postal directories and newspapers often referred to it as the Argyle Hotel – which must have caused some confusion.

If you look to the left of the sign for the Argyll Hotel, you will see another ghost sign, dating from around the same time, for MARSH, SON & GIBBS, LTD (2).

After Brunel had driven a mile-and-three-quarter tunnel through the high ground between Box and Corsham, revealing seams of Bath Stone on

a hitherto unexpected scale, quarrymasters moved in to exploit them. By the mid-1860s, over 100,000 tons of stone was being extracted annually, and the local economy was largely dependent on the industry. As the century progressed, wasteful and often ruinous competition between the various firms led to a series of mergers. One of the companies formed as a result was Marsh, Son & Gibbs. It was established in 1887 and owned or held the lease of quarries at Hartham Park, Pickwick, Corsham, Kingsdown and Limpley Stoke. An office was opened at York Street in Bath, and in 1897 the company supplied the stone for the statues around the newly-excavated Roman Baths.[6] In 1902, when it took over Tildesley & Co, a stone and granite business in London, a limited company was formed, and new offices were opened at Railway Place, adjoining the Argyll Hotel.[7]

Bright though the future may have seemed, the newly-formed company soon ran into trouble. Less than a year later, Richard Marsh, who seems to have been the driving force behind the enterprise, died after an accident, aged 62.[8] The following year, there was a slump in the stone industry.[9] The company soldiered on, but in 1908 Francis Gibbs, who had assumed control of the quarrying side of the business after Marsh's death, was declared bankrupt.[10] The company was officially wound up two years later and its assets were taken over by the Bath & Portland Stone Firms Ltd.

Beneath the sign for Marsh, Son & Gibbs, which is still clearly legible, are traces of what appears to be another sign, with black lettering. It is, however, too indistinct to make any sense of it.

Go through the tunnel at the east end of the station, cross the footbridge over the river, turn left along the road for 50m and, just past the pedestrian lights, look across to see a ghost sign for ANTIQUES & PINE, the legacy of a shop closed some 20 years ago, and now converted to a coffee shop (3).

Cross at the pedestrian lights and, as you follow the pavement round into Claverton Buildings, you will see a sign on the corner for SPRING GARDENS ROAD (4). This is not so much a ghost sign as a sign for a ghost road, its name recalling pleasure gardens abandoned over 200 years ago. The road, though – or at least the path

whose course it followed – was already centuries old by the time Spring Gardens opened in 1735.

Until Pulteney Bridge was built in the 1770s, the only way across the river – except by ferry – was the medieval bridge at the bottom of Southgate Street, which linked Bath with Widcombe. From Widcombe, a path led north through riverside meadows to Bathwick Mill, the ruins of which can be seen in the photograph on page 57. The fields around the mill were used to grow much of the produce sold in Bath's markets, and, while some of this would have been taken across to the city by ferry, much would have been carted down to Widcombe, across the old bridge and up Southgate Street.

Even before the fields near the mill were given up to create Spring Gardens, the riverside path was a fashionable place for visitors to take a stroll, and the opening of the gardens only enhanced its popularity. Later, it was along this path that Catherine Morland – accompanied by Henry and Eleanor Tilney – set off for a walk to Beechen Cliff in Jane Austen's *Northanger Abbey*.[11] By then, however, Spring Gardens were more or less defunct. Following the opening of Pulteney Bridge, work started on Laura Place and the streets radiating from it in 1788, so that the gardens were overlooked by what amounted to a building site. In 1795, Sydney Gardens opened at the far end of Great Pulteney Street, and, although Spring Gardens struggled on for a while, the end came with a grand gala night on 30 August 1798.

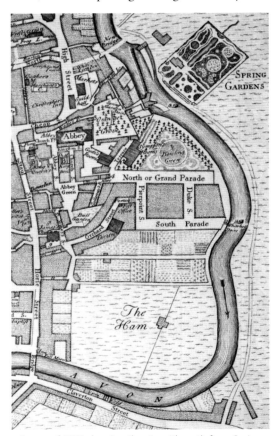

A map of 1775 showing the riverside path from Spring Gardens to Widcombe

GHOST SIGNS OF BATH

Even more far-reaching changes were soon to affect the riverside path. Plans for an imposing crescent on the site of Spring Gardens came to nothing, but in the early nineteenth century rows of mean streets were built a little further downstream. Known as the Dolemeads, they were on land that regularly flooded and soon became notorious as the city's worst slums. They lasted less than a century, before being swept away by the council and replaced by new houses built on high revetments to protect them from flooding. By then, two bridges had been built across both river and riverside path – North Parade Bridge in 1836 and St James's Railway Bridge five years later.

Curiously, given that Spring Gardens closed in 1798, the path or road alongside the river does not seem to have been called Spring Gardens Road until almost a century later. The first reference to it appeared in the *Bath Chronicle* on 26 February 1891, but even 14 years later some of the city's councillors claimed not to have heard of it, as this exchange from 1905 indicates:

> At the Bath City Council on Tuesday, when the minutes of the Housing of the Working Classes Committee were under discussion, Mr Peacock inquired where and in what parish Spring Gardens was situated?
> Mr Hearse: 'In Lyncombe and Widcombe.'
> Mr Peacock: 'I have never heard of Spring Gardens Road in Widcombe. I always thought it was in the parish of Bathwick.'
> Mr Powell: 'It extends from Widcombe slip to Grove Street.'
> Mr Peacock: 'I have never heard of it. Spring Gardens Road is in the parish of Bathwick. Spring Gardens Road is the name given to something else.'
> Mr RA Moger was appealed to, and said that the land in question was adjoining the Mission Hall in the Dolemeads, and facing the new road which is called 'Spring Gardens Road'.
> This answer was not sufficient for Mr Peacock, for at a later period in the meeting he said he wanted to know if Mr Moger was right in his answer to him just now (laughter). 'I want to know if he is sure he is right', added Mr Peacock, amid renewed laughter.
> Alderman Phillips: 'You had better put him on oath.'[12]

If the councillors could not agree where Spring Gardens Road was, there seems little hope of anyone else coming up with a definitive answer. That reference to the 'new road' is intriguing, though, especially as, comparing a map of 1904 with one from over 50 years earlier, it looks unchanged. On the 1904 map, however, it is marked as Spring Gardens Road, whereas on earlier maps it is not named, indicating that it was not known as such until shortly before that first reference in the *Bath Chronicle* in 1891. This puts the likely date for the sign on the wall in Widcombe somewhere in the late 1880s or early 1890s – although it has clearly been repainted since. Today, it marks not the start of one of Bath's most historic footpaths – or, depending on your point of view, one of Bath's most obscure and disputed thoroughfares – but a ghost road, for Spring Gardens Road was severed, just north of its junction with Claverton Buildings, by the construction of Rossiter Road in the 1970s.[13]

Walk along Claverton Buildings to N° 24, four doors along from the Ram (5) to see:

This overlays an earlier sign with the same wording. Much of it has faded to nothing, but if you look to the left of SURGICAL and above PHOTOGRAPHIC you may make out traces of the earlier lettering. As can be guessed from the services on offer, as well as the style of both sets of lettering, the signs date from after the First World War. Arthur Doble established a chemist's here in the 1920s, and later handed over to his son, Hugh, who was still here in the 1970s.

The next sign, seven doors along at 6 Sussex Place, is a good deal trickier to see, and, try as you might, it is unlikely you will make out more than a few words (6). The only ones that can clearly be seen lie to the right of the first-floor window – LADIES TAILOR. Similar lettering appears to the left of the window, but, having been covered with white paint at some stage, what it says has so far eluded us. Equally indistinct is the name of the proprietor, which appears in larger letters between the first and second-floor windows. The problem is not helped by the number of tailors who occupied these premises over the years. The 1872 *Directory* lists William T Jordan as a tailor and draper here. He was still here in 1888, but by 1892 a tailor called John Snell had taken over. He left in 1903 and was succeeded by George Henry Chapman.

Although it is difficult to make out much of the lettering between the first and second floors, there seem to be a G and an H at the beginning, with

MAN at the end. Tentative identification of the sign as reading GH CHAPMAN led us to try to find out something about him, and the discovery of a tragic tale.

George Henry Chapman was born in Corsham in 1871. His father was a stonemason, but he decided to become a tailor. By 1901, he was living as a lodger on Camden Road in Bath and working for a tailor in the city. A couple of years later, he moved to 6 Sussex Place to set up in business on his own. He was a bachelor, and the 1911 census listed only one other person living in the building – a lodger called Henry Cole, who was a plumber. George Chapman's

tenure of 6 Sussex Place seems to have been a successful one, but it came to an untimely end in August 1926:

> At the coroner's inquest at Bath yesterday, relative to the death of George Henry Chapman (54), a master tailor, of 6 Sussex Place, Widcombe, Bath, who was found dead in a workroom at his place of business on Tuesday morning, a verdict of 'suicide by coal gas poisoning while of unsound mind' was returned by the coroner (Mr FE Shum).
>
> Frederick Jeffrey Chapman of The Cleeve, Corsham, Wilts, brother of the deceased, said he had lately been suffering from acute melancholia, and had been staying with him in the hope of deriving some benefit. The inquiries of the Trade Board regarding the wages of his employees appeared to have affected him adversely, although witness and his legal adviser had effected a settlement of the questions at issue.
>
> Inspector James, of the Bath Police Force, said he found Chapman's body lying in a fireplace in a workroom on the premises. The head was covered by a rug, and a gas heater for warming irons was close to his face.
>
> Mr JM Harper, police surgeon at Bath, said he considered death had occurred quite twelve hours before the discovery of the body. Death must have been very rapid. Everything was in order in the room, and some very good work was being done there.[14]

Whatever the cause of his melancholia, it is unlikely that he was worried about money, for he left almost £4,000.[15] The shop was taken over by Mrs Dorothy Date, who ran a draper's there until the 1940s. She was succeeded by a 'fancy draper' called Mrs R Ollis, who was still there in the 1970s.

Next door, at 7 Sussex Place – the end of the row – is an even more illegible sign (7). The white band between the first and second floors – partially removed to make way for a new lintel above the first-floor window – is a feature of a number of buildings in Bath, and was generally painted to cover up a sign. In some cases, the sign can be made out, in some cases it cannot, while in others – such as this – the vague outline of a few letters are all that survives. These are almost  impossible to see, even with the sun shining on them, but, if you look at the left-hand side, you may be able to make out the curve of a P or an R – or possibly a D – with another one just left of the windows.

For much of the twentieth century, there was a dairy here. In 1901 it was owned by George Dunn, by 1914 he had handed over to Mrs AM Pyatt, but by 1925 W Silcox & Sons had taken over. They were not only dairy farmers at Violet Bank Farm on Prospect Road, off Widcombe Hill, but also potato merchants, with a warehouse at Widcombe Wharf. When they took over 6 Sussex Place, it became a fruiterer's and greengrocer's as well as a dairy. At some stage, they renamed it Prior Park Dairy, and this is the name that was painted on the sign. We know this because in 1975, when Sussex Place was listed, the listing included the information that 'the endmost house retains a painted sign on the front and side reading PRIOR PARK DAIRY'. Sometime in the last 40 years, despite the ghost sign being specifically included in the listing, therefore, it seems to have been painted over. As for the part of it that wrapped around the side of the building, all trace of that seems to have been scrubbed clean away.

On a brighter note, you can, from here, look across to the White Hart, built by Ralph Allen around 1730 and sporting a fine newly-painted sign by Tobias Newbigin, who also painted the titles on the front cover of this book.

We now turn to Widcombe Baptist Church, with four Biblical texts writ large on its roof (8). Given that the church which had them painted is still active, we were initially dubious whether they could be considered as ghost signs, but, after probing their history and discovering why they are fast fading to nothing, our qualms also faded.

The four texts, in large white letters, are followed by chapter and verse in much smaller letters. The text on the south elevation – partially visible from here – is YOU MUST BE BORN AGAIN. The others are PREPARE TO MEET Your GOD (on the east), WE HAVE REDEMPTION THROUGH HIS BLOOD (on the north), and CHRIST DIED FOR OUR SINS (on the west).

The church they adorn has an intriguing history. Built by the Independents (who later became the Congregationalists) around 1820, it was taken over by the Wesleyan Methodists in 1834. Disappointing attendance figures led them to give it up only four years later, and in 1838 it was taken over by the Church of England, who used it until St Matthew's Church at the bottom of Widcombe Hill was consecrated in 1847. Two years later, a group of Baptists who had seceded from the

Looking down on Widcombe around 1920, with the texts on the church roof clearly visible.

Baptist Providence Chapel on the Lower Bristol Road took it over. They acquired the freehold in 1868, and the congregation still worships in the church today.

The locks at Widcombe around 1900, with the stern exhortations on the church roof unmissable by any bargees passing through them.

In June 1903, as part of a major refurbishment, the Biblical texts were painted on the roof 'to be seen from surrounding hills and the Cliff'.[16] It is hard to imagine a more auspicious location for them. They could be seen not only by anyone travelling through Widcombe, but also by bargees passing through the nearby locks, while passengers on the Great Western Railway had a grandstand view of them. How many generations of impressionable children, noses glued to the carriage window as their train drew slowly across St James's Bridge, felt a shiver of apprehension as they took their portentous sentiments on board?

They certainly left their mark on a young boy called John Haddon, who, when he came to write his *Portrait of Bath*, began it thus:

Our point of view, in several senses of the phrase, determines what we see. When I was small my parents sometimes took me to Bath on a real puffing, clanking train and my first impression of the city was a message in huge white letters which said 'We Have Redemption Through His Blood' and changed, as we drew into the station, to 'Christ Died for Our Sins'. I was greatly impressed at being addressed in this way from what I now know to be the roof of an Ebenezer chapel and I would probably have been even more affected if I could have seen the roofs on the other side which change from information to admonition – 'Ye [sic] Must Be Born Again' and 'Prepare To Meet Thy God'. I did not really understand the message but it gave me the impression that Bath was a pretty stern place which shouted at you from the roof-tops.[17]

Today that shout has grown somewhat muted, as rain, weather and lichen have taken their toll. Although repainted many times over the years, the texts now seem to be fading away, and it is unclear whether they will be repainted again.

In the late 1950s, the building was reroofed with asbestos slates, which had to be left for at least two years before the texts could be reinstated. When repainting started in 1961, however, an objection was lodged with the council, and the ensuing controversy attracted the attention of the national media. Permission to proceed was eventually granted, 'and the texts which had been used to the salvation of several in the past once again proclaimed the Word of God to all who saw them'.[18]

When the building was reroofed in the 1990s, the new slates once again had to be allowed to weather. The Widcombe Association's archive records that, when the texts were eventually repainted, someone on Widcombe Hill, whose house overlooked the church, objected to the council's planning department, which diplomatically decreed that the lettering could stay, but that, when the building was reroofed again, the texts should not be reinstated.

If you carry on round the corner, you will come to a Biblical text which is in no imminent danger of disappearing. In its early years, the Ebenezer Chapel had a canalside beerhouse for a neighbour. Known as the Canal Tavern, it was clearly a thorn in their side, and when it came up for sale in 1910 they took the opportunity to acquire and demolish it. In its place they built new rooms for their Sunday school, with a celebratory text carved on the corner: 'Instead of the thorn shall come up the fir tree and it shall be to the lord for a name'.

Cross the road, carry on over the canal and, when you come to 20 Caroline Buildings – at the end of the second row of buildings – look up to see a faded red band above the first-floor windows (9). Until comparatively recently, two faded lines of lettering could be made out. Originally, the top line read DOWNS

while the second read EMIGRATION AGENT. They dated from the 1880s, when William Francis Downs ran an emigration agency here. He also had an office at 12a Burton Street. By 1895, he had moved to Lower Weston and become a shipping agent. Today, the letters have faded almost completely away.

Carry on to the corner of Pulteney Avenue, where you will see an expanse of white paint over the entrance and side window of the shop at 8 Pulteney Terrace (10). This too may seem to offer slim pickings, but if you time it right – when the late summer afternoon sun slants across the side wall – you should be able to make out most of what was a fairly elaborate sign. Starting off in the middle of the side wall, the main set of lettering reads:

MILK
DELIVERED TO ALL PARTS OF THE CITY
TWICE DAILY
FROM OUR OWN ...

And there it ends, in mid flow, the last line covered by a modern sign for Pulteney Avenue. On either side are smaller sets of lettering: that on the left reads NEW LAID EGGS; that on the right PURE DAIRY BUTTER.

There was more lettering above the entrance, but, even though some of the white paint has peeled away, revealing fragments of florid script, none of it can be made out. It is almost certain, though, that one of the words would have been SILCOX, for this dairy, like the one at Sussex Place, was owned by William Silcox & Sons, who were here from around 1900 to the mid-1960s, when the shop became a turf accountants.

Carry on, and, just after crossing the end of Lime Grove, you will see an impressive terrace of three- and four-storey houses on the right. In the late nineteenth and early twentieth centuries, this was boarding house territory *par excellence*, and if you stop at the gatepost of Nº 5, 'Fernleigh', you will see a sign whose faded elegance recalls those long-lost days

(11). In the mid-1880s, Francis Wilkinson, an auctioneer, acquired this house, along with the one on the right, for his wife Mary to open a private boarding house. At the time, the address of the two houses was 25 & 26 Pulteney Gardens; they were renumbered 5 & 6 Pulteney Road in the early 1900s. An idea of the sort of clientele Mrs Wilkinson attracted can be gleaned from a letter published in the *Bath Chronicle* in 1896:

> Sir, – Allow me to call attention through your columns to a matter of some local interest if not importance, viz., the state of the Pump Room windows. It may seem ungracious in one who has recently experienced the many advantages, which this city offers an invalid, to point out a slight defect, but perhaps my assurance will be accepted that I do so in no carping spirit. It is now the end of May, and it needs no expert to discover that in the case of the Pump Room windows 'Spring Cleaning' has been forgotten.
>
> WJ Salter
> (BA Oxon)
> Fernleigh, Pulteney Gardens, May 30, 1896[19]

Mrs Wilkinson died in 1908 and by 1910 both Nº 5 & Nº 6 – with Nº 6 newly named 'Islay' – had become private houses.

The next set of signs line the banks of the canal, harking back to its nineteenth-century heyday as a vital part of the city's commercial life. We last saw the canal when we crossed over it at Widcombe. Since then it has climbed up through five locks, so to return to it we must do some climbing ourselves. Carry on to the railway bridge, turn right through an archway beneath it and follow a footpath and steps up to the towpath.

Delightful though the view that greets us at the top of steps is today, in the nineteenth century this was a dirty, noisy and distinctly unpicturesque area. The charming garden with private mooring opposite was a coal wharf, and the building to the right of it – now an architect's office – was the coal warehouse and offices. To the left, the canalside building with a funnel-type chimney – part of which also houses an architect's office – was a malthouse. Remarkably, both buildings still have ghost signs on their walls – very faded ghost signs, admittedly – as does the imposing three-storey Georgian building at the back of the malthouse. And, as its sign is the earliest of the three, that is where we will start.

Turn right and, just past the top lock, turn left across a footbridge. Carry on up to Sydney Buildings, cross and turn left along the raised pavement for 100m. After passing the three-storey detached Georgian building across the road at N° 21, look back to see a ghost sign – or rather a palimpsest of two ghost signs – on its side wall (12). What appears to be the later sign reads TANNERS. As for the earlier sign, only three letters – larger than those on the other sign – are legible: a J at the start, a A behind the S of TANNERS, followed by a C (or possibly an O).

Sydney Buildings was renumbered in 1902, and this building, formerly N° 11, became N° 21. It dates from around 1814 and by 1832 had been taken over by Frederick Spencer, who also owned the adjoining coal wharf. In the late 1860s, the house and business were taken over by George Dike, who stayed until the mid-1880s. As the style of both sets of lettering clearly dates from the early nineteenth century, they must therefore have been painted between 1814 and 1832.

Turning to the 1826 *Directory*, we find a 'J Tanner, Flour Factor' listed in Sydney Buildings. No number is given, he does not appear in the 1819

Directory nor in the 1829 *Directory*, and we have found no other reference to him. We do not even know his first name. But he was almost certainly responsible for at least one of the signs. As for the other, it remains a mystery. The J at the start could be the J of J Tanner, but, while the AC could be part of the word FACTOR, there is space for only four or five letters between the J and the AC, which rather discounts that theory.

On which inconclusive note, take a look at the former malthouse and coal warehouse from this side before heading back down to the canal in search of their ghost signs.

Before you reach the coal warehouse, however, look between the first-floor windows of the building to the right of it to see what appears to be a painted rectangle with possible traces of lettering. This is the back of N° 25 Sydney Buildings (which was originally N° 14) and looks like another ghost sign, although we have failed to positively identify any letters or discover any leads as to what it may once have read.

Unfortunately, the sign on the north wall of the coal warehouse is almost as illegible. Not only has it faded badly, but it is now virtually hidden by a large evergreen shrub (**13**). It originally read:

SOMERSET

COAL WHARF

F. SPENCER[21]

This was established by Frederick Spencer, mentioned earlier in connection with the sign on 21 Sydney Buildings. In 1832, he placed an advertisement in the *Bath Chronicle*:

Somerset Coal Wharf, Sydney Buildings, Bathwick

SPENCER and COMPANY
Respectfully Offers to the Public the Best
SOMERSET COALS at Tenpence per Cwt. (for Cash)

They have adopted a mode of conveyance from the Somerset Pits likely to enhance the public benefits of WATER CARRIAGE, and they confidently hope for general approval and support. They anticipate that the public will approve a scheme tending in some degree to check those scenes of fraud and cruelty so frequently perceivable on the roads in and near this city.

To show the quality of Coals on Sale, SPENCER and COMPANY respectfully entreat probation. In making their arrangement for the supply of Coals to Bath, they have sought to avoid that deterioration of quality caused by the common mode of carriage; and as this choice was only to be obtained by an expensive outlay, they are the more earnest in desiring to merit the approbation of their Friends. A customer desiring Coals from any particular Pit can be supplied accordingly.[22]

This, for anyone familiar with the history of the canals around Bath, may come as something of a surprise. It had been possible to carry coal from the Somerset coalfield to Bath via the Somersetshire Coal Canal and the Kennet & Avon Canal for well over 20 years. Both canals had been constructed at enormous expense. Yet, as this advertisement indicates, much of the coal destined for Bath was still being carried by road, with all the problems of theft and mistreatment of horses that seems to have entailed. The 'expensive outlay' Spencer & Co had to make was presumably for a fleet of boats, although there were also the tolls charged by the canal companies to take into consideration.

Frederick Spencer's investment clearly paid off, and four years later he added another string to his bow by becoming sole licensee in the area for 'kyanising' wood, a process which had recently been invented by an Irishman called John Kyan. In an advertisement in 1836, he announced that he was 'laying down tanks at the Somerset Coal Wharf ... for immersing and preparing Timber, Cordage, Canvass, etc, according to the Patent Process'.[23]

The remnants of the sign on the side of the old coal warehouse

Kyanised wood was very popular for a time, and was used extensively by Brunel – most famously for the original skew bridge over the Avon west of Bath station – but fell out of favour in the 1850s.

Frederick Spencer was still at the wharf in 1861, employing three clerks, six labourers and a boy. He was then aged 54 and, according to the census, was also blind. He later retired to Weston Super Mare and the business was taken over by George Dike. By the early twentieth century, however, it had ceased to be a coal wharf, and the premises were used by a succession of carpenters, builders and decorators.

The next sign, on the former malthouse, although it has largely flaked away and is partially obscured by a tree, can still be made out (14). It reads HUGH BAIRD & SONS LTD, MALTSTERS and dates from around 1934 when the malthouse was taken over by Baird & Sons, a Glasgow firm which also owned a much larger malthouse on Broad Quay. The building is around a century older, however, and, in an advertisement from 1843, the Bath Brewery on

Kingsmead Street boasted of 'its well-known MALT-HOUSE situate on the Banks of the Canal'.[24] In 1898, when the building was advertised for sale, it was described as

> the Substantially Built 30-QUARTER MALTHOUSE, eligibly situate at Sydney Buildings, Bath, with frontage to the Kennet & Avon Canal, and Stage for unloading grain. Also Stabling, Coach-house, and Harness-room adjoining (at present converted into a shop). The Premises comprise Malt Kiln with tiled floor, Furnace with improved air tubes, Heater, and Reek Disperser, Two Working Floors, virtually underground, rendering them capable of being worked all through the summer, Large Stone Cistern. There are 9 Malt Bins, ranging in capacity from 200 to 90 Quarters each, with ample Storage for Barley.[25]

It was taken over by HJD Blake & Sons, which later became Tucker & Blake's, before Baird & Sons took over in 1934. After they gave up the malthouse in 1973, it was converted to offices and residential accommodation.

Carry on along the canal, walk up the steps to Bathwick Hill, cross at the zebra crossing up to the right and turn left downhill. As you turn right along Sydney Wharf, you will see across the road, on the side wall of 18 Raby Place, a ghost sign for SEERS COAL OFFICE (15). If you look closely, however, you will see traces of other sets of lettering, some of which are only really visible under certain lighting conditions, and none of which is decipherable in its entirety.

Taking the only reasonably straightforward one first – COAL OFFICE has been painted twice, with the two sets of lettering not quite in line. Then, if you look at the top line, you will see, behind the second E of SEERS, two smaller letters – M and O. To the right of the R you may also be able to make out an L. If you come down below the top line,

and look to the left, you can make out BUILDER in the same smaller letters. Finally, if you look under the first E of SEERS, you will see, in letters midway in size between the two other sets, the start of the word PUBLIC.

Although there are traces of other letters, these are all that we have managed to decipher, leaving the challenge of working out what all this means for someone else to take forward. Who the builder might have been we do not know; as to what was 'public', the most likely explanation is that it was a weighing machine. Public weighing machines were once common in towns and cities throughout the land, and were used to weigh carts laden with goods, especially coal. The 1886 Ordnance Survey map shows two weighing machines on the wharf opposite, where coal was landed, on the site now occupied by retirement flats.

This is the wharf which, in the late nineteenth century, was owned by Charles William Seers, who lived at 18 Raby Place.[26] In 1890, his father bought him a half share in the coal merchant's business owned by George Dike (who had taken over Spencer's coal wharf in the 1860s

---

SEERS, late DIKE,

COAL FACTOR,

TOWN OFFICE—

6, WOOD STREET,

(QUEEN SQUARE),

Wharves { RABY PLACE - -
{ WESTMORELAND (G.W.R.) STATION, **BATH.**

Somerset, Forest of Dean, Derby, Welsh and Anthracite Coal always in Stock.

Telephone—No. 23.

An advertisement from 1897

GHOST SIGNS OF BATH

and moved here in the 1880s). They traded as Dike & Seers at the wharf opposite 18 Raby Place until 1894, when Seers bought Dike out and changed the name of the business to CW Seers. In an advertisement from 1897, Seers described himself as a coal factor, with wharves at Raby Place and the GWR's Westmoreland goods station, and an office at 6 Wood Street. He also acquired some wagons, registered with the Midland Railway, with his name painted on the side, to deliver coal to the Midland station in Bath.[27] But, impressive though all this may have sounded, the reality was somewhat less alluring. He had no previous experience of the coal trade and his over-rapid expansion, combined with a lack of capital, proved his undoing. In 1904, he sailed for Canada, leaving his father to wind up his business affairs and settle his liabilities.[28]

He returned to England in 1909 and took a job as a clerk at thirty shillings a week. It was not long, however, before he was dreaming of making it big once more, and the following year he went into partnership with a Charles Brookman. They opened an office at 2 Bladud Buildings as the Midland Collieries Direct Coal Supply Syndicate, and Seers' father gave him an advance of £100 to get the enterprise off the ground. This time, his nemesis was even swifter. Only three months after setting up the business, Brookman did a runner, taking the £100 with him. Seers was declared bankrupt and the following year he sailed from Liverpool to start a new life in New York.[29]

Continue along Sydney Wharf, and, after passing the building on the corner of Raby Mews, turn to look at the ghost sign on its back wall **(16)**. This is another palimpsest, but one that offers no problems of interpretation. The more prominent of the two signs reads

CLEVELAND

ARMS

USHERS ALES

This, somewhat surprisingly, is the earlier sign. The later one, which is much more faded, reads

THE

RENDEZVOUS

CLUB

The concrete post which obscures part of this extremely unusual sign is a recent addition, having been erected around 15 years ago.

The Cleveland Arms was built around 1831 by William Robinson, a local brewer. Less than ten years later, Brunel drove his Great Western Railway directly beneath it, proving, if nothing else, that it had been well built. In 1852, when it was advertised for sale, it had 'a very desirable piece of land at the back ... upon which a good brewery or several cottages might be erected'.[30] It was bought by William Stockham, who took the hint and built a brewery. He died in 1860, aged 46, after which the pub was run by his widow, Mary Ann, and later by his son, Charles. In 1892, it was taken

over by Joseph Phipps. After Phipps' died in 1910, aged 65, his widow, Louisa, continued to run the pub, assisted by her daughter, Annie, while her son George ran the brewery. In 1926, it was purchased by Ushers of Trowbridge, who closed the brewery, painted the first of the two signs on the side wall and set about transforming it 'into an up-to-date house – in fact a model establishment to meet present-day requirements'.[31]

Six years later, however, they applied to transfer its licence to the Trowbridge House on Coronation Avenue, which only had a beerhouse licence. The Cleveland Arms, they had decided 'was a substantial and valuable property in a part of Bath which had ceased to make any particular progress in the way of development', whereas an increasing number of new homes were being built near the Trowbridge House.[32] The application was granted and the Cleveland Arms closed, but in October 1933 it was bought by Harry Lever, ex-landlord of the White Hart at Ford, who reopened it as the Rendezvous Club, and painted a new sign over the old one.[33] He was granted a licence to serve alcoholic drinks with meals, but the club soon became notorious as an after-hours drinking den. Less than a year after it had opened, the police raided it and closed it down. According to the *Bath Chronicle*, 'the raid took place on the night of Bath's match against the London Welsh and several well-known rugby footballers were among those whose names were taken by the police.'[34]

After standing empty for a time, in 1937 the building was taken over by the Church Army as a 'Work-Aid Home', before being bought by the South-Western Gas Board in 1949 and converted to offices.[35] It has since been converted again to provide student accommodation.

Carry on along Sydney Wharf, turn left over the railway and then right. Cross Sydney Road, turn left and then right into Sydney Gardens, and follow the path as it curves round the back of the Holburne Museum. To the left of a modern toilet block, you will see – neglected and unloved – a cast-iron gentlemen's urinal dating from 1914, the year after the gardens opened as a municipal park. Behind the modern toilets, you can pick your way past rampant shrubbery to find, fenced off and embowered

in ivy, an even more neglected and unloved cast-iron convenience for lady visitors, installed at the same time. Their centenary seems to have gone unmarked, and they must surely be two of the least known, least regarded and least cared for Grade II-listed buildings in Bath. A little further on, though, is a listed

building that has fared somewhat better – a gardener's cottage or lodge dating from around 1840, now used as an education centre, but in the early twentieth century a cloakroom for visitors to the gardens, and still with a fragment of a painted sign over its entrance (17).

Head out of the gardens and cross two sets of traffic lights to the left-hand side of Bathwick Street. Walk up the street, taking a look at the painted strip between the first and second-floor windows of the Barley Mow (betokening a hidden ghost ghost sign, perchance?), before turning left into Daniel Street and left into Sutton Street to look at two

fast-fading ghost signs on the Pulteney Arms – PRIVATE & PUBLIC BARS, with a manicule, by the main entrance, and SMOKE ROOM, with traces of earlier lettering, by the side door a little further along (18). Both look to date from the nineteenth century, but some

caution may need to be exercised, as in the 1960s the pub was revamped in a thoroughgoing Victorian style, complete with gas lighting. So, despite all appearances to the contrary, they may be much more recent than they look, but if so they are very convincing. Before moving on, it is worth looking up to see yet another possible ghost sign – in the form of another strip of white paint running the width of the building, but with no trace of any lettering beneath it.

For the final ghost sign, cross Sutton Street, head along to Great Pulteney Street, cross over and carry on along Darlington Street to the archway near the end (19). This was the entrance to Darlington Mews, where, as the advertisement below indicates, carriages and horses could be hired by nearby residents. By the early twentieth century, however, as horses gave way to cars, stables and coach houses gave way to garages, and here on Darlington Place is a particularly fine example of a garage sign from the 1940s.

Written vertically on the left is the word GARAGE, with the rest of the sign to the right:

DARLINGTON MEWS.
(OPPOSITE BATHWICK CHURCH.)
B. NEWNHAM
(Brother-in-Law to the late Mrs. MOODY), and
JAMES LOVENBURY,

MOST respectfully announce to their Friends and the Public that they have taken to the Old-Established Business carried on by the late Mrs. MOODY, at Darlington Mews ; and in asking for a continuance of the favours so liberally bestowed upon their predecessor, beg to assure those who may patronize them that, by punctuality, moderate charges, and strict attention to orders, it will be their endeavour to merit the same.

Neat Landau Fly Carriages, Britzkas, Phaetons, Gigs, &c., with Steady and Respectable Drivers.

Job and Saddle Horses Let to Hire by the day, week, month, or year.—Horses taken in to bait or to stand at Livery. Good Loose Boxes and Lock-up Coach Houses.

Orders received at 13, Argyle Buildings ; at RADNEDGE'S Dairy, Argyle Buildings; or at the Mews. (70

An advertisement from 17 July 1845

SERVICE

CARS SERVICED & GARAGED

REPAIRS & OVERHAULS

BATTERIES CHARGED

Then, to the left of a DUNLOP STOCK logo:

TEL. 4388.

And to the right of the logo:

A.E. BARTLETT MIMC

SERVICE GARAGE Sydney Mews.

Why Mr Bartlett should have given this address is curious, as Sydney Mews is the lane across the road, to the left of St Mary's Church. Perhaps he thought people would not know where Darlington Mews was, and so opted for a more familiar address, even though it was not strictly accurate; perhaps he thought it sounded better; or perhaps his garage was indeed across the road on the site now occupied by modern houses, but the only place he could find for a sign was here. In which case, you would expect to see an arrow – or at the very least a manicule pointing across the road, so that unsuspecting customers did not turn down through the archway. Someone must know, but, if they do, we have not managed to come across them, so on yet another inconclusive note we end this tour of Widcombe and Bathwick.

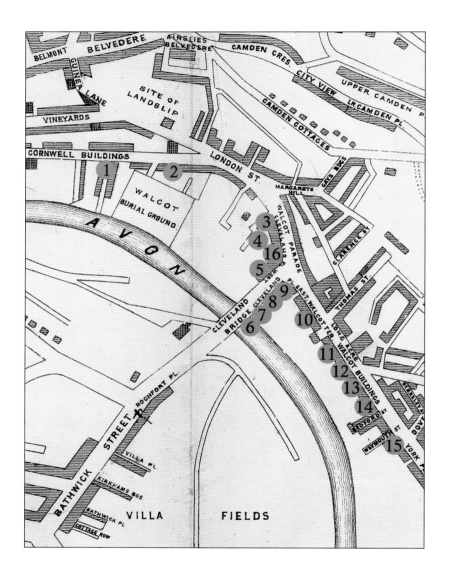

5

WALCOT

Ideally, this walk should be undertaken in the late afternoon – from around 4.30pm on – between mid-April and mid-August, although, given the rich variety of ghost signs it yields, if you cannot do it then, you really should not give it a miss. It also differs from the other walks in that it takes an out and back trip along a busy road. As you will see when you walk it, however, this is the only way in which all the ghost signs can be seen.

Start by heading out of town along Walcot Street. The first ghost sign is just beyond the Bell Inn, at the gated entrance to St Swithin's Yard, on the right, where flats now occupy the former Walcot Schools (1). As you

look through the gates you will see the sign – or rather signs – on the wall on the right. Although it may seem incredible today, countless numbers of children would have passed these large signs advertising cigarettes – Wills' Gold Flake and Players – as they walked through the gates of their school every day. The old adage about getting them young certainly applied here. There are at least two generations of signs here, with the earlier lettering for the two brands of cigarette still dimly visible. One unusual feature is that a part of each sign is much clearer than the rest of it. This is probably because an advertising hoarding was mounted on the wall at a later date, partially obscuring the signs and preserving a part of each of them from the ravages of sun and rain.

The commercial history of this building – 128 Walcot Street – does not indicate why tobacco was advertised so prominently here.[1] It was a grocer's shop from the late nineteenth century until around the time of the First World War. In 1919, a 'general dealer' called William Bave took it over, but from the late 1920s to around 1950 it was a confectioner's. In 1952, Charles Fletcher – described simply as a 'shopkeeper' – was here, but by 1961 it was home to Borthwick Meat Imports, and by 1973 the Fatstock Marketing Company had moved in. Quite where the signs fitted into this continuum is unclear, although we do know that in 1949 there were plans for a new sign, which, 'under new advertisement regulations, Bath City Planning Committee [regarded] as injurious to amenities'.[2] Unfortunately, we do not know what sort of sign this was, or whether it eventually appeared.

Carry on, crossing the end of Walcot Gate, and two doors along, at 142 Walcot Street (formerly 20 Cornwell Buildings), look up to see one of Bath's most rewarding ghost signs, which evokes the spirit of a Walcot Street long gone (2). This is another palimpsest, with its two layers – dating from the mid-1870s and the late 1880s respectively – both clearly legible. The later one, which is easier to decipher, was for someone with several strings to his bow. Flanking his name – W WHITE, writ

large – are his various trades: LOCK & BRIGHT SMITH, GENERAL IRONMONGER on the left and GAS FITTER, BELL HANGER &c on the right, with WORKSHOPS AROUND THE CORNER, and a manicule, below.

William White was born in Charlton in Somerset, but by the time of the 1861 census, aged 26, he had settled in Walcot, married a local woman, fathered four children, and was working as a brightsmith, employing a boy and a man. As his business prospered, he moved to Cornwell Cottage behind Cornwell Buildings, his two daughters became schoolteachers, one of his sons became a lawyer's clerk, while the other – Arthur – worked alongside him. Around 1887, he opened the shop at 20 Cornwell Buildings. He later took over a nearby marine stores and opened another shop in Upper Borough Walls, but in 1901 appeared before the bankruptcy court:

William White ... an ironmonger, late of Cornwell-buildings, Walcot, and carrying on business at the Upper Borough Walls, trading as White and Son, came up for his public examination ... A series of questions were put to the debtor ... and in answer to them [he] said he started business 40 years ago as a blacksmith. He was able to pay his creditors up to last year, and had never been in difficulties before. He started an ironmonger's shop in Cornwell-buildings about 14 years ago, and carried on that business up to the time he took the other in the Upper Borough Walls. He carried on both businesses for a time, but subsequently gave up the one in Walcot. He should have been more successful with the Upper Borough Walls business had he not had the Walcot one dragging on. His shop in Cornwell-buildings was not a success. He took the shop in the Upper Borough Walls for the purposes of bettering himself. At about that time he reckoned he had £300 in goods and things. He had his son in the business, and he made arrangements to pay him wages – about £2 10s a week, but he started paying him 30s a week ... He had not filed an account of receipts and payments for the last two years because he did not know how to do it. He kept accounts which he understood himself, and he did not think he should ever have to explain them. When he was ill the accounts went back, and he could not pick them up ... His son managed all that went on in the shop at the Borough Walls. He looked at the accounts there sometimes, but never thoroughly examined them. For four years he carried on the business of a marine store dealer in Walcot-street. It was broken up through the premises being wanted for the Walcot Schools. He paid off the creditors of the man who had this business previously to the amount of 5s in the £. Then a distress was put in, and he had to buy the things under the hammer. He lost money at the marine stores. Had he been able to get rid of the Walcot premises when he went to the Borough Walls he believed the latter would have been a profitable concern, but the fact of having so many premises and leases at Walcot handicapped the Borough Walls business which had to pay for them.[3]

When the official receiver asked for a cash account to be filed, William White's solicitor replied that 'he did not think [he] could do it; he was an old gentleman of 67, and more or less illiterate.' In response, the receiver suggested that he 'make out the best account he could; he simply asked for a bare statement of receipts and payments', and it was agreed that he should 'have skilled assistance' to provide this.

When the 1901 census had been completed a few weeks earlier, William White, now a widower, was living with his son Arthur and his family at 7 Sion View, off the Wells Road. He seems to have moved back to Cornwell Cottage, however, for he appears once more, in a sad story from 1903 concerning the body of a new-born child discovered at a house in Alfred Street:

William White, blacksmith, of Cornwell Cottage, Cornwell Buildings, said he was cartaker [sic] at the Walcot Mortuary, and was there when DC Lovell brought the body of a baby on August 25th. He was also there the next day when the body was examined by Mr Dunlop.[4]

Now for the earlier set of lettering, which is somewhat trickier to decipher, and only really visible in good light. Fortunately, it only consists of a few words. In the centre, underneath W White's name, and in similar-sized lettering, is the name HW HOOPER. Unlike the lettering used for White's name, however, the lettering used for Hooper's is sans serif. To the left of this, underneath the list of White's trades, is the single word AUCTIONEER, while to the right is the word APPRAISER.

Henry William Hooper's career, although more varied, was no less fraught than William White's. In the 1871 census, he was recorded as an upholsterer living at 19 Cornwell Buildings, but by the time of the 1877 *Directory* he had become an auctioneer and furniture broker, with his name emblazoned on the wall of N° 20 Cornwell Buildings. The reason it was painted here seems to have been because N° 19 was set back from the street, behind other buildings, so a deal with the occupier or owner of N° 20 was necessary to get his name in the public eye.

Unfortunately, he was soon to gain notoriety of a more unwelcome kind. In 1878, at Corsham Petty Sessions, 'Henry William Hooper, of Bath, auctioneer, was fined £1, including costs, for disorderly conduct at the Queen's Head, Box, and refusing to quit the premises'.[5] Whether this incident prompted him to move away from Bath, his home town, is not known, but by the time of the 1881 census he was living at Woodborough near Pewsey and working as an upholsterer. He later moved to Seend and then to Devizes where he took up auctioneering once more. A report from 1889 gives an insight into his business practices:

At [Westbury] Town Hall, on Monday … a case of great interest to auctioneers was heard. Mr Henry William Hooper, auctioneer, of Seend and Devizes, was summoned, at the instance of the Inland Revenue Department, by Mr C Collins, Supervisor, for hawking without a licence, contrary to the Act passed in August 1888, consolidating the law relating to hawkers' licences … The facts of the case are these: Mr Hooper holds an auctioneer's licence, and in December last he had a sale by auction at the Duke Inn, Bratton. At the close of the sale the surplus stock he removed thence in a waggon, hired by him of the landlord (Mr Hobbs), to the Ludlow Arms Inn, Westbury, three miles distant, where he held another sale; and after that he took goods from that town in a waggon, hired of Edward Scull, to the King's Arms Inn, Dilton Marsh, where he held a further sale on December 12. Handbills announcing these were produced, and defendant held that he had a perfect right to sell at these places, the hired rooms being his

Details of the palimpsest sign on 142 Walcot Street

place of business for the time being. The Supervisor showed that by the Act any auctioneer selling at his own place of business where he resides, or anywhere else in that same town, did not require a hawker's licence, but in this case defendant's place of business was at Seend and Devizes, and that to sell as he there was selling required a hawker's licence. The Bench took the same view, and ... inflicted a fine of £5 and costs, or a month's imprisonment.[6]

By 1891, he was living on Northgate Street in Devizes with his wife, daughter, and three sons, the eldest of whom was working as an upholsterer and furniture dealer. Ten years later, however, his wife had died and he was back in Cornwell Buildings, working as an upholsterer and living with his youngest son, aged 15, who was described as an upholsterer's assistant. In 1904 his name appeared in the *Bath Chronicle* once again:

> Henry William Hooper, of 21 Cornwell Buildings, was summoned by Francis Horace Moger, Clerk to the Urban Sanitary Authority, for that on or about the first day of January, 1904, there existed a nuisance within the meaning of the Public Health Act, 1875, at 22 Cornwell Buildings, arising from insufficient closet accommodation and defective paving. Defendant said that the work was being proceeded with and he asked for an adjournment for a week. Mr Moger offered no objection, the work being well in hand and the application was granted.[7]

The 1911 census lists him as living alone, aged 65 and working as a caretaker – possibly having taken over the post at the mortuary chapel previously held by William White.

A few doors along, at 5 London Street, is a gallery where Nick Cudworth's atmospheric and evocative landscapes, portraits and still lifes are on display. You may also spot a print of the painting of Cleveland Terrace featured on the front cover, which Nick Cudworth generously allowed us to use – a view which summons up all the allure of one of Bath's most famous sets of ghost signs. To see them for yourself, carry on for another 100 metres and look up at the side wall just past the Methodist Chapel (3). These signs date from the first decade of the twentieth century, when Herbert John Archard ran a grocery store and sub-post office here. Born in Trowbridge around 1874, he was brought up in Bradford on Avon, where his father was a cloth worker. He too became a cloth worker for a time, before moving to Bath with his two sisters around 1899 and opening a grocery store at 8 Margaret's Place. This was across the road from Cleveland Terrace, facing the west end of Walcot Parade, where a gateway now leads into Hedgemead Park. When Margaret's Place was demolished in 1902, he moved to 6 Cleveland Terrace, taking over a provision merchant's and sub-post office from Sydney Tucker. He also married in 1902 and a year later his wife gave birth to a daughter.

For ten years, all went well, until, one September evening in 1912, 'a fire of considerable fierceness ... occurred in Walcot':

The premises involved were those occupied by Mr HJ Archard and his family at 6 Cleveland Terrace ... Mr Archard, who carried on business as a grocer and provision merchant, has been the occupant of the premises for the past ten years. A portion of the shop was used as a sub-post office, and was known as the Cleveland Place Office ... All the occupants of the house were at home at the time of the outbreak. Being Thursday, business had been suspended at one o'clock and the shop and post office closed. Mr and Mrs Archard, with their daughter Ruby Archard, aged nine years, remained in the house the whole afternoon and evening with Mr Archard's father, who is nearly 70 years of age. In the evening they were joined by Miss Archard, Mr Archard's sister ... and a friend, Mr W Kay. The child went to bed at eight o'clock as usual, occupying a room at the back on the second floor. It was while the other occupants of the house were having supper in the dining room, which is at the back of the shop, that the first intimation was given that something unusual had happened. Suddenly, and without the slightest indication, the light of two gas jets, with which the room was fitted, failed, and the room was plunged into darkness. Under the impression that something had either gone wrong with the gas meter or the main, one of the company opened a door leading to the basement of the premises at the back with the idea of investigating the cause of the failure of the light. Immediately the door was opened a volume of dense smoke confronted the opener. The smoke came from the basement which was used as a storage place for stock. That a fire had broken out was only too evident, and at this moment the flames

A distant view of N° 6 Cleveland Terrace around 1905, with a sign for NESTLÉ'S MILK on the right, and signs for HJ ARCHARD'S DEVONSHIRE DAIRY and BOVRIL on the left, all of which have survived, at least in part. To the left of the top-storey window is another sign, on which the word PALACE can be seen. This may have advertised the Palace Theatre of Varieties in the Sawclose, but appears to have been painted on a board, and is long gone.

had a firm hold of the back portion of the building, for they were rising fiercely and smoke was gathering in volume and density. There was no time to be lost.

The saving of the child was the first consideration, and Mr Kay immediately rushed upstairs to rescue the little girl. He was met by much smoke, and not knowing which bedroom she was occupying, and the house being in total darkness, he was unable to discover the little girl. However, Mr Archard, her father, quickly followed Mr Kay, and, rushing into the bedroom, snatched the child from the bed and brought her downstairs in his arms ...

An alarm had been raised, and the Bath Fire Brigade were called at 10.26 ... On their arrival, they discovered that the fire had got a firm hold of the back portion of the premises, flames and smoke issuing from the ground floor and top windows. Several supplies of water were quickly got to work and poured onto the burning building ... Pipes were carried to the roof, and so directed as to cut the fire off from the adjoining premises. This was successful, and the conflagration was confined entirely to the back of N° 6, Cleveland Terrace. The flames dashed up through the house and quickly penetrated the roof, which in a comparatively short space of time completely collapsed, and as the tongues of flame leapt high into the air the effect, according to onlookers, was one of great brilliance against the clouded sky.

The whole of the back portion, from basement to roof, was gutted. Of the top storey nothing is left but the main walls, while the staircase is charred and burnt from top to bottom ... Considerable damage has been done both by fire and water, and the loss, we are informed, is only partially covered by insurance. Every room in the house has suffered, and the rooms at the back and their contents have been completely ruined.[8]

The shop never re-opened. Herbert Archard moved his business to temporary premises nearby, but, less than four months later, the *Bath Chronicle* reported that

Opposite: The Nestlé's sign has survived remarkably well.

Above: The sign for Archard's Devonshire Dairy not only has other lettering showing through underneath, but has had a window inserted, while the Bovril sign has been covered up.

Below: A photograph from 1981 when the Bovril sign could still be seen.

some inconvenience was caused on Wednesday through the Cleveland Post Office, Walcot, not opening its doors as usual for the transaction of business. A notice has been posted in the window stating that all postal business will be transacted at the head office, York Buildings. Up to within a few months ago the office was carried on, combined with a grocery and provision business, at Cleveland Terrace, and when these premises suffered considerable damage by fire the business and the post office were transferred to temporary premises at Nelson Place East. The proprietor of the grocery business and the sub-postmaster was Mr HJ Archard, who, we are given to understand, has gone abroad. He was at his premises on Tuesday, and closed the post office in the ordinary way at eight o'clock in the evening.

We understand that Mr Archard had made all arrangements to take his wife and family abroad, but had omitted until the last moment to notify the postal authorities of his intended departure. On Tuesday night he inquired of the authorities whether he could get the post office transferred, but he was informed that it was then too late to make the necessary arrangements. In consequence the office had to be closed, as already stated. It was taken over by the officials on Wednesday.[9]

And that is the last we hear of him. He had been in Bath less than 15 years; his first shop had been pulled down, his second had burnt down. It is hardly surprising he wanted to try his luck elsewhere. What is astonishing is that the signs painted on the walls of 6 Cleveland Terrace during his time there should not have only survived a devastating fire but still present an impressive display over a century later.

The sign at the back of Nº 3 Cleveland Terrace in 2010 (above) and 2015 (below), showing the old and new configuration of drainpipes which partially hide it.

Turn down Cleveland Cottages, beside 6 Cleveland Terrace, and look up at the back of the building three doors along to see a ghost sign for a PLUMBER, GAS & HOT-WATER FITTER (4). There was a plumber at 3 Cleveland Terrace for a very long time. George Watts set himself up here as 'plumber, bath & water-closet erector, painter, glazier and general contractor' around 1890. Shortly before the First World War, his place was taken by George Hewitt, who was here until the 1940s. What is curious is that the sign is at the back of the building, down a narrow cul-de-sac where few people would have ventured, and, even if it was intended to be seen from across the river, that was some distance away.

Head back up to the street and turn right along Cleveland Terrace. As you pass Nº 1, at the far end of Cleveland Terrace, you are walking past one of Bath's most intriguing ghost signs. Although it can be made out from below, to appreciate it fully you need to see it from the raised

GHOST SIGNS OF BATH

pavement opposite, which you will be walking along later, so discussion of it will be deferred until then.

Carry on round the corner into Cleveland Place West, and, two doors along from the Curfew Inn, look up to see a slab-serif sign proclaiming FUNERALS FURNISHED (5). This one is something of a puzzle. Cleveland Place West was built in the late 1820s, and in 1835 N° 9 became a museum, many of whose exhibits, such as minerals, shells, and 'natural and artificial curiosities', were for sale. It closed in the early 1840s when the proprietor, Charles Empson, relocated to 7 Terrace Walk.

It seems highly unlikely – although not impossible – that he was responsible for the sign on the building, but tracking down a more plausible candidate is no easy matter. 'Funerals furnished' was a popular phrase in the nineteenth century, yet meant different things to different people, as a sample of advertisements from the *Bath Chronicle* will demonstrate.

In 1837, Charles Edwards, 'cabinet maker, upholsterer, estate and house agent' at 3 Margaret's Buildings, offered 'funerals furnished'.[10] In 1843, Ford & Merrett, 'cabinet-makers, carpenters and undertakers' of 21 Beauford Square offered the same facility.[11] The following year, however, Parton & Company of N°s 2 and 3 Milsom Street, after announcing a 'display of foreign articles for ladies' costume', and drawing attention to their 'show room [containing] a most fashionable assortment, in rich satins, cachmeres [sic], shawls, scarfs, cloaks, mantles, &c,' and their 'linen-drapery, hosiery, haberdashery, and furnishing goods' ended by adding, 'family mourning and funerals furnished'.[12]

So the sign on 9 Cleveland Place West could have been put there either by a cabinet maker or by a draper. However, not only were the majority of advertisements offering 'funerals furnished' placed by drapers; there were two such establishments across the road in Cleveland Place East. In 1856, the *Bath Chronicle* carried an advertisement from George Angell's Walcot Drapery Establishment at 3 Cleveland Place East offering 'family mourning and funerals furnished', and in 1861 it carried a similar advertisement for B Moor's Family Drapery Establishment at 1 Cleveland Place East.[13]

Step forward Absalom Read, tailor, entrepreneur, and the most likely person to have had the sign painted on N° 9. Born around 1806, he worked as a tailor, and in the early 1840s moved, along with his wife, a milliner called Maria, ten years his junior, to 9 Cleveland Place West. Between 1846 and 1848, WH Bailey from London placed advertisements in the *Bath Chronicle* offering to treat those with varicose veins or hernias by fitting them with his patent surgical stockings or trusses, and requesting them to call on him at 'Mr Read's, Cleveland Place'.[14] This seems to show something of an entrepreneurial spirit on Absalom Read's part, the sort of spirit that may have led him to advertise 'funerals furnished' to passers-by. Wishful thinking,

perhaps, but, until a more likely candidate is discovered, the best we can come up with. If he did announce his presence in this way, however, it was a very short-lived one. He had gone by the early 1850s, leaving no trace – except perhaps for the ghost sign – behind.

Cross at the lights to Cleveland Place East, turn right and walk to the lodge at 3 Cleveland Bridge. Here we have another mystery, which is odd, for this time we have a name and what appears to be a trade – HARRIS GENERAL COAL (6). Cleveland Bridge was built in 1827 and the style of the lettering suggests that this sign was painted no later than around 1840. There is, however, no trace of a Mr Harris or anyone else selling coal here during this period. The wording of the sign is also unusual. At first we assumed that the word following 'COAL' (which has either been scrubbed off, or disappeared when the stone on which it was painted was replaced) was 'MERCHANT' or 'DEALER'. There are two problems with this, however. First, no instances of coal merchants or coal dealers in Bath describing themselves as general coal merchants or coal dealers have been found. Second, neither 'MERCHANT' nor 'DEALER' would fit into the space available.

There is, however, another possibility. In 1836 a soup kitchen 'for the benefit of the poor' was set up in this lodge, where it continued to operate until around 1842. Another charity established at around the same time was the GENERAL COAL FUND, also known as the

'GENERAL COAL AND POTATOE [sic] FUND'. This aimed to supply 'the Poor of Bath with Coal and Potatoes, during the months of January, February, and March, at one-third of the market price'. In December 1838, the committee reported that 'besides relieving 4,406 families, amounting to 17,091 individuals, they have also supplied many sick and aged persons with soup ... from personal knowledge of their destitution'.[15]

Given that the aims of these two charities were so similar – and indeed overlapped – it seems probable that they co-operated with each other and may even have operated in tandem. If so, what better place to paint a sign advertising the operations of the GENERAL COAL FUND to the well-heeled residents of Cleveland Place and the folks rattling across Cleveland Bridge in their carriages, and hoping thereby to solicit subscriptions from them? And, as it happens, 'FUND' would fit quite neatly into the space at the end of 'HARRIS GENERAL COAL' – although who HARRIS was unfortunately remains a mystery.

Heading back along Cleveland Place East, you pass the Eastern Dispensary of 1845 – counterpart to the Western Dispensary whose entrance sign featured in the third walk – with DISPENSARY chiselled in stone. A little further along are some of the ghostliest signs in Bath, a fading remnant of the cacophony of competing claims on the attention of passers-by that once characterised the city's streets. None of what is left is easy to read, especially from below, although you will have the chance of seeing these signs more clearly when you walk back along the high pavement of Walcot Parade.

For now, though, walk along to N° 5 and look up. Above the second-floor windows you may be able to decipher BATH & WEST

Left: N° 5 Cleveland Place East, showing signs reading BATH AND WEST OF ENGLAND and ESTABLISHMENT.

Below: A close-up of the BATH AND WEST OF ENGLAND sign on N° 5 Cleveland Place East.

Bottom: N° 6 Cleveland Place East in 1981, showing the sign – since removed – for the BATH & WEST OF ENGLAND COLLEGE OF CHEMISTRY & PHARMACY.

Opposite: A postcard from around 1910, showing the college sign on N° 6. The college had yet to expand into N° 5, so there is no matching sign there, although the unrelated sign reading ESTABLISHMENT can be seen above the first-floor windows. Finally, on N° 4 is the sign for HC Broad, Chemist & Pharmacist.

OF ENGLAND, while above the first-floor windows is the word ESTABLISHMENT (7). The two signs are unrelated: the lower one can be seen, already somewhat faded, on the postcard above from around 1910, its significance unknown, while the upper one dates from after the First World War. There was once a matching sign above the second-floor windows of Nº 6 – to the right – which read BATH & WEST OF ENGLAND COLLEGE OF CHEMISTRY & PHARMACY. Still visible in the early 1980s, it has since been cleaned off, and only the faintest trace remains. This college was established at Nº 6 in 1907, and later expanded into Nº 5, before moving to Bristol in 1929, where it formed part of the Merchant Venturers' College, and later of the College of Advanced Technology. In 1966, it moved to Claverton Down as part of the University of Bath.

Next door, at Nº 4, are a couple of ghost signs which have largely faded to nothing (8). First of all, at the very top, the word CHEMIST can just about be deciphered, although there are indications that this may have been painted over an earlier sign or signs. The postcard above shows that this sign read CHEMIST HC BROAD & PHARMACIST.

Immediately below it, just above the windows on the third floor, is the first line of a later sign, which covered much of the building. Although only odd letters are visible, it has been possible to piece together much of what it says.

The top line reads K.J.C. McCLENNAN F.C.S. M.P.S. Below it, between the two third-floor windows, WHOLESALE & RETAIL

GHOST SIGNS OF BATH

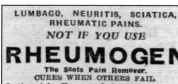

Above: An advertisement from 1936.

Opposite: The faded signs on N° 4 Cleveland Place East.

Below: A sign on the side wall of N° 3 Cleveland Place East in 1981. Only faint traces of it remain today.

appears. Then, above the second-floor windows, are some words of which only a few letters remain. ... URIN ... can be seen to the right of the left-hand window, and ... ENSING to the right of the other window. This could have read MANUFACTURING & DISPENSING, with the word CHEMISTS below, now painted over. Below the second-floor windows, the words RHEUMOGEN Ltd appear in large letters, with FOR in small letters to the left and another word, almost totally obliterated, to the left of that. This may have read 'Agent for Rheumogen Ltd'.

This all dates from 1936. Kenneth John Cable McLennan was for many years the proprietor of Laird & Son's chemists in Edinburgh, and later director of Burgoyne, Burbidges & Co, a chemical company then based in London but now relocated to India. After developing Rheumogen, described as a cure for lumbago, neuritis, sciatica and rheumatic pains, he moved to Bath in 1936 and took over the chemist's shop at 4 Cleveland Place East. He died two years later, in a Bristol nursing home, at the age of 58, and the business was acquired by a Mr Swain.

On the side wall of 3 Cleveland Place East, to the left of N° 4, is the merest shadow of a ghost sign reading J PYKE & SONS, MILLINERS & FANCY DRAPERS (9). It was still legible in the early 1980s, but has since been cleaned off, and only a trace remains – you may still be able to make out the word FANCY.

John Pyke was born at Sampford Courtenay in Devon around 1841. At the age of 18 he came to Bath as an assistant at Stokes, Bryan & Roadway's drapers at 17 & 18 Cheap Street and the Abbey Churchyard. Nine years later, he established his own drapery business here. When he died in 1922, the business was carried on by two of his sons, but by 1934 it had been taken over by P Kent & Co.

If you carry on a little way to look up at the façade of Nº 3, you may see, above the second-floor windows, letters spelling out CANTON HOUSE. (Don't worry if you can't – you will get a better view later from Walcot Parade.) This is where things get confusing. The letters look as

though they date from around 1900, when John Pyke was here, but there is no record of him calling his business Canton House. However, in the early 1900s, there was a milliner's shop four doors to the left, at 2 Canton Place, kept by a Miss Kate Price, and in 1904 a series of advertisements in the *Bath Chronicle* referred to it as Canton House. These are the only references to a Canton House in Bath we have so far discovered, and the mystery as to why the sign was painted on Cleveland Place East must for the moment remain unsolved.

From unsolved mysteries and signs scrubbed almost away, we turn to something altogether more satisfying. A little way along the London Road, at the end of Walcot Terrace, a bust of Aesculapius, God of Healing, looks down from above the entrance to WF Dolman & Son, Funeral Directors (10). Below it is the date 1837, and above the date can just be made out the letters ABLIS, which once formed part of the word ESTABLISHED. Further down, just above the funeral directors' sign, it is possible to make out THE BATH.

For elucidation of these enigmatic fragments, we must turn to the side of the building, and one of Bath's most recondite ghost signs. Unfortunately, it is one of those signs that really needs to be seen with the sun on it, but, because it is hemmed in by tall buildings, the sun rarely, if ever, reaches it. With a little patience, however, it is possible to make out

THE BATH EAR & EYE INFIRMARY

This infirmary was, as the date over the entrance indicates, established in 1837, although its original home was not here but in one of the lodges on Cleveland Bridge. It was originally known as the Walcot Ear & Eye Infirmary, and was a charitable institution, supported by public subscription, and providing 'medical and surgical relief' to those who could not otherwise afford it. It clearly fulfilled a need: in 1840 the *Bath Chronicle* reported that, in the previous year, 132 people had been admitted 'for diseases of the ear' and 319 'for diseases of the eye'.[16] Its success rate – 66% 'cured' and 14% 'improved' – was impressive, with only 29 cases deemed 'incurable'. It was, according to the 1846 *Directory*, 'open to the poor every Monday, Wednesday and

Above: The head of Aesculapius and a sign which once read ESTABLISHED 1837.

Below: Above the present-day sign, THE BATH can just be made out.

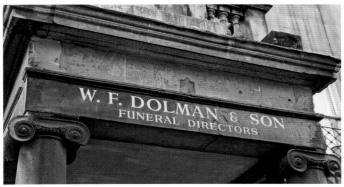

The sign for THE BATH EAR & EYE INFIRMARY on the side of the building

Saturday between 11 and 12 o'clock', although anyone severely afflicted – provided they lived in Bath – could be treated in their own homes.

In 1847, the infirmary moved 'from Cleveland Bridge to Walcot Terrace, where an elegant and commodious building had been fitted up for its purposes, at a considerable expense'.[17] To mark the occasion, it changed its name to the Bath Ear & Eye Infirmary. This upset another charitable institution, the Bath Eye Infirmary, which had been founded in 1811. The governors of the Eye Infirmary, which had itself just moved from Pierrepont Place to Bladud's Buildings, were so concerned that people would muddle up the two institutions that they placed a notice in the *Bath Chronicle*:

> In consequence of the Institution formerly called the 'Walcot Ear and Eye Infirmary' (which has lately been removed from Cleveland Bridge into another part of Walcot) having adopted the name of 'The Bath Ear and Eye Infirmary', confusion has arisen in the minds of many from the similarity of the designations of the two Charities, and the Committee of the last-named Institution having declined to take the necessary step to obviate the evil which was represented to them, the Committee of the BATH EYE INFIRMARY feel it incumbent upon them to call the attention of their Subscribers to the circumstance, and to inform them that Mr WILLIAM ROGERS is the only authorised Collector for this Institution.[18]

The move from Cleveland Bridge to the more imposing premises on Walcot Terrace seems to have been a success, but it was not long before the infirmary started to run into the sort of cash-flow problems experienced by many such charities. In 1854, the *Bath Chronicle* reported that, during the previous year, 645 patients had been admitted to the infirmary, and that a total of 9,384 people had been treated since it had been established 17 years earlier. It added, however, that

> the funds, notwithstanding the strictest economy, have been insufficient to meet the expenditure ... and, unless the assistance of the public is afforded, the Committee fear they will have to curtail extensively the operation of the Charity. This, it appears, is the only institution in the West of England where diseases of the ear are specially treated, and its doors are open to the necessitous not only of Bath, but of every locality.[19]

This appeal seems to have done the trick, for the infirmary on Walcot Terrace continued to operate for another 60 years. In 1914 it moved to 17 Charles Street to become the Bath Ear, Nose and Throat Hospital, which later relocated to 27 & 28 Marlborough Buildings, where it remained until closure in the 1960s, its role being taken over by the Royal United Hospital.

The building on Walcot Terrace, meanwhile, was taken over by William Dolman, described in the 1920 *Directory* as a 'cabinet maker and dealer in antiques'. The following year's *Directory* listed him as a 'cabinet maker', a year later he was a 'furniture dealer', but by 1923 he had become a 'furniture dealer and undertaker', thus establishing the business still operating today.

Before moving on, it is worth considering the extraordinary history of this diminutive building, which may have been put to a far different use before becoming an infirmary. It was certainly here by 1810, for it appears on a map published that year, but was probably much older, and, as the remains of what appear to be a bath have been discovered beneath the floor, it seems to have been built as a bath house.

It would not have been the only cold bath house in the city. There was a well-known cold bath near the river in Widcombe, which was demolished in 1966, and one below Marlborough Buildings, which appears on a map of 1800 but had disappeared by the 1850s. Although it may seem strange that there is no similar documentation for this cold bath, this may be because it catered for a somewhat different clientele. It may, in fact, have been a bagnio, a type of establishment very popular in Georgian London, whose attractions were not confined to bathing. A reference in a long-forgotten play called *The Maid of Bath* lends some weight to this theory. The play, written in 1771 by Samuel Foote, salaciously dramatised the sexual intrigues surrounding Elizabeth Linley, the 'Maid of Bath'.[20] Among the many in-jokes about people and places in Bath is one concerning the nephew of a Bath alderman who has set up 'a bagnio at the end of Long Acre' – the name by which the row of buildings across the road has been known since the eighteenth century. Obscure references in satirical comedies cannot, of course, be taken as historical fact, but the possibility that one of Georgian Bath's more disreputable establishments was located here cannot be discounted. We know there was at least one bagnio in Bath around this time, because of a court case in 1782 which attracted national attention. The *Bath Chronicle's* coverage of it makes extraordinary reading:

> A gentleman residing near Chippenham became acquainted with a pretty young widow in the neighbourhood, paid his addresses to her, and prevailed upon her to accompany him to Bath, that they might be 'made one flesh'. The lady assented, they went to a bagnio at Bath, where a person dressed in canonical habiliments (a female) and called the Archbishop, officiated and performed the marriage. A little time developed the artifice, and convinced the lady she was still a widow.[21]

The report goes on to deal with the accusations and counter-accusations at great length, leaving us with a tantalising glimpse of another side to eighteenth-century life in Bath. How many descriptions of trips to the Pump Room or Abbey, by fastidious visitors to the city, would we willingly exchange for a no-holds-barred account of a night of unfrocked frolics and unfettered fun at this shrine to blasphemy, cross-dressing and who knows what other dark delights? And did it all take place here? We will probably never know.

Carry on to 4 Walcot Buildings, once the Black Dog beerhouse, which closed in 1917 (11). A lodge of the Royal Antediluvian Order of Buffaloes – better known as the 'Buffs' – met here and the initials A O B flanked the windows

The former Black Dog beerhouse in 2005

on the first floor. Until the building was cleaned in 2014 these were still clearly visible on the soot-blackened stonework, but, although 4 Walcot Buildings now shines forth in all its pristine splendour, the letters can still be made out if you know where to look.

Two doors along, at 6 Walcot Buildings, is a sign for THE WALCOT FRUIT & POTATO STORES which poses no such difficulties (12).

If you look carefully, however, and the light is right, you can make out a ghost sign beneath the ghost sign. The wording is the same, but the letters are larger and slightly lower down. There was a greengrocer's and fruiterer's here from the late nineteenth century until the 1960s, with some of the produce grown in greenhouses at the back, and, while the choice of phrase may seem quirky, 'fruit & potato stores' were once common throughout the country.

Four doors along, we come a recently uncovered fascia-board sign, behind glass, with the name MILLS clearly visible, as well as some other letters which have not stood the test of time so well (13). The likelihood is that they form the first part of the word CONFECTIONER. What is visible is only the central part of the sign, and MILLS would probably have been preceded by WILLIAM. William Mills was born at Southleigh in Devon in 1827. In 1850 he married Esther Miles from Englishcombe, and the following year's census lists him, aged 24, as a confectioner at 10 Walcot Buildings. This gives a probable date for the sign of around 1850-51. He was still here in 1881, but, when he died four years later at 6 Larkhall Place, he was described as 'William Mills, late of 10 Walcot Buildings, aged 58'.[22]

Now we move along to 19 Walcot Buildings, and another fascia board sign, but one that is anything but straightforward (14). On top, 'J BUCKNALL' appears in a style which is best described as displaying a disarming lack of pretension. It also appears fairly recent. Beneath it can be made out 'R.C. BUCK'. Beneath that is another name, of which only 'A & ………M' are fully visible. Flanking these three names are, on the left, the words 'Fancy Goods', and, on the right, 'Tobacconist'. Finally, over the door, is a sign for a LIBRARY.

Taking these in order: no record of a J Bucknall has been found, but Reginald Claud Buck is listed in the 1952 *Directory* as running a toy shop here. As for the 'Fancy Goods' and 'Tobacconist' signs, they may date from the early twentieth century, when Mrs Lucy May was a newsagent, stationer and toy dealer here. The sign over the door, however, probably dates from the nineteenth century, when Henry Hyams ran a library here.

Henry Naphtali Hyams was born in Warsaw around 1820. In 1844, at the age of 24, after emigrating to England, he married Harriet Palmer of Bath, some five years his junior, and set up as a stationer at 1 Piccadilly, further out along the London Road. By 1855, he had moved to 19 Walcot Buildings and opened a bookshop and circulating library, where he also sold newspapers and stationery. He and his wife had three children: Matilda, who died in infancy, George and Rachel. His wife died in 1863, and his son George died three years later, at the age of 20, leaving Rachel to assist to him in the business. Sometime after 1871 he remarried Elizabeth Hayward from Cold Ashton. After his death in 1880, Elizabeth and Rachel continued to run the business for a time, but by 1887 the shop had been taken over by a newsagent called Charles Hockey.

Although the earliest set of lettering over the window seems to match the sign for the library over the doorway, however, it is far from certain that it does so. All that can be made out clearly are 'A &', and then, after a long gap, the letter 'M'. It looks as though the letter in front of the 'M' is an 'A', and it is possible that the letter before that is a 'Y', which would indeed form part of the name HYAMS. The 'A' and

'&' at the beginning do not tie in, however, as none of the members of the Hyams family had a first name beginning with an 'A'. Moreover, if, as seems likely, there was just one other letter after the 'A', that would leave a very long gap before the word HYAMS. This suggests, despite appearances to the contrary, that this set of lettering does not date from the same time as the library sign. Trawling through directories, however, has failed to come up with another possible candidate, so this part of the sign must remain, for the present at least, a mystery.

It is with a sigh of relief, therefore, that we carry on to 27 Walcot Buildings, and a set of signs that present no such difficulties (15). These pet shop signs date from  between 1957 and 1961 when the London Road Pet Stores opened here, in what had previously been a glass and china shop.

Now it is time to retrace our steps along the London Road, crossing at the pedestrian lights by 16 Walcot Buildings, and climbing the flight of steps at the end to Walcot Parade. Here you have a grandstand view of the ghost signs across the road, which you have already seen from ground level – with one exception. As mentioned earlier, from down below it is hardly worth bothering trying to make out the signs on 1 Cleveland Terrace – the soot-blackened building which now houses a property letting agency (16). From up here, though, it is a different story. This is one of Bath's most fugitive signs, but, when the late afternoon sun shines on it, it acquires a lenticular quality, and its shape – and meaning – shift depending on where you view it from.

As you head west along Walcot Parade, you will see, above the second-storey windows of Nº 1, the words

WALCOT

TEA WAREHOUSE

with the merest hint of something else underneath. Carry on past Nº 1, however, and look back, and you will see

WALCOT

FURNITURE WAREHOUSE

From the east ...

... from the west ...

If you look at the building from directly opposite, meanwhile, you will see the word WALCOT clearly enough, but the rest will appear a muddle, only decipherable if you have looked at it from both sides first. This fortuitous visual phenomenon makes this ghost sign a thing of great rarity. We can only hope that, whatever happens to the building, the bands above the second-storey windows are never tampered with, for cleaning, restoration

... and from directly opposite

or refurbishment would almost certainly upset the delicate balance which holds the two sets of lettering in curious equilibrium.

As for dating them, Cleveland Terrace was built in the late 1820s, and the 1833 *Directory* lists Edmund Rawlings as a tea dealer and grocer here, so it is likely he was the first occupant, and had a sign painted on stone that shone nearly as bright as when dug from the quarry. Dating the second sign is more problematic. By 1852, Nº 1 Cleveland Terrace was occupied by a cabinet maker called James Beckett. He was succeeded by Robert Lanham and Adam Fussell, who were also cabinet makers. A more likely candidate, however, is Edward Witcombe, a former valet from Rode, who in 1872 set himself up as a 'furniture broker' here.

That concludes the fifth walk, but, if you walk to the west end of Walcot Parade, you can, if you wish, turn right uphill to start the next walk along Camden to Larkhall.

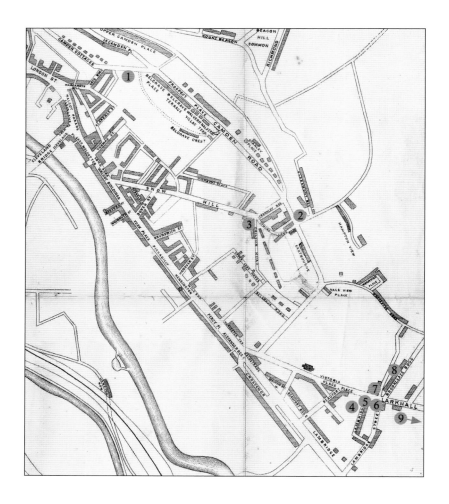

6

CAMDEN & LARKHALL

This walk starts where the last one ended, at the west end of Walcot Parade, from where a climb up Margaret's Hill will, after 300m, lead to Gay's Hill House and one of Bath's most celebrated ghost signs (1).

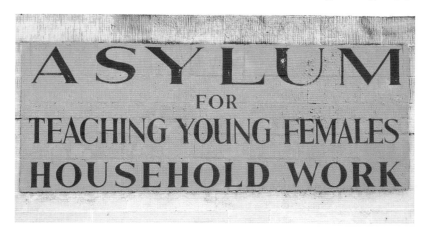

There can be no more eloquent expression of the gulf between rich and poor in the early nineteenth century than this sign.

It dates from 1819, when a meeting was held at the Guildhall 'to establish an asylum for the reception of young females, children of the poor inhabitants of Bath, Walcot, Bathwick, and Lyncombe and Widcombe, to be instructed in religious duties, and to be trained up as useful household servants'.[1] After 'some liberal donations and subscriptions were entered into', it was agreed that those admitted to the asylum should be 'unprotected females, not less than 12 years of age nor above 14', and that their training should 'qualify them for situations of inferior domestic service'.[2] The word 'unprotected' gives the clue to why the asylum was needed. 'Unprotected' girls, without the means of supporting themselves, and with none of the skills that would enable them to find employment, were in danger of being drawn in the *demi monde* of prostitution, crime and utter destitution. There were several similar institutions in the city, most of them caring for older girls and women, of which the former penitentiary in Walcot Street, with PENITENTIARY CHAPEL still carved in large letters above its first-floor windows, is the best-known example.

The institution at Gay's Hill House was known by several names, including the Asylum for the Maintenance and Instruction of Young Females in Plain Needlework and the Asylum for the Maintenance and Instruction of Young Females in Household Work. For a time, it was one of the most fashionable of the many worthy causes competing for the patronage of the great and good. It attracted titled patrons, and charity balls and concerts held to raise funds for it were well subscribed. By 1827, however, it was in trouble. There had been an outbreak of typhus in the asylum, and it had been necessary to hire nurses to care for the girls. In order to save money, the number of girls who could be accommodated was reduced from 22 to 16.[3]

At a meeting 'of the friends and subscribers to the asylum' on 17 April the following year, the Rev Harvey Marriott, referring to 'the efficacy of the moral and religious instruction, which the Guardians of the Institution had ever deemed the most important part of its object', made a passionate plea for more funding:

> Every child, at this period when crime is on the increase, placed in this 'Preventive' charity, may be looked upon as rescued from the mass of evil. This is particularly applicable to a society like the present, appropriated for the religious instruction of females; upon whose moral character and conduct the state of society has so much depended, that, according to its prevalence or otherwise in that sex, the experience of the past proves that society at large has been either good or evil. The objects of this charity are not selected from among those of good character *only*, but from those whose forlorn and destitute condition exposes them the most powerfully to temptation.

He concluded by expressing the hope that, 'in this Christian land, the exposed child of penury and domestic ill would not put forth her appeal in vain'.[4]

This seemed to do the trick for a time, but four years later there was another crisis. On 22 March 1832, the *Bath Chronicle* reported that,

> yesterday being the day set apart for the National Fast, business was suspended, and divine service was performed at the churches and other places of public worship in this city. Collections were made in the churches in aid of that excellent institution, the Asylum for the Maintenance and Instruction of Young Females in Household Work, Gay's Hill, Upper Camden Place, whose funds are almost exhausted. We trust that the inhabitants of this city will stretch forth their hands to save from extinction a charity which is calculated to do so much inestimable good.[5]

A week later, it reported that the collections had raised over £377, and expressed the hope that 'this timely aid ... will have more than a temporary effect, and that the efforts of the benevolent will be used to fix it on a permanent basis'. It also revealed that, since its establishment in 1819, 94 girls had been admitted to the asylum. Of these, 61 had been placed 'in respectable service', eight had been discharged for ill health, three had been expelled for misbehaviour, five had died and 17 were still there.[6]

Curiously, this is the last we hear of it. What happened to it, or to the 'timely aid' it had received, or indeed to the girls remaining within its walls, must, unless further information comes to light, remain a mystery – as must the question of why its sign has managed to survive for over 180 years.

Carry on uphill, and, when you reach the top of Gay's Hill, look to the left to see a white-painted two-storey building (Nº 25), the location of one of Bath's most recently uncovered – and recently re-covered – ghost signs. This was once a pub called the Rivers Arms, and the early nineteenth-century sign that lurks beneath its façade is featured on pages 268-73.

Turn right along Camden Road and after 500m you will come to the corner of Fairfield Road, and a sign for a GROCERY & PROVISION STORES (2). There is a similar sign round the corner, while above the

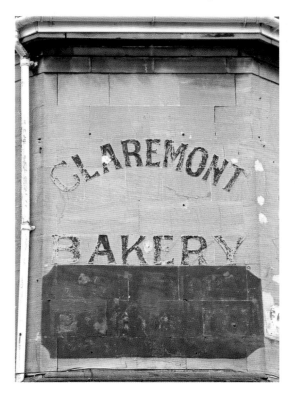

entrance is a sign for CLAREMONT BAKERY, with a painted-out panel below it, in which POST OFFICE, along with some other indecipherable lettering, can be seen.

The post office sign is probably the earliest. There was a post office here in the late nineteenth century, but by 1914 it had moved to 1 Claremont Terrace, across the road, where it remained until recently. By the 1930s, the shop on the corner of Fairfield Road was Batstone & Sons, Bakers and

Grocers. Later it became a general grocer's, run in the 1950s by Gerald Whiteley and in the 1960s by D & P Harrison.

Before moving on, you might care to turn to page 259 for a photograph of another lost ghost sign which may lurk beneath the paintwork on N°s 2 to 5 Claremont Terrace.

Turn down Tyning Lane and, as you take the first left into Chilton Road, you will see a sign for a FAMILY GROCER on the fascia board

of N° 1 (3). The first known occupant of this building was Thomas Powney, who was listed as a carpenter in 1872, but who by 1886 had become a grocer. In 1888, the business was taken over by George Francis, and it remained a grocer's until comparatively recently. The longest recorded tenure was that of Arthur Tiley, who was here from the mid-1920s to the late 1960s.

Walk along Chilton Road, and after it bears right downhill, take the first left along Belgrave Road. At the crossroads, carry straight on along Dowding Road, take the first right down Holland Road, and turn left at the end along St Saviour's Road.

Although, compared with the earlier walks, this one has so far offered relatively slim – and well-spaced out – pickings, all that is about to change, as we approach one of the most fascinating, and least-known, clusters of ghost signs in Bath.

Stop opposite the end of Victoria Place, and, looking ahead, compare the buildings on the right with those in the photograph opposite, which dates from around 1910 (4). The former Victoria Bakery – still sporting an impressive weathervane – survives as a takeaway, and the building next to it is still there, but beyond that modern buildings have sprung up on the site of what was once the office of Burden & Clark, builders, whose name was painted on the hoarding beside it.

The firm was founded around 1880, as Burden & Giddings, by James Burden and Thomas Giddings. Thomas Giddings died in 1903, and by 1907 James Burden had gone into partnership with Harry Clark. It was around this time that the office fronting St Saviour's Road was built. Prior to that, the business operated from the yard behind it, which is still there, and is still known as Burden's Court, as you will see if you go round the corner into Lambridge Place. You will also see, if you look up at the end wall of the building overlooking the yard, the faded shadow of what must once have been a very imposing sign. This building, 17 Lambridge Place, was originally the home of Thomas Giddings, and later became the home of James Burden's son, George, who followed him into the business.

Nº 17 Lambridge Place had been home to a building firm long before Thomas Giddings lived there, however. Although the 1819 *Directory* recorded it as the home of 'T Field Esq', by 1826 George Williams, a carpenter and joiner, had moved in. By 1833, he was describing himself as a builder, and he remained at Nº 17 until around 1872, when David Rawlings, another builder, took over. So, when Burden & Giddings arrived around eight years later, they were taking over a well-established builder's yard.

The sign on the side of Nº 17 once covered most of the upper part of the wall, but much of it has flaked away, and, although the names of the proprietors would doubtless have appeared at the top, all that can now be made out with any certainty is:

...LDER

CARPENTER &

FUNER...

... which presumably once read 'BUILDER, CARPENTER & FUNERAL DIRECTOR'. There is, in addition, a small white-painted rectangle which covers the rest of the last word, and which appears to contain further indecipherable lettering. White paint also appears to have been applied to the lower part of the wall, and there are markings which suggest there may have been writing here too, but this is by no means certain. It also does not seem very likely. The sign on the top part of the wall would have been visible not only from Lambridge Place, but also – with only single-storey buildings standing in the way – from St Saviour's Road and Larkhall Square. Any words on the lower part of the wall would only have been visible from within the yard.

The partnership seems to have been dissolved during the First World War, as in the 1917 *Directory* George Burden is listed as being in business on his own as 'builder, decorator and undertaker'. This gives us the clue to the likely date of the sign, for, had it been painted earlier, 'builder' and 'carpenter' would have been plural rather than singular. George Burden's son later took over the business, which was still operating from here in the 1970s.

Head back to St Saviour's Road, turn right and look at the building on the corner, which sports a ghost sign – Player's Please – above the entrance (5). Player's adopted this slogan in 1924, and looking back through

the directories, we find that, at that time, Albert Webb had a newsagent's here. After he died in 1929, the business – now listed as a tobacconist's – was carried on by his widow. By 1952, Jill Whiteford and her husband had set up a ladies' hairdresser's, newsagent's, stationer's and tobacconist's here. By 1960, this had been scaled back to become Jill's Hairdresser's, and today it is Ma Cuisine.

Carry on to the corner of Upper Lambridge Street and look below the window of the chemist's to see the next ghost sign – OILCAKE, GURGEONS, SHARPS (6). Not items you'd be likely to find in the average shopping basket today, so a little elucidation is in order. Oilcake was – and still is – made from the fibrous matter left after seeds such as rape and linseed had been pressed for their oil and was fed to livestock. As for gurgeons and sharps, a guide to *Old Country and Farming Words*, published in 1880, has this to say:

> Meal is undressed flour; it is separated into flour (the finest part), seconds, middlings, and even thirds; then blues, boxings, sharps, gurgeons, scuftings, pollards (fine and coarse), and bran.[7]

If you carry on round the corner you will see two more ghost signs– PURE SCOTCH OATMEAL below the window and, above it, the magnificent, if somewhat distressed, sign seen below:

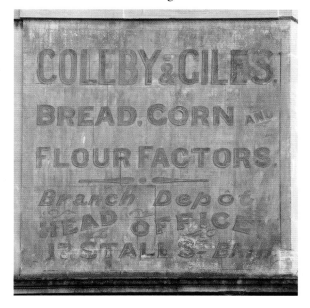

This, then, was a place where flour milled in Bath – both fine and coarse – could once be obtained. And the business it recalls was one of the best-known – and most ill-starred – in the city.

Sometime between 1809 and 1819, Christopher Frost established a 'flour and bread company's warehouse' at 17 Stall Street. He 'disposed' of the business in December 1825 and went travelling, not for pleasure but in an attempt to evade his creditors. He was unsuccessful, and, three years later, the *Bath Chronicle* revealed that

> Christopher Frost, formerly of Bath, Somersetshire, baker; then of the city of Naples, Italy; then of New York, North America, in no business; then of his Majesty's ships Wellesley and Victory, seaman; and late of Rose and Crown Court, Sun Street, Finsbury Square, in the county of Middlesex, in no business, [was] a prisoner in the Debtors' Prison for London and Middlesex.[8]

Frost's business in Stall Street had been taken over by John Rutter, a Quaker from Witney in Oxfordshire, who expanded into the corn and seed trade, and built the original Camden Flour Mill on the Lower Bristol Road.[9] Sixteen years later, it was at Camden Mill that he met his death. At the inquest,

> G Rawlings, the captain of one of Mr Rutter's boats, deposed that he was in the coal yard of Mr Rutter's wharf, Lower Bristol Road, about seven o'clock in the morning. There was one cart on the engine, which, having been weighed, deceased took another cart from the yard, and was leading it toward the engine-house, when the horse plunged and hit him against the wall of the house. The horse was not frightened, and witnesses could not account for the accident. After deceased had been jammed against the engine-house, he fell down, and the wheel of the cart passed over the lower part of his bowels ... Witness ran and picked up Mr Rutter. He was quite insensible, and was put into a wheel-chair and taken to his house almost immediately ... Mr Rutter was 68 years old next birthday.[10]

He was succeeded by his sons, John and Samuel. John, who remained a bachelor, later became a gentleman farmer at Wick Farm, Saltford, where he lived with other members of his extended family, leaving Samuel to run the business. In 1853, Samuel married Mary, 'eldest daughter of the late John Coleby of London' at the Friends' Meeting House in Uxbridge. He brought Mary's brother, Henry, down to Bath to manage the business, and later went into partnership with him.[11]

That accounts for the first of the two names on the sign. The route by which Samuel Giles came to Bath is not only more convoluted but also less clear. According to his obituary, he 'was a member of a good old family of Friends, his father being at one time in a large way of business in London. After serving his apprenticeship in the grocery trade, he entered the establishment of Messrs Peek Brothers, one of the largest tea houses in London.'[12] At the time of the 1871 census he was a grocer's assistant, aged 19, at The Pavement in York. Three years later comes the first reference to the firm of Coleby & Giles in Bath – with no mention of Samuel Rutter.[13] A year later, Samuel Giles returned to York to marry Elizabeth Pumphrey, and by the time of the 1881 census was living at Bewdley Villa on Prior Park Road. The same census records that Henry Coleby, described as 'a corn dealer employing 13 men', was living at 17 Stall Street with his second wife (his first marriage having ended in divorce).

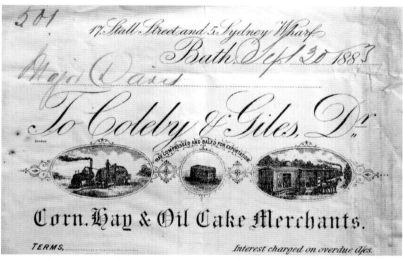

A billhead from 30 September 1883, shortly after Henry Coleby's retirement

Two years later, however, the *Bath Chronicle* reported that the partnership between 'Henry Coleby and Samuel Giles, trading as Coleby and Giles at 17 Stall Street and Sydney Wharf', had been dissolved, and that Henry Coleby had retired.[14] On the face of it, this seems surprising,

as he was only 43. Six months later, however, he died at Cotham Grove in Bristol, which suggests his retirement was due to ill health.

Samuel Giles continued to trade under the name of Coleby & Giles, but in 1884 was faced with another setback, when a fire broke out at the back of the premises in Stall Street. It started on the third floor, where a steam-powered chaff cutter was located, and which was 'full to the ceiling with hay'. Although considerable damage was caused, and a great deal of hay lost, the fire was prevented from spreading by several policemen 'tossing huge armfuls of burning hay into the street below, and now and again playing water upon it to prevent its igniting the fire escape and the lower portion of the house'.[15]

The business was soon back on course, and over the next few years Samuel Giles opened branches in Westgate Street and Twerton, and in 1892 added the one in Larkhall, dating the sign here precisely. Two years later, however, the *Bath Chronicle* reported his death at the age of 43:

> It is with feelings of deep and unaffected regret and sincere sorrow for his widow and mourning family that we record the death ... of Mr Samuel Giles, proprietor of the old established corn, bakery and confectionery business ... of Coleby & Giles. The end came on Sunday morning after a severe and painful illness of but a few days' duration. Few men were better known or more popular in the city than Mr Sam Giles, his genial, hearty manners and kindly disposition made him a general favourite, while his business enterprise and straightforward, honourable dealing had won for him the respect and esteem of his fellow citizens. He was ever ready as well to promote any movement for the welfare of the city, as to do a neighbourly or friendly act, and there is too much reason to fear that his death was hastened by his endeavours to render aid and relief to the sufferers by the recent floods. He was out with ... others in a boat distributing provisions to the poor people in the Dolemeads who could not leave their homes by reason of the flood, and in the performance of this work of mercy he got thoroughly drenched. This brought on a chill, and yesterday week he was obliged to take to his bed, his illness developing into congestion of the lungs and liver, and terminating as above stated.[16]

His widow, Elizabeth, carried on the business, but the Larkhall branch was last listed in the 1896 *Directory*. She moved to Redland in Bristol to live with her parents and the company was eventually wound up around 1908, with Charles Shapland taking over the bakery at 17 Stall Street.

You may wish, before moving on, to take this opportunity of calling into the Titfield Thunderbolt Bookshop across the road. Named after one of the finest Ealing Comedies, filmed just south of Bath on the Camerton & Limpley Stoke Railway in 1952, this specialises, as you might guess, in transport books, but also has a selection of local books.

After that, take a quick look at the butcher's on the corner of Lambridge Buildings (7). You will see that the modern street name partially covers an early and very faded painted version of the name. Above it, you will see a sign bracket with the merest hint of a rectangle painted on the stonework behind it. The sign that hung from the bracket was that of the White Lion Inn, closed in 1959. It may have been preceded by a painted sign on the wall itself, but, if it was, it was a very long time ago and there is very, very little of it left.

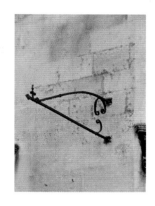

Far richer pickings await at 10 Brookleaze Buildings – which lies on the far side of Larkhall Square, to the right of the drinking fountain (8). Above the plat band between the ground and first floors is something quite splendid, quite early and quite odd – because it is on the wrong building. Turning to the 1841 census, we find 'James Parsons, Slater & Plasterer' – a listing that corresponds exactly to the ghost sign on Nº 10 – at Brookleaze Buildings. He also appears in the following two censuses, before dying, at the age of 74, in 1864. The problem is that in each case he is shown as living at Nº 7 Brookleaze Buildings, not Nº 10. Having checked a map drawn up by council surveyors in the 1850s, held in Bath Record Office, it is clear that the house numbers along here were the same then as they are now – so how to account for this anomaly?

Surprisingly, this sort of thing was not that uncommon, and came about because some landlords would not allow their tenants to paint

signs on their walls, while some were quite happy for them to do so, presumably in exchange for some small remuneration. So it seems that James Parsons, anxious to promote his business, having been forbidden to paint a sign on his own house, did a deal with the owner of one three doors along. Originally, the sign may also have indicated that prospective clients should call at N° 7 rather than N° 10, but, if it did, that part of it has long disappeared.

Head back to Larkhall Square and turn left along St Saviour's Road for 500m to the Bladud's Head pub in Lower Swainswick, and some ghost signs discovered in 2013 – another glimpse of the riches that often lie hidden beneath layers of paint or render (9). In this case, the signs have not only been preserved but restored by local artist Pete Cashman, who also painted the modern pub sign.

The Bladud's Head beerhouse was opened at 1 Catsley Place in the late 1840s by John Cooper. The 1851 census shows that he was running it with his wife Jane. By the time of the 1861 census, the beerhouse keeper was Isaac Hales, and John Cooper was living on his own a few doors away at 5 Dead Mill Lane and working as a labourer. Ten years later, however, he had remarried and was back at the Bladud's Head.

The licensing sign on the side wall indicates the position of the original entrance, which was moved when the beerhouse was extended into the two adjoining cottages. The border round the lettering was not part of the original sign, which would have included the licensee's name at the top. Faint  traces of lettering can just be made out, although whether they form part of John Cooper's or Isaac Hales' name is not clear. They do, however, give some idea how faded the rest of the lettering may have been before it was enhanced.

As well as the licensing sign – and more prominent because of its position on the corner – is a chequerboard, and, while the licensing sign is a fantastic discovery, this, because of its rarity, is in another league altogether. The Chequers is not only one of the commonest, but also one of the oldest pub names there is.[17] By the eighteenth century, the word was virtually a synonym for a pub, and many pubs, when they first opened, seem to have been called the Chequers by the licensing authorities when those applying for a license did not suggest an alternative. There were at least 24 pubs called the Chequers in Bath at one time or other in the late eighteenth century, although many of them were renamed after a couple of years.

It has also been suggested that chequerboards were painted on the walls of buildings to indicate that they were pubs. One such sign, painted on the side door of the Methuen Arms in Corsham, has long been known, but no other examples were known in the Bath area, so there was no way of

knowing whether this was common practice or simply the whim of an eccentric landlord. Within the past five years, however, two more examples have come to light in Bath – one in 2011 on Upper Camden Place, since covered up, whose location you saw earlier – and now this. All three date from the first half of the nineteenth century. This is clearly something that demands further research, as, despite being a relatively recent phenomenon, there seems to be virtually no information on it. It would be fascinating to know, for example, how widespread it was, and whether its purpose was to assure the illiterate that a particular building was a pub or to indicate that certain people – such as masons or possibly Freemasons – were particularly welcome there. A further mystery is the roughly-painted mark beside it – an eye within a triangle perhaps, or some kind of mason's mark? This does not seem to be a sign that will give up its answers readily, but makes a splendid way of rounding off the walk – especially if the Bladud's Head happens to be open. And, if you turn to pages 241-42, you can read about the chequerboard sign on the Methuen Arms in Corsham, where we consider another possible reason for it having been painted.

There is also the option, if you are still up for some more ghost signs, of carrying on past the Bladud's Head to start the next walk through Bailbrook and Batheaston.

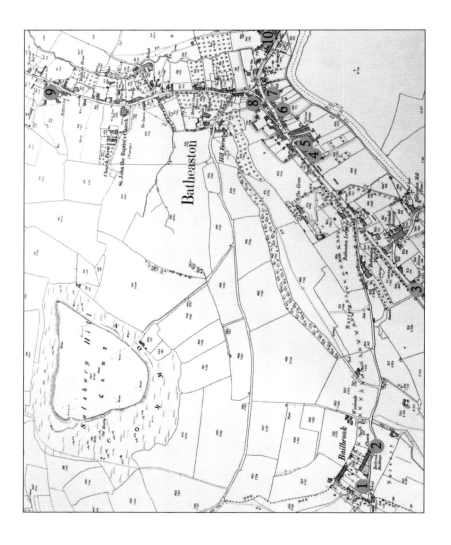

7

BAILBROOK, BATHEASTON, BATHFORD
& BATHAMPTON

This walk – devoted almost exclusively to bakers and beerhouses – starts where the last one ended, at the Bladud's Head pub in Larkhall. To get there from the city centre, take the N° 7 from the bus station and get off in St Saviour's Road just before the Bladud's Head (the stop is known as Linen Walk). Carry on past the Bladud's Head, following the road as it curves right, and turn right up Ferndale Road. Cross the Gloucester Road and carry on along Bailbrook Lane. After passing the old school, you will see a turning on the left with a post box in the wall (1). If you look to the left, over the door of N° 35 you will see a ghost sign:

The sign is incomplete, but one of the words it originally included would have been beer, for this was a beerhouse.

According to the present owner of the property, Thomas Beale bought what was then described as a 'tenement and shop' for £110 in 1828.[1] In the 1851 census, he was listed as a gardener, aged 48, with his place of birth as Chetly, Worcestershire, which does not exist – this could, however, be a misspelling of Chatley, which is between Worcester and Droitwich. His wife, Mary, aged 25, was from Walcot, and was listed as a shopkeeper. Three other people were also living in the house: Mary Brown, a widow, described as a 'former laundress', aged 87; Sarah Morley, a single woman, described as an 'annuitant', aged 19; and George Morley, aged 1.

The following year's *Directory*, however, lists Thomas Beale as the landlord of the King's Arms at Bailbrook. Whether he had taken out a beerhouse licence since the census or omitted to tell the census enumerator about his sideline is not known. In 1857, he made the first of several appearances in court, when he was

> summoned for having his house open for the sale of beer after ten o'clock on the night of the 15th January. PC Young stated that he

visited defendant's house at 20 minutes past ten on the above night, and although he knocked at the door, and called out 'police' several times, he was for some time refused admittance. At length the landlord opened the door, and he found five men in the tap room drinking and smoking, who left when he (the officer) did.

Defendant produced his license, which stated that he was at liberty to keep his house open till 11 o'clock, and the Bench dismissed the case.[2]

Round one to Thomas Beale – and no doubt there was carousing aplenty at the King's Arms that night. But PC Young did not have to wait long to settle the score; just over a year later,

Thomas Beale, beerhouse-keeper, Bailbrook, was summoned for refusing to admit the police into his house. PC36, Young, stated that, on Good Friday afternoon he was passing the defendant's house, when he heard voices inside, and the sound of dominoes rattling on the table. He knocked at the door, and someone inside asked, 'Who is there?' He replied, 'Police; open the door'. He remained knocking at the door 17 minutes by his watch, when he was admitted; but there were no persons in the house but the landlord, his wife, and servant,

Defendant stated that he did not hear the knocking, he being in the garden at the rear of the house.

Fined 10s and costs.[3]

By the time the 1861 census came round, Thomas Beale had given up gardening and was described as a 'grocer &c' – still no mention of the beerhouse. His age was recorded as 62 – meaning that, unless he had aged 14 years since the 1851 census, one of them must have been wrong. His place of birth was given as Chasely – which, like Chetly, does not exist. The conclusion has to be that Mr Beale was less than co-operative when it came to answering questions from people like census enumerators. By this time, he had four children, aged between 3 and 9 – or so he said – and, although the former laundress and the annuitant had gone, George Morley, now aged 11 and described as a 'visitor', was still there.

Four years later, he made his final appearance in court, this time for

having his house open for the sale of beer after the permitted hours ... PC Pitman deposed that he visited the house at half-past 10 o'clock – which was half an hour after the legal hour – and found about a dozen people there drinking and smoking. The landlord was sitting with them. The defendant, in answer to the charge, said his clock had stopped and he did not know the time.

Fined 10s and costs.[4]

He died less than three years later, on 12 August 1868, and the King's Arms was taken over by a French polisher called James Bolwell. It survived until 1958, when it closed and became a private house.

Carry on along the lane to the tin church (2). Although we have so far avoided including lost ghost signs in the main part of this book, relegating them to a separate chapter at the end, in this case we are making an exception. In 1855, the vicar of Batheaston, the Rev TP Rogers, wrote to the Dean of Christ Church Cathedral, Oxford (who held the advowson of Batheaston) asking for funds to build a church at Bailbrook. This, he explained, was a matter of some urgency, as the residents of Bailbrook were 'for the most part an unsatisfactory and disorderly set'.[5] He mentioned no names, but Thomas Beale's would almost certainly have been on a list of the principal offenders. The vicar's plea fell on deaf ears, and it was not

until 1892, 37 years later, that the tin church was built in Bailbrook.

It continued in use until the mid-1960s, after which it lay derelict until taken over and converted to a home-cum-studio by an artist called Graham Boys in 1977. In March 1994, work started on the Batheaston bypass, a hugely unpopular scheme that would cut a swathe out of Solsbury Hill and alter the character of the Avon valley east of Bath forever. Although the project was eventually completed, battles between campaigners and developers, and treetop occupations by activists camped out on Solsbury Hill, set a new benchmark for environmental campaigns and changed the government's road-building policy, at least in the short term. To support the campaign, Graham Boys painted STOP IT! on the roof of the church, a message which was visible right across the valley. Unfortunately, several years ago, the roof, by now very rusty, had to be replaced, and the sign went as well.

Carry on along the lane for 75m, turn right through a kissing gate, follow a path past Bailbrook House, carry on down to the London Road and turn left. After 500m, you will see a building on the right, at right angles to the road, and a modern building, with two garages on the ground floor, set back beside it (3). This development is known as Miller's Place, but until 2012 it was the Waggon & Horses. Although, from this side, there is nothing to indicate it was once a pub, if you carry on and look at its back wall you will see a painted sign dating from when Courage's owned it.

The Waggon & Horses, like the King's Arms, started life as a beerhouse, and the story of how it got its name is a curious one:

Mr Emerson had the mill at Batheaston ... near the bridge. He sent two wagons each with four horses to Shepton Mallet, one of them being in charge of a carter named Brown. Coming back the men took the horses for water at the trough near the Swan at Dunkerton. The hosses [sic] were so thirsty, that they rushed for the water. Brown was crushed against the trough and his thigh was broken. He had to have his leg off. Mr Emerson treated him right well. He bought Brown a cork leg and put him in one of two houses where Edward Ashton used to have the coach horses. He got a licence for him and set him up and had painted a fine sign on which were the Waggon and Horses.[6]

In 1843, the beerhouse featured in another report concerning a wagon and horses:

As two teams belonging to Mr Brown of Wormwood were ascending Batheaston Hill, on their way to fetch coals, some person fired a gun on the right side of the road, which caused the horses in the first wagon to take fright. They galloped off at a rapid pace, and continued their progress until they arrived opposite the Waggon and Horses beerhouse at Batheaston, when the traces became unhooked, and, by some means, got entangled round the legs of the horse in the limbers, and threw him down, cutting him in such a manner as to disable him for work for a long time, if not altogether.[7]

James Brown, the Waggon & Horses' first landlord, died in 1856 and the beerhouse was taken over by Charles Davis, who, like Thomas Beale, soon attracted the attention of the local constabulary. On 10 May 1860, the *Bath Chronicle* reported that

Charles Davis, keeper of the Waggon and Horses beerhouse, Batheaston was summoned for opening his house for the sale of beer before the hour of half-past twelve on the morning of Sunday last. PS Milburn, who laid the information, said he was in plain clothes near the defendant's house, in company with a policeman in uniform. Seeing two men and a female enter the house, he went in, and found the parties he had seen enter sitting in the bar, and a quart cup on a shelf near, half full of beer, with froth upon it. Defendant told the officer that the parties in the house were friends from Bath. PC Edwards corroborated Milburn's statement, and added that Mrs Davis followed him out to the door, and said to him, 'I hope I shan't hear of this again. I will give you any money if you won't summon us.' In reply to the charge, however, defendant contended that the parties were friends of his. Fined 20s and costs.[8]

GHOST SIGNS OF BATH

A year later, after a game of skittles turned nasty, the Waggon & Horses once again featured in the *Bath Chronicle*:

> Chas Weaver and Wm Fielder were skittling at the Waggon and Horses, Batheaston ... The former, on losing to the latter, not only refused to pay him, but struck him when he asked for the money. A summons resulted, and Weaver was fined 1s and costs. Several companions, who gave evidence, were refused their expenses.[9]

The Waggon & Horses was eventually taken over by George's Brewery, which built a single-storey extension (since demolished). After George's was taken over by Courage's in 1961, the new owners painted the sign which still survives. It later passed through the hands of several pubcos, including Innspired, Punch Taverns and Pub-folio, before closing in 2012. The photographs on the right show it in the 1940s and being convrted to housing in 2015.

Carry on along the London Road, which eventually turns into the High Street, and look out for N°s 226 and 228 on the right (4 & 5). There are tantalising fragments of two nineteenth-century signs here: on the plat band of 226, the plaster on the right has fallen away to reveal four letters – TERS, while painted on stone above the fascia board of 228 is the lower part of the name GARRAWAY.

The 1840 Tithe Map apportionment lists Maria Garraway as the owner of both these properties.[10] In the 1841 census, she is recorded ⌐ widow, occupying N° 228 with four of her children, while a bak⌐

Left: Letters on the plat band of N° 226 High Street

Below: The bottom part of the name GARRAWAY on N° 228

James James is recorded as occupying N° 226. Maria Garraway had been a widow for nine years, her husband's death having been reported in the *Bath Chronicle* in April 1832:

> Mr Garraway of Batheaston, baker, of Batheaston, committed suicide, by hanging himself in an outhouse adjoining the premises which he occupied. The awful fact was discovered by one of his own children, who went to call him to dinner; when the body was perfectly lifeless. It is reported that pecuniary embarrassments led him to commit the dreadful act ... The deceased has left a wife and six children.[11]

Sixteen months earlier, the *Chronicle* had reported the bankruptcy of 'John Garraway, Batheaston ... baker and grocer'.[12] Although we cannot be certain that this was Maria Garraway's husband – as Garraway was a common name in Batheaston – it is likely that he was; the disparity between the six children he was reported to have left in 1832 and the four listed in the 1841 census can be accounted for either by the two eldest having left home, or, at a time of high child mortality, by one or more of them having died.

The 1841 census suggests that, after her husband's death, Maria Garraway came to an arrangement whereby James James took over N° 226 and carried on the bakery business, while she ran the grocer's shop with the help of her children. In the 1846 *Directory* she is listed not only as a grocer but also as a postmistress, but whether this was a new departure or something she had done for some time and failed to mention to the census enumerator is not clear. By 1851, James James had gone and N° 226 was occupied by a nurse called Ann Stevens and one of her charges, along with three lodgers. Maria Garraway, now aged 65, was still listed as a grocer at N° 228, and was assisted by her daughter Matilda, aged 23. Two of her sons were also involved in the business: William, aged 32, as a 'letter carrier' (or postman), and John, aged 26, as a baker.

Maria died in 1857, aged 73, and her daughter took over the post office. John continued to work as a baker, and in 1865 managed to get on the wrong side of a business rival:

> John Hill, a baker, of Batheaston, was summoned for threatening to shoot John Garraway, another baker, of the same village, with a revolver. Mr Wilton appeared for the complainant, but the defendant did not appear, and sent his wife. The case, however, was proceeded with. It appeared that the parties were drinking with others in a public-house, and a dispute arising, Hill took a revolver from his pocket and said he would give Garraway the contents. But his arm was seized by another man present. It further appeared that Hill is a very excitable man, and in the habit of carrying a revolver to the terror of his neighbours. The magistrates accordingly issued a warrant for his apprehension. On Monday the defendant was brought up and bound over to keep the peace for one month, himself in £20 and two sureties of £10 each.[13]

John Garraway died two years later, at the age of 44 and Matilda had to give up the shop because of ill health. By 1871 Alice Garraway, aged 21, had taken over the grocery business and post office, and was living at N° 228 with her twelve-year-old sister. She was from a different branch of the family: her father had been born in Swainswick, before moving to Bath to run a baker's and confectioner's in Walcot Buildings. In 1875, the grocery and post office was taken over by Robert Bence, who in the 1880s moved the business further along the High Street.

The Garraway family were at N° 228, therefore, from sometime before 1830 to 1875, which makes it difficult to date the sign which partly survives on the building. As for the sign on N° 226, there is very little to go on: ... TERS could come at the end of many words, but one word it cannot come at the end of is BAKERS, and the only trade we know to have been associated with this building is baking. The writing looks as though it may date from the early nineteenth century – perhaps even before John Garraway acquired the building – and, as records for that period in villages such as Batheaston tend to be sketchy in the extreme, it may only be when more of the sign is revealed that sor light can be shed on the mystery.

Six doors along, you come to Avondale Place, and beyond it, another lost inn – the White Hart, closed in 2007, although with no ghost sign. Carry on along the High Street, and, just after passing the old post office at N° 258, you come to the old bakery – with a ghost sign reminiscent of the one on the chemist's in Larkhall – at N° 262 (6):

CORN BRAN
GURGEONS
BARLEY MEAL
&c

This was Hill's bakery, which moved here from premises next door but one to the George & Dragon in Stambridge Buildings around 1890. The business had been founded by John Hill from Minchinhampton – the same John Hill who, in 1865 had attempted to shoot John Garraway after a disagreement in a pub. He died in 1873, aged 52, and the business was taken over by his son, Rowland, who moved it here around 1882. Rowland Hill seems to have been as excitable as his father. In July 1888, for example, he was fined ten shillings for punching a newspaper boy 'because he would not give him a paper for nothing'.[14] A few months later, he was summoned for being drunk and disorderly after he 'ran out of his house shortly before twelve at night and created a disturbance in the street'.[15] He did not appear in court, but was represented by his sister, 'who said he was ill in bed', and was fined twenty shillings in his absence. The following year, he was summoned 'for removing three pigs from the county of Wilts into Somerset ... without a licence':

> At 10.30pm the attention of AS [Acting Sergeant] Edwards was attracted by the squeaking of pigs, and on investigation he found that the defendant had purchased some pigs at Atworth, and that they were being driven to Batheaston in the defendant's trap. Defendant was anything was polite when questioned as to his license, and first of all drove away in a hurry. Ignorance of the necessity of obtaining a license was pleaded as an excuse. Defendant was fined 20s and

costs, or 14 days' imprisonment, because of his bad behaviour to the police.[16]

Just over four months later, he was dead. Around 6.20 on the evening of 2 December 1889, he went out into the backyard. He had already suffered a couple of fainting fits and cut down on drinking as a result, but, when he failed to return, his wife went out to look for him and found him lying dead against the wall. He was 38.[17] His widow, Louisa, was left with five young children to look after, but, like Maria Garraway, she rose to the challenge and ran the bakery for over 30 years, before handing over to her son William, who continued running it until around 1950.

Carry on to Nº 280 High Street, opposite the turning to Penthouse Hill (7). We did not originally intend to include the sign for DAFNIS SUPPLY STORES on this building, because it is not a true ghost sign. As in several other places around Bath, the name is only visible because letters once screwed onto the building have been removed. A visit on 14 October 2015, however, found another ghost sign in the process of being created. Picca-  dilly Antiques, which had occupied the building until a few weeks earlier, had moved out, and their name was in the process of being painted out in preparation for the conversion of the shop to a café – as seen in the photograph above.

The building was first recorded as a shop in the 1881 census, when William Leader from Lymington in Hampshire was running a grocer's here. By 1952, it had been taken over by Rupert Dafnis as the Dafnis Supply Stores. This closed in 1999, and Piccadilly Antiques opened in 2001.

Across the road, at the bottom of Penthouse Hill, is a ghost sign painted on wooden boards (8):

DREWETT BROS

SHOEING FORGE & GENERAL SMITHS

CARPENTERS & WHEELWRIGHTS

FENCING & GATES OF ALL DESCRIPTIONS ... Established 1727

George Drewett was born in Tinhead, Wiltshire in 1853, and grew up in Edington. The son of an agricultural labourer, he became an agricultural labourer himself, before marrying Elizabeth Taylor, the niece of John Dingle, schoolmaster and registrar of Batheaston, in 1876, and taking over the forge on Penthouse Hill.

In 1949, with the forge still being run by his descendants, the *Bath Chronicle* ran a feature on it:

> While the Pump Rooms speak of Beau Nash and diamonds scintillating on costly satins, the old forge at Batheaston has an atmosphere of quiet simplicity.
>
> Established in 1727 and later taken over by the Drewett family, who are still its owners, the forge has served many horses in the Bath district.
>
> The forge is practically unchanged, with the walls hung with horse shoes and the smouldering remains of a fire in the furnace. Mr Francis Drewett told a reporter something of the history of the forge.
>
> He and his three brothers, Albert, Henry and Charles Drewett, are its present owners. Mr Francis Drewett can remember when they shoed as many horses in a week as they now do in a month.
>
> The First World War brought heavy trade and mule shoes were hammered on the anvils for the pack mules in France ...
>
> Leading from the forge into the furnace room is a door much scarred and indented with letters.
>
> Originally the Drewetts made iron casts of names for local craftsmen, and wishing to make tests, plunged the implements into the door to see the effect.
>
> That is done no longer because the casts can very well be bought much cheaper, made in a way that entails less work.
>
> Mr Francis Drewett said he allowed an hour for shoeing a horse, and charged between 14s and 26s. The iron is obtained from Bristol

because it takes too much time and costs too much money to 'double' – melt down old shoes for new ones.

Now the brothers rely on the making of gates, trailers and motors for their income.

Apart from a brief respite a year ago, when an American film director used the forge as a 'set', Mr Drewett said that business has continued much the same.[18]

Today, the forge is home to Garden Requisites, a company established by John and Hilary Thurman to produce garden arches, pergolas and trellises, but whose range now also includes items such as porches, door canopies and fireguards.

For the next ghost sign, head up Penthouse Hill, carry on for half a mile, and, as you approach Seven Acres Lane, look up at the side wall of the house on the corner (9). This sign, for the Coopers Arms, dates from after 1923, when George's acquired the Bath Brewery and its estate of

tied houses. In 1871, there was a grocer's shop here, run by Annie Young, but, sometime between then and 1881, a cooper called William Cook moved up from the High Street and turned it into a beerhouse. When he died in 1885, aged 53, after a short illness, the owner of the building ran into opposition from local residents when he tried to get the licence transferred:

Mr EB Titley made an application on behalf of Mr John Symes, the owner of the Coopers Arms, Batheaston, for the transfer of the license … to a person named Fitzwilliam Geo Hunt. The late landlord of the house, Wm Cook, had died, and there was no one to apply for a transfer in the usual way ... Mr Melhuish, of Batheaston, presented a memorial signed by the ratepayers of Batheaston, praying that the license should not be transferred because there were enough licensed houses in the village, besides which the house was too small for the purpose to which it is adapted, and the memorialists also urge their memorial on moral grounds.[19]

Despite this, Fitzwilliam Hunt did take over the Coopers Arms. By 1894, however, he had moved twelve doors away to become landlord of the Northend Inn, handing the Coopers Arms over to Henry Painter. In 1911 the licence was transferred to Albert Blakemore, who was only here for three years before Herbert Holloway took over. His son, Harry Holloway, later recalled what life at the Coopers was like:

> Living in the pub with the living quarters mixed with the licensed quarter I got to know the regulars well. It was Mr Crook Harding who had everyone in the parish with a nickname. The coal merchant was Crocodile Shearn, the dairyman Ratty Bailey, Monger or Codger Lewis was cattle drover and rag gatherer ... Shab Lantern Ames and Chog Rawlings were market gardeners, and Swede Lewis worked in the gardens. Wingee Harding was road man, Jacky Jasper was Mr John Rawlings, the local builder, Tommy Eye and Bill Eye, their name being Ricketts, came down from St Catherine once a week to do their shopping and always came in the pub, and after they'd had a few pints they used to start singing, and

> Tommy would go round the room shadow boxing. Then they would go off home, but very often they would get so far, start quarrelling, have a fight, then go home as happy as could be ... Bank Holiday at the pub was always great days for people having a good singsong, which was carried out in a very orderly manner. Everyone sat round while the singer sang his song and only came in and sang the chorus. One of the noted singers was Target Green who was a bellringer. Others were

Jacky Jasper, Wingee Harding, Nobby Harding. Maurice Rickett was the Jazz Band Drummer, Bill Rhymes on his mandolin. Monger Lewis used to sing The White Squall, and what a row and plenty of action! Bill Jones the thatcher would sing a song about a girl with her hair tied up in blue ribbon, and he would sing for about half an hour in a very gruff voice and one tune, and this used to be a good evening.[20]

Herbert Holloway's wife, Edith, died in 1925. He later remarried, and, after he died in 1938, the licence was transferred to his widow, Mrs Virtue Holloway.

The Coopers Arms finally closed in the 1950s, leaving the Northend Inn as the only pub at this end of the village. In 2008, when the Northend Inn's owners applied to convert it to a private house, local residents – in marked contrast to the memorialists of 1885 – were outraged, organising meetings, protesting to the council and succeeding in getting the application refused. The Northend reopened, but closed again in 2010. Another application was submitted, objected to – and withdrawn. Then nothing – until 2015, when the owners applied for a certificate of lawfulness, claiming that, as they had been using the pub as a private house for over four years, the council had to accept this as a *fait accompli* – which they did. You pass the former Northend Inn – Nº 41, with not even a ghost sign to recall its illustrious past – as you head back to the High Street.

Today, Batheaston, which ten years ago had five pubs, has just two, which, bizarrely for a village which is so spread out, are next door but one to each other. To find them, head back along Northend, but, when the road swings right down Penthouse Hill, carry on down a narrow alleyway and a flight of steps. Turn left along the High Street at the bottom and soon the George & Dragon and the White Lion will come into view.

There are no ghost signs as such here, but, if you look above the entrance of the George & Dragon, you will see a gas lamp with a sign for HOME BREWED BEERS (10). This may seem like a survival from the  distant past, but the George & Dragon was the last pub in the Bath area with its own brewery, which only closed in 1960.

This row of buildings dates from the early nineteenth century, but it is not clear when the George & Dragon opened as a beerhouse. The first record of it comes in 1848, when George Bevan, a 'beer-house keeper of

Batheaston', was fined ten shillings for serving after hours.[21] However, it is likely that it opened some years earlier. At the time of the 1841 census, 14 Stambridge Buildings – the right-hand side of what is now the George & Dragon – was occupied by George Bevan, a mason, and his wife Hannah, a shopkeeper. Although we do not know whether they had yet obtained a beerhouse licence, in the 1851 census George Bevan is described as a mason and grocer, and his wife as a shopwoman. Failure to mention the licence to the census enumerator in 1851 suggests that there may well have been a similar omission ten years earlier.

As George Bevan was a mason, it may seem odd that he did not call his beerhouse the Mason's Arms – a popular name at the time – especially as there were no other pubs with this name in the village. Perhaps it was down to his sense of humour, as his name was George and his wife ran the pub while he was out at work. The first reference to it as the George & Dragon comes in a report of a fire from 1852:

> On Monday night last, between ten and eleven o'clock, an alarming fire broke out in a wheat mow, in a barton, near Batheaston, in the occupation of Mr G Bevan, of the George and Dragon Inn, in that place. As soon as the occurrence became known, the most active efforts were made by the neighbours to extinguish the flames, and though they could not save the stock from destruction, they succeeded in preventing the fire from injuring the contiguous property. The West of England fire engine was despatched to the spot in time to lend assistance. We understand that Mr Bevan's property is not insured. It will be seen by our police report, that the fire was the work of an incendiary, who has confessed his guilt, and is committed to take his trial.[22]

It turned out that the fire had been started by a man called George Morley from Bathwick, who thought the rick belonged to a Mr Yeeles, who had had him confined to the stocks a few weeks earlier for drunkenness. When he discovered his mistake, he confessed so that no one else would take the blame.

By 1871, George Bevan had expanded the George & Dragon into Nᵒ 13 and was employing his son Alfred as a maltster. Two of his others sons, Albert and Charles, had taken over Duncombe Farm at Colerne, with 243 acres, and were employing six men. When George Bevan died in 1878, his estate included not only the George & Dragon, but also six cottages on Bannerdown Road. The sale realised £1,340, with George's son Albert paying £765 for the George & Dragon.[23] Albert Bevan did not take over the pub straight away, but leased it out until 1894, when he moved back from Colerne to Batheaston. He was landlord of the George & Dragon until his death until 1921, although for the last seven or eight years of his life it was run by his wife Matilda, as he was an invalid. Matilda continued to run it until her death nine years later, when it was taken over by her eldest daughter, Kate. By the end of the Second World War, it was one of only four pubs in the Bath area still brewing their own beer, and featured as such in a report in the *Bath Chronicle*:

> It is surprising to many visitors that nearly all the beer consumed in Bath comes from outside the city. Since the closing of the Bath Brewery we have now left only four houses ... where Bath-brewed beer is on sale. These are the Ram Brewery, Widcombe, and the Long Acre Brewery, Walcot, belonging to the Withers family. The two others are Mr Bevan's house, the George & Dragon (though more frequently known as Bevan's) at Stambridge, and Mr Stride's, the Burnt House, Odd Down.[24]

The George & Dragon outlasted them all, brewing its last batch of beer in 1960. Kate Bevan's youngest sister, Ada, later recorded her memories of life of at the pub, starting with the day she arrived there with her father, Albert Bevan:

> My father came to the George and Dragon from Duncombe Farm, Colerne, when I was small, but he kept on the farm ... Lots of people came into the George and Dragon I can remember. They were a nice crowd we had ... Most people were market gardeners ... Of course, we brewed our own beer, and we grew the barley, too, at Duncombe ... We made our own malt in the malthouse at the back. This was a fine building with great beams, now destroyed ... We made about 300 gallons [of beer] at a time, and it could be kept as long as you liked, or run off at once.[25]

So the gaslit sign above the entrance to the George & Dragon is a reminder not just of the last home-brew house in the area, but also of a remarkable brewing and pub-owning dynasty.

That is it as far as the ghost signs of Batheaston are concerned, and there is a bus stop, with regular services back to Bath, across the road. There are, however, two more ghost signs not that far away – one in Bathford and one in Bathampton – so, if you want to take them in as well, carry on along the London Road, staying on the left-hand side. At the roundabout, cross and carry on under the railway bridge. After crossing a footbridge, bear left up Bathford Hill. After 500m, turn left along Ashley Road, and after 75m you will see Nº 3

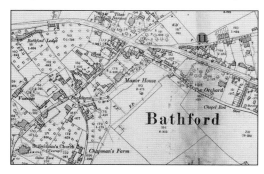

on the left, with a ghost sign on a blocked window on the ground floor (11). USHERS ALES AND STOUT is still legible; underneath is what looks as though it may read IN BOTTLES AND ON DRAUGHT or something similar.

At the time of the 1861 census, William Brooks, a 26-year-old blacksmith from Monkton Farleigh, was living here with his wife Ann. In 1866, he took out a beerhouse licence and in the 1871 census was listed as blacksmith and beer retailer. He called his pub the Smith's Arms. After he died in 1897, there were a couple of other landlords until Henry Mulcock took over around 1908. Shortly afterwards he had his photograph taken with his family outside the pub, and it shows that at that time the sign on the blocked window read PINCHIN'S XXX BEER ALE & STOUT.[26] Pinchin's Brewery was at Box, and was taken over by Usher's in 1924. In 1932, Henry Mulcock retired and the licence was transferred to a Mr CH Greenaway. The Smith's Arms closed two years later, on 16 January 1934, and was subsequently converted to two dwellings.[27]

Head back down Bathford Hill and turn right across the footbridge. Just before the railway bridge, cross and follow a footpath which climbs up to the line and crosses the railway bridge

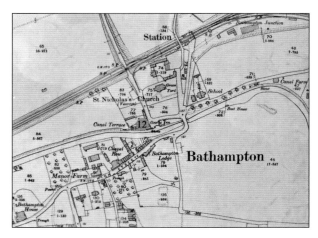

before heading down to a field on the other side of the river. Follow a track diagonally across the field, at the end of which is a level crossing over a railway line. Head along the lane on the other side, at the end of which you will see the George Inn, with ghostly lettering above its door (**12**).

It is not known when the George became an inn, although the building looks to date from the seventeenth century, while its west wing, added after the canal opened, has a datestone of 1815. The earliest reference to the inn we have come across is from 1823, when 'Mr Edmund Shaw, landlord of the George Inn, Bathampton [died] in his 36th year'.[28] It is another landlord whose name appears above the door, however – William Knee, who died on 22 March 1873, aged 82, and was, according to his obituary in the *Bath Chronicle*, 'formerly of the George Inn, Bathampton'.[29]

It took some time to track this elusive Mr Knee down. Not only did a trawl of the census returns for Bathampton fail to come up with anyone of that name, we also drew a blank with the directories – until we checked one for 1833, which did indeed list a William Knee as landlord of the George Inn. Further confirmation came from the 1832 electoral roll, which listed William Knee of Bathampton as the 'occupier of a house at a rent of £50 and upwards'. Whatever happened, he must have left by 1841, because of his non-appearance in that year's census. Which makes it very odd that the *Chronicle*, in their obituary, mentioned only an inn he had left over 30 years earlier. It also dates the sign over the door of the George to between 1823 (when Edmund Shaw died) and the early 1830s, when William Knee was at the inn.

To return to Bath, take the steps up to the canal and turn right along the towpath.

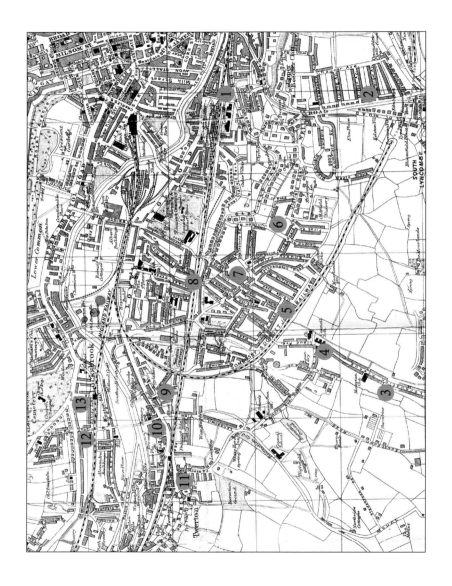

8

BEAR FLAT, OLDFIELD PARK, TWERTON & LOWER WESTON

This walk through the western suburbs of Bath is not only longer than the previous walks – with, in several instances, a considerable distance from one ghost sign to the next – but many of the signs are much more recent than those previously visited. There are, however, some real gems waiting to be discovered in this part of the city. One option, for those whose time – or enthusiasm for walking – is limited, is just to visit the more interesting signs by car or bus. Those who do opt for the full tour, however, will discover, amid the ghost signs, hidden corners and surprise views across to the Georgian terraces on the northern slopes of the city.

All that said, however, the first sign comes so close to being a non-event that we thought long and hard about whether to include it all. But for the sake of completeness ...

... cross Churchill Bridge at the bottom of Southgate Street, bear right along the Lower Bristol Road, cross at the pedestrian lights, and turn left along Oak Street. At the end, continue up a path and the first ghost sign – such as it is – is on your left as you climb the steps to the Wells

Road (1). This is – or was – an advertisement for the *Bath Chronicle*. If you look at the lurid yellow paint on the top part of the wall, you should be able to make out, to the left of the rubble stone, the letters EV, and to the right, the letter G. These formed part of the word EVENING  – the time of day when the *Chronicle*, then daily, appeared. Above this, we are reliably informed, the words LOCAL NEWS could until recently be made out. The sign, however, seems to be fading fast, and, try as we could, we could not see them. Perhaps you will have better luck.

Carry on up the Wells Road, cross at the pedestrian lights, go up an alleyway between houses and turn left along Magdalen Avenue. Turn right up Magdalen Road and at the end, with the horse trough ahead, turn right up Holloway. When you reach the shops at Bear Flat, cross to the left-hand pavement and carry on in the same direction along Wellsway.

When you come to Milton Avenue, look above the fascia board over the entrance to the showroom on the right-hand corner, and you will see traces of what appear to be several sets of lettering (2). Unfortunately, these are now so fragmentary as to have so far eluded elucidation. If you look to the left of the entrance, however, you will see, to the left of the tall window, some lettering – the rest of which disappeared when the window was inserted – which can be read fairly easily. There are two sets of lettering – red and green. The red letters spell out the following:

HOL ...
Family
Devonsh ...
& Pure...
to all p ...
COWKEE ...

Of the green letters little remains – DAI towards the top and two or three indistinct letters, the first of which may be a D, further down.

This was a dairy, built in 1899 on land which had previously formed part of Holloway Farm, whose name it took, and the first three of the red letters would have been part of the word 'HOLLOWAY'. Further down, 'Devonsh...' was obviously 'Devonshire' and would probably have been followed by 'cream'; 'to all p...' would have been part of the phrase 'delivered to all parts of the city' or something similar, and 'COWKEE...' would have been 'COWKEEPERS'. None of this may seem that exciting, but, in terms of the window onto the past it opens up, this is one of the most interesting ghost signs in the city.

Imagine a time when Wellsway was a dusty highway with fields on either side. Bath was out of sight in the valley below, but the road would have been busy with coaches and carts bound for the city, as well as wagons laden with coal from the pits around Radstock. It was also the venue for an annual fair, established in the middle ages, which, at one time stretched from where you are standing to the Bear Inn, but dwindled away in the early 1800s. By 1821, for example, the *Bath Chronicle* reported that

> Holloway Fair, on Monday, was but thinly supplied with stock, which varied considerably in price; beasts from £7 to £14 a head. One pen of lambs sold as high as 25s per head. Pigs were heavy of sale.[1]

Nineteen years later, the report was not only briefer but had a comic finality to it:

> Holloway Fair, which took place on Thursday last, was attended by a very small number of persons. It was only a shade above being no fair at all.[2]

And that is the last we hear of it.

Fragmentary lettering above the fascia board of 75a Wellsway ...

... and to the left of the entrance

Despite the demise of the fair, most of the land on either side of the road remained undeveloped, with only a handful of buildings set amid the fields – the old Bear Inn at the top of Holloway, Elm Place opposite where you are standing, Devonshire Buildings further up – and Holloway Farm.

How long the farm had been here is difficult to say. By the mid-nineteenth century, however, the lease was held by John Carey. In August 1862, when an annual treat was held at St Mark's Schools in Widcombe,

> the children, about 300 in number, assembled at their schoolroom ... and after parading the lower portion of the town, proceeded to a field connected with Holloway Farm, kindly lent for the occasion by Mr Carey. By the consent of the Guardians the children were accompanied by the juvenile fife and drum band from the Union Workhouse. After a good tea and a plentiful supply of cake, the youngsters enjoyed themselves in various ways, the sports being kept up with considerable spirit by the respected master, Mr Hillier.[3]

When the children enjoyed a similar treat six years later, however, the field was 'lent by Mr Butler of Holloway Farm'.[4]

John Butler was born around 1822 in Batcombe, Somerset, the son of a yeoman farmer. By 1851, he had moved with his wife Sarah to Farmborough, where he had a 105-acre farm and employed three men. He was still there in 1861, but by 1868 had moved to Bath and leased Holloway Farm, with 80 acres. The 1871 census shows that he was employing two men and two boys. He died in 1880, aged 56, and his widow took over the running of the farm, assisted by her three unmarried daughters, Mary, Isabella and Elizabeth, aged 32, 29 and 20 respectively. In 1888, Elizabeth married a farmer called Robert Brunt from Wellow, leaving Sarah to continue running Holloway Farm, with the help of her two elder daughters, until her death in 1896 at the age of 74.[5] By then, however, major changes were under way.

In 1877, the Bath & West of England Society had held the Bath & West Show at Holloway Farm. When it was staged there again in 1891, the *Bath Chronicle* marvelled at 'the canvas town, with its vast agglomeration of contents, which covers the broad expanse of Holloway Farm'.[6] A week later, reviewing the show, the *Chronicle* sounded a more plangent note:

> With regard to the future, it is doubtful whether, should the Society decide to revisit Bath, suitable ground within its confines will be available. The speculating builder is invited to commence operations in the fields which on the present and past occasion have been free for use, and doubtless he will readily respond, as he will be, we conclude, under no more restriction in covering this beautiful site with commonplace tenements than the others where he has left traces of his enterprise and of his ingenuity in getting as many houses as possible in a given space. It is to be regretted that these pleasantly-situated meads could not be secured with the view of adding to the open spaces of the city and dedicating them to the public. The fiat, however, has gone forth, and rural Beechen Cliff, which has been a charm for generations, is doomed to become the home of the modern utilitarian type. The loss to the city will be great whatever may be the gain to individuals.[7]

Five months later, when Holloway Farm was sold at auction for £11,000 to George Hancock, managing director of the Bath Stone Firms Ltd, the *Chronicle* lamented that

that portion of the Beechen Cliff Estate known as Holloway Farm has been sold at the building price value, and the hope of seeing it converted into

Bear Flat in 1888 showing Holloway Farm

GHOST SIGNS OF BATH

a park for the dwellers on the south similar to that enjoyed by dwellers on the east and west has been extinguished ... A playground is needed for this quarter of the city now more than ever, but where to find a convenient site is not easy to discover ... Under these circumstances we hope it is true what we hear, viz., that there is a chance of obtaining a portion of the Holloway Farm Estate for a recreation ground. The new owner is a gentleman residing in Bristol: he has, we understand, signified his willingness to part with a portion of the land for the public use should the authorities desire to secure it.[8]

For the time being, though, nothing happened, and Sarah Butler and her daughters continued to run the farm. Not until 1896 – the year of Sarah's death – did things start moving in earnest, with an advertisement in the *Chronicle*:

TO BUILDERS AND OTHERS
The BEECHEN CLIFF ESTATE, Wells Road
Eligible BUILDING LAND to be LET on Ground Rents. This fine estate, now known as HOLLOWAY FARM, is about to be developed for building purposes: it is suitable for the erection of small Villa Residences of an inexpensive character, although there are many fine sites adapted for the erection of a larger class house [sic], and persons contemplating building a residence for own [sic] occupation would rarely find a more desirable position. The estate commands fine views from all parts: it lies high and dry, and the locality is a remarkably healthy one.[9]

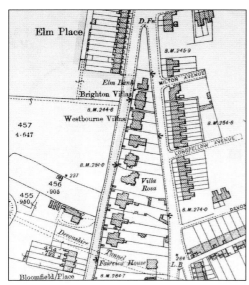

By 1904 houses had been built on the site

Given its previous comments, it is hardly surprising that the *Chronicle* greeted this news with barely disguised distaste:

We understand it is intended to encourage the erection of a small and inexpensive class of modern house with all the latest sanitary and other improvements, and to give to each house a large plot of land. This scheme should meet the wants of a large section of the public, viz., clerks, shop assistants, and the better class of artizans and others to whom it is important to be as near as possible to their places of business. We are still strongly of the opinion that the land should be secured (if possible) by the Corporation, but failing that are very glad to hear that the owners intend to avoid the evils of overcrowding the land with houses.[10]

Two years later, the council resolved to ascertain the terms upon which a portion of the land could be acquired to create a park, and later purchased eleven acres, at £300 an acre, to lay out Alexandra Park.

As the fields of Holloway Farm disappeared beneath streets of suburban villas, however, the Misses Butler continued to work as farmers and dairykeepers, and were described as such in the 1900 *Directory*. By then, however, Holloway Farm had been demolished, and they had moved into Milton House, with a purpose-built dairy adjoining and sheds at the back, to which their cows, now moved to pastures beyond the new houses, would walk down Milton Avenue for milking.

Mary and Isabella retired in 1905 and the business was taken over by Joseph Derriman from Cerne Abbas, who in the 1911 census was described as a 'dairyman (milk retailer)'. Mr Derriman retired from business in the 1940s, and the dairy closed, but he continued to live in Milton House until his death in 1966 at the age of 88. Today, Milton House offers award-winning bed & breakfast, while the old dairy offers replacement windows.

Walk back a little way along Wellsway, cross at the traffic island, carry on across Bloomfield Road and turn left. At the end of Elm Place, turn right down a footpath. After 200m, at the end of the playing field, turn left along another path and, when you come to the Two Tunnels path (which follows the course of the old Somerset & Dorset Railway), turn right along it. After 600m, drop down off the path to Monksdale Road and turn left. Follow Monksdale Road uphill, turn right at the top along The Oval, and then first right along Chestnut Grove to Coronation Avenue, where you will see the next ghost sign – on N° 132 – ahead (3).

Coronation Avenue was named in honour of the coronation of Edward VII in 1902. At first, N° 132 seems to have been a fish and chip shop. Frederick Stone, described as a 'fishmonger, etc', was here in 1910 but, by the time of the 1911 census, Elizabeth Hobbs, a 'fried fish shopkeeper' had taken over. Around 1916, Robert Hall opened the

Coronation Dairy here, which he continued to run until his death in 1933. His widow stayed on at N° 132, but the dairy – still recalled by a particularly evocative ghost sign – closed.

Head downhill past the Trowbridge House (to which the licence of the Cleveland Arms, visited in Walk 4, was transferred in 1932), and, opposite the green-domed splendour of Oldfield Park Junior School, on the corner of Lymore Avenue, you will see a former corner shop with a white-painted panel over the door (4). Although there was clearly a sign here, we have been unable to make it out. For over a century, however,

this was a post office and corner store. In 1911, it was being run by Herbert Tucker, then aged 26. He was still here over 40 years later, before passing the business on to a Mr Harris. It eventually closed around 2004 and has since been converted to residential accommodation.

Carry on down Claude Avenue, continue along Bridge Road, and at the end turn right along Cynthia Road. After passing the top of Herbert Road, look for the next ghost sign up on the right (5). Given that this building only dates from the early twentieth century, what remains of the sign has an extraordinarily elusive quality to it. Some of it, at least, is clearly legible – ST KILDA'S RD on the south-facing wall, and E WEEKS ... DAIRYMAN on the west. Look closer and, on the west-facing wall, you will make out GROCER, in black, between the two other sets of lettering, and – if the light is right – DAIRY, in red, above DAIRYMAN, with PROVISIONS in smaller letters behind it. There are hints of other words as well, which we have not managed to decipher.

So it looks as though there are at least three sets of lettering, and, not surprisingly, the shop here changed hands several times. The

original occupant was Charles Sealy, who also ran the grocer's shop at 17 Monmouth Place visited in Walk 3. By 1923, FW Atkinson was running a grocery store here. In 1932 Ernest Weeks moved in and established St Kilda's Rd Dairy, but kept the grocer's shop going. After he retired in the 1940s, it went back to being just a grocer's, under a succession of owners, until, like other corner stores, it succumbed to competition from the supermarkets.

At the end of Cynthia Road, turn right up St Kilda's Road and left along Melcombe Road. As you carry on, the road swings left past a large redbrick building. Although it sports no ghost signs (as far as we are aware), this little-known building deserves a mention because of the role it played in Bath's commercial, industrial and transport history. Built as a bakery by Twerton Co-operative Society in 1913, it was served by a private siding from the Somerset & Dorset Railway, which ran behind it, and in its heyday up to four wagons of flour and six of coal were delivered here weekly.[11] The coal yard also provided domestic coal for Co-op customers. In 1922, the Twerton Co-operative Society merged with the Bath Co-operative Society to form the Bath & Twerton Co-operative Society, making the bakery and coal yard even busier. Coal trains continued to serve the siding until November 1967, 20 months after the withdrawal of trains over the Somerset & Dorset line.[12] Melcombe Court flats were later built on the site of the coal yard, and, after the bakery closed in 1971, it became a CRS milk depot. Today, renamed the Old Dairy, it is home to business units.

At the end of Melcombe Road turn right along Beckhampton Road. Carry on as this curves left along Oldfield Lane, carry straight on past the Moorfields pub and turn left, opposite St Alphege's church, along Second

Avenue. Carry on across King Edward Road and, when you come to Junction Road, look to the right to see, on N° 32, a sign for the Norton St Philip Dairy (6). This company was established shortly before the First World War, and by 1914 N° 32 Junction Road, previously occupied by Gane & Son, nurserymen, was a branch dairy run by William Batten. Although the company continued to expand, by the late 1930s, despite having seven other branches in Bath, it had disposed of the one on Junction Road, which became the Junction Road Stores. This closed by the early 1950s, and the building became a private house.

Bear left along Junction Road and turn left into Winchester Road. At the end, cross and carry on along a footpath, turn right at the end and, after turning left along Shaftesbury Road, cross the zebra crossing and turn right into Moorland Road, where you will find not only a choice of cafés but also the Oldfield Park Bookshop, with a comprehensive selection of local (and not so local) books. Take the first right along Livingstone Road to see, on the right, a very attractive pair of ghost signs on N° 15 (7). This

building was originally a private house, but by 1947 Donald Wyatt had established a bicycle and pram repair business here. In the 1952 *Directory* it was listed as Williams Cycle Agents, with Donald Wyatt as proprietor, but by 1961 JC Hare Ltd, cycle agents and dealers, had taken over. They continued to run the business until comparatively recently. Despite the style of lettering of the sign on the left harking back to an earlier period, therefore, both signs almost certainly date from after the Second World War. although the one on the right can be no later than 1957, when BSA Cycles Ltd – a subsidiary of the Birmingham Small Arms Company – was sold to Raleigh.

Carry on along Livingstone Road, turn left into Stanley Road West and in the distance you will see a sign for GASARC ENGINEERING, a company still very much in business (8). As you approach it, however, you will notice that it has been painted over a ghost sign for

STANLEY ENGINEERING CO
MECHANICAL ... ENGINEERS
MACHINERY STOCK HOLDERS

The Stanley Engineering Company was founded around 1911 and its original premises were in Manvers Street. In 1924 it took over the old Griffin Engineering Company's factory on the corner of Oldfield Lane. After the Second World War, it expanded into the premises now occupied by Gasarc Engineering. One unusual feature of the company was that, in 1919, it acquired a private railway siding on the GWR to the east of where Oldfield Park station was later built, which remained in use until 1966.[13]

Incidentally, although Stanley Road West led to the Stanley Engineering Company's works, this was coincidental. The road was named when it was constructed in the early 1890s in honour of Henry Morton Stanley, who had become a national hero after finding Dr Livingstone near Lake Tanganyika in 1871. Livingstone Road dates from around the same time. Originally, it was known simply as Stanley Road, but was renamed Stanley Road West after the Second World War to avoid confusion with another Stanley Road off Manvers Street. Although this other Stanley Road was renamed Railway Street when the Southgate area was redeveloped, Stanley Road West still retains its now pointless suffix.

Carry on past the Gasarc Engineering Works, turn right at the end and right again, and, after crossing the railway, turn left along a footpath. This curves away from the railway towards the end of Bellotts Road, which you cross to head along another footpath by a garage. Carry on when you come to a road, with Twerton Cemetery on your left, but, as the road curves, go past wooden posts on the right to cross the Two Tunnels Path and head along Inverness Road (9). At the end, turn to look back at a ghost sign on the last house on the left:

W BAILEY
MASON, BUILDING CONTRACTOR
ALL KINDS OF TILE HEARTHS ... FLOORS &c [FIXED?]
ESTIMATES GIVEN ...

Inverness Road dates from between 1892 and 1894, and, as Walter Bailey was the first to occupy this house – and painted his calling card on the

side – it seems likely that he built it. It was standard practice at the time, when a builder put up a number of houses, for him to live in one himself. This ghost sign, then, is in a class of its own: not only did it tell passers-by that Mr Bailey, mason and builder contractor, lived here; it showed the sort of work of which he was capable.

Walter William Bailey was born in 1853 at Eltham in Kent. In 1871, aged 17, he was living with his widowed mother, who was a laundress in Lewisham, and working as a mason. By 1876, he had moved to Bath, where he married Fanny Gane from Combe Down. They settled at Upper Trafalgar Place under Beechen Cliff, and, while he worked as a mason, Fanny worked as a dressmaker.

What happened next is unclear, but, by the time of the 1891 census, he was living as a boarder in the house of a stonemason called John Floyd on Locksbrook Road, while his wife was staying with her aunt at Sevenoaks in Kent. The 1901 census, however, shows him and Fanny reunited and living at 1 Inverness Road, with a nine-year-old daughter, Winifred. Although we have no way of knowing, it may have been that Fanny had gone to Sevenoaks a decade earlier so that her aunt could care for her in her confinement. Moving forward to 1911, we find that the family had moved to 37 Ringwood Road. Walter, now aged 58, was still working as a mason and builder, although Fanny, three years his senior, was an invalid, being cared for by Winifred. Fanny died a year later. After his retirement from the building trade, Walter Bailey worked as a caretaker at East Twerton Schools, He died, aged 72, in 1924.

Turn right along Burnham Road and then left along the Lower Bristol Road. After passing Bathwick Tyres on the left, look across to Avon Buildings to see a rather splendid sign on a derelict building (10).[14] There are, in fact, two signs rather curiously intermingled here. At the top, E DILLON & SON appears in two versions. Then come two different signs, one overlaid on the other: PURVEYORS / OF / PRIME / ENGLISH ... and FAMILY / BUTCHERS. Finally, there is what appears to be a phone number, again in two versions, but both so far gone as to be indecipherable.

Edward John Dillon was born, the son of a butcher, in 1857 at Millbrook Place in Widcombe. He had two older brothers: George, born 1849, who became a cabinet maker, and Henry, born 1853, who trained to become a butcher. His father had other ideas for Edward, however: in the 1871 census he is recorded, aged 14, as a tailor. This seems not to have been to his liking, and by the time of the 1881 census he had joined the Royal Navy as a Stoker (2nd Class) and was on HMS Griffon somewhere

east of the Bahamas. A year later, however, after a spell in Haslar Naval Hospital, he was invalided out of the navy and returned to Bath, where he moved in with his parents, who were now living at 8 Brunswick Street, and married Lucy Butler from Oxfordshire.

His father was still working as a butcher, but his brother Henry, who was also living at 8 Brunswick Street, had become a music teacher – or 'professor music' [sic] as he was described in 1881 census. Instead of following in his father's footsteps, however, Edward worked as a tobacconist for a time. By 1887 he had moved to 4 Dover Place, and, while the 1888 *Directory* lists him as a butcher at 3 Denmark Terrace in East Twerton, by the time of the 1891 census he had abandoned butchery, at least for a time, and moved to Circus Mews, where he was working as a Bath chairman. This may seem like a curious career move, but by this time not only had his father – now aged 72 – retired from butchery to work as a Bath chairman, but his brother George had given up cabinet making and set up a Bath chair factory called Dillon & Co in New Orchard Street. Edward's other brother, Henry, the music teacher, had died two years earlier at the age of 35.

By 1900, Edward had moved to 61 Locksbrook Road, where that year's *Directory* lists him as a 'chairman and waiter'. In the following year's census, however, he is described as a 'butcher & general dealer'. At the age of 44, he had made his final career move, and to ensure the future of the business had engaged his son, Edward Blashford Dillon, aged 15, as an assistant.

Three years later, he moved to 10 Avon Buildings, converted what had been Fred Batten's grocery store to a butcher's and had an elaborate sign painted. The business prospered, and by the time of the 1911 census, not only was his son working for him, but so were two of his daughters, Lucy and Elsie – even though they were not acknowledged on the sign.

Edward Dillon went on to become president of the Bath Butchers' Association, which in 1927 held a special dinner to mark his 70th birthday. Replying to the toasts and congratulations he had received, he reminisced about his career:

> Mr Dillon told the company that he started when he was just ten years old with his uncle in New Bond Street. He dealt with skewers in a round block in Hampers Passage. Hampers kept the premises now occupied by Ealands. He thought winters were colder then. A few years later he went in to the merchant service and the Navy, which filled the middle part of his life ... As the name of Dillon had been so long on the roll [of the association] he hoped that his son and family would carry it on.[15]

He died, aged 77, in 1935, but by then the business was being run by his son, who carried it on until the 1960s, when it was taken over by a Mr Norris and later became Eastaugh's Butcher's.

Carry on along the Lower Bristol Road, turn left under the railway and continue along Twerton High Street. After passing the Twerton Chippy, look up at the gable end a little way along to see BREWERY in faded lettering above the first-floor window (11). You may also just be able to make out the words WHITE HART written in a semi-circle above it. This sign dates from sometime before 1899 when the White Hart pub and brewery closed.

'BREWERY' can still be made out on the side of the building ...

... as can 'WHITE HART BREWERY' on the extreme left of the plat band

If you carry on to the front of the building – now split into three houses – you will find something even more interesting – a palimpsest of two ghost signs on a plat band running the length of the building. Although neither is legible in its entirety, enough has survived to provide a fascinat-

ing glimpse into a forgotten world, where tipplers and temperance campaigners were avowed enemies.

It starts off straightforwardly enough, with WHITE HART in two versions. Then comes BREWERY in black, which, towards the end, is overwritten with the start of another set of words in blue: TEMPLAR INSTITUTE & RESTAURANT Headquarters TWERTON LODGE, followed by four more letters that look like LOOT. Underneath it, enough of the black lettering survives to make out what looks like WINES and possibly the start of the word BEER.

Further along 'TEMPLAR INSTITUTE & RESTAURANT' can be made out ...

... as can 'Head Quarters TWERTON LODGE'

After the White Hart closed, the Bath Brewery, which owned it, put it on the market for £500, but, after it failed to find a buyer, disposed of it to the Twerton Lodge of Good Templars for £355. The Order of Good Templars was an organisation founded in the United States in 1851 to promote total abstinence, and is still active today. The Twerton Lodge was fired with a missionary zeal to stop Twerton drinking, and 'directly they got into possession [of the White Hart] they burnt the old vats and other things connected with alcoholic liquor they found on the premises.'[16] Despite their enthusiasm, the institute lasted only until 1908, when the Templars moved out of the building, which was converted to three cottages the following year.[17]

Head back along the High Street and, after going under the railway, cross the Lower Bristol Road at the lights and head in the direction of the city centre. By the Golden Fleece pub, turn left along Fielding's Road, and, when this swings right into a supermarket car park, carry on along a footpath. After crossing a footbridge over the river, carry on in the same direction up Station Road. Just before the junction with Newbridge Road at the top, look for a ghost sign reading CHEMIST on the single-storey extension on the left (12). This is on the back of what is now a clock & watch repairers, and dates from the late 1930s when Reg Pointing opened a chemist's here, which was taken over by Mills & Mills in the mid-1960s.

For the final ghost sign, turn right along Newbridge Road to the Weston Hotel, which has some magnificent, but – given the prominence of the building – surprisingly little-known ghost signs (13). They are, it has to be admitted, more than a little faded, but enough of them survives to indicate that they represented sign-writing of the highest order.

The first of them can be glimpsed on the side wall, above the single-storey extension. Only the first part of the sign can be read from this side of the road. You have to cross over to see that it originally read WESTON HOTEL, although the last two letters have been sacrificed

to make way for a door. Moving to the front of the building, WESTON appears to the left of the porch and HOTEL to the right, while, above the porch's second-storey window is the word FIRKINS. Finally, around the corner, on the east-facing wall, WESTON HOTEL is written above the second-floor windows, although this sign has almost disappeared.

The large building at the back of the hotel was built as an assembly room at the same time, and has a carved sign high in the gable end reading GEORGE BIGGS 1890.

George Biggs was a big player on the Bath pub scene in the late nineteenth and early twentieth centuries. Starting off with the Crown Brewery in New Orchard Street, he went on to acquire a string of pubs, two of which – the Royal Oak in Larkhall and the Weston Hotel – he had built.[18] The Weston – originally intended to be called the Shakespeare – opened in September 1890, the lease being taken by Michael Clune, of Mortimer & Clune, wine merchants of Bristol.[19]

So far so good. It is when we come to the name painted on the porch that things turn murky. To say that George Firkins is a man of mystery is an understatement, and tracking him down has not proved easy. He was born in 1843 in Bristol, the son of a sawyer. By 1871, he was living in Shoreditch in London, working as a shoemaker, and married with

GHOST SIGNS OF BATH

Above: The sign for FIRKINS above the entrance to the Weston Hotel

Opposite top: The sign on the west wall of the hotel, with the last two letters sacrificed to make way for a door

Opposite below: George Biggs' name on the datestone of the former assembly room at the back

two children. By 1881, now described as a boot manufacturer, he had moved to Bow, but ten years later he was in Plymouth, 'living on his own means'.[20] The 1891 census was carried out on 5 April, and soon afterwards he moved to Bath to take over the Weston Hotel, for on 19 November, the *Bath Chronicle* reported that

> another of the enjoyable smoking concerts promoted by Mr Firkins at the Weston Hotel, took place on Monday. There was a large attendance, and the high-class programme gave great satisfaction ... Mr Firkins intends, we believe, to hold these concerts at intervals throughout the winter months.[21]

Less than a year later, on 29 September 1892, George Firkins died at the age of 49. Two months later, the *Bath Chronicle* reported the death 'at the Weston Hotel [of] Frances, second daughter of the late George Firkins, aged 23'.[22] There was to be one final reference to a man whose association with the Weston Hotel had proved so tragically brief. In November the following year, the *Chronicle* reported that a concert had been 'held in the Assembly Rooms adjoining Firkins' Weston Hotel'.[23] Apart from these four brief mentions of George Firkins, however, we know nothing. His widow, Priscilla, was listed as the licensee of the Weston Hotel in the 1894 *Directory*, but she had gone by the following year. She later married a 'railway engine painter' called William Taylor and settled in Swindon, leaving only the name above the entrance to the Weston Hotel as a reminder of one of Bath's shortest-serving landlords.

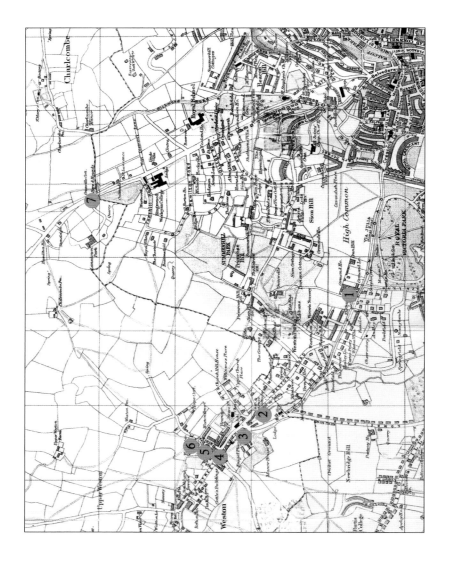

9

WESTON VILLAGE & CHARLCOMBE

This chapter is in two parts – a walk through Weston village, followed by a visit to a pub on Lansdown which lies within the parish of Charlcombe. The walk starts at the top of Park Lane, at the north-western corner of Royal Victoria Park. On the west corner of Park Lane is a little-known milestone set into the wall, indicating that the GWR station was a mile and a half away.[1] Not a ghost sign, as the letters were incised and filled with lead, but an interesting survival none the less.

A little way along Weston Road we come to the first ghost sign, on the single storey building on the right:

NURSERYMAN SEEDSMAN & FLORIST (1)

This was the shop for Weston Nursery, which was established shortly after the opening of Royal Victoria Park. The first reference to it comes in 1837, when it was owned by James Salter and John Scammell.[2] They owned a similar nursery, the shop for which also survives, on the London Road. Known as Kensington Nurseries, its name can still be seen on the pediment, although, as the letters are incised, it does not qualify as a ghost sign. By 1840, George Wheeler had joined the partnership,

VICTORIA NURSERY,
WESTON ROAD, and
KENSINGTON NURSERY,
LONDON ROAD.

MESSRS. SALTER and SCAMMELL beg leave most respectfully to inform the Nobility, Gentry, and the Public in general, that they Sell every kind of VEGETABLE and FLOWER SEEDS, &c., at both their Nurseries ; likewise a general Assortment of STOVE and GREEN-HOUSE PLANTS, consisting of Fine
CAMELLIAS, CAPE ERICAS, GERANIUMS,
AMARYLLIS,
And many other select and elegant Plants now in cultivation. All the most approved
DAHLIAS,
At Prices as low as those quoted in any Nurseryman's Catalogue of the Season.

☞ SALTER and SCAMMELL having no Shop in the City, Orders left for them with Mr. LONG, Hair Dresser and Perfumer, No. 7, OLD BOND STREET, will receive the most prompt attention.

An advertisement in the *Bath Chronicle* on 26 April 1838

but in October that year the partnership was dissolved, with Scammell taking Kensington Nurseries, and Salter and Wheeler taking the Weston Nursery.[3] Two years later, Wheeler retired, leaving Salter to carry on alone until he handed over to James Griffin in 1846.[4]

BATH NURSERY AND SEED ESTABLISHMENT.

JAMES GRIFFIN,

(Successor to J. Salter,)

NURSERYMAN, SEEDSMAN, AND FLORIST,

WESTON ROAD, & 2, NEW BOND ST., BATH.

The Public are respectfully assured that every attention continues to be paid to the different departments of the Nursery and Seed Business, and that no pains are spared to procure every article, new or otherwise, both genuine in quality, and true to kind.

Separate Descriptive Catalogues of the principal divisions of the Business, may be had (post-free) on application. They are as follows :

AGRICULTURAL SEEDS, comprise all that is good, and saved from the most genuine stocks.

HORTICULTURAL SEEDS, contain all the choicest vegetable, herbs, &c., Imported and Home Grown.

FLOWER SEEDS, include all the best and newest kinds, known either in this or Foreign Countries.

DUTCH FLOWERING BULBS, imported from Haarlem every Autumn.

SPRING BEDDING PLANTS, all the newest and best kinds.

Forest Trees, Fruit Trees, Flowering Shrubs, Evergreens, American Plants, &c., &c.

Hot House, Green House, Orchidaceous Plants, &c., &c.

EXPERIENCED GARDENERS AND BAILIFFS RECOMMENDED.

Edward Carpenter acquired the nursery in the late 1850s.[5] He was there until his death in 1874, when his son Henry took over.[6] After Henry Carpenter's death in 1902, the nursery passed to John Milburn, previously superintendent of Royal Victoria Park.[7] He was there until his death in 1942, when his son John Boucher Milburn took over.[8] After the nursery closed, most of its land, which lay behind villas further along Weston Road, became the site of a housing development called Linden Gardens.

Above: The remains of the sign on the former nursery

Opposite: An advertisement from 1852

Below: An advertisement from 1914

JOHN MILBURN, F.R.H.S.,
NURSERYMAN AND FLORIST.
VICTORIA NURSERY, WESTON ROAD, BATH.
LATE OF KEW GARDENS.
18 years Superintendent of the Royal Victoria Park and Botanical Gardens, Bath.

Carry on along Weston Road. After 300m follow the main road as it bears right into Weston Park, and take the first left to continue along Weston Park (2). As the road starts to drop down into Weston village, you come to the Old Crown on the left, where you will see a sign for HOME BREWD BEER to the right

of the first-floor window. There is also part of an old licensing sign above the entrance, but it is the other sign that is of particular interest. It looks to date from the early nineteenth century and can be no later than 1862, the year the Old Crown – or the Crown as it was then – stopped brewing beer. On 30 October 1862, the *Bath Chronicle* carried the following advertisement:[9]

CROWN INN, Weston, near Bath.

MR. H. EVE is favoured with instructions from Mrs. MIZEN to SELL BY AUCTION, on TUESDAY Next, Nov. 4th, 1862, commencing at One o'Clock precisely, the whole of her BREWING PLANT, which comprises—Seventy Gallon Copper Boiler, Mash Tub, Underback, Working Round, 5 nearly new Store Pieces, from 185 to 680 gallons each, Three Pockets Hops, Hop Strainer, Wort Pump, Piping and Taps, Gutta Percha Piping, Buckets, and Spring Trap and Harness.

On View the Morning of the Day of Sale ; and any further Particulars may be obtained at the AUCTIONEER'S Offices, 4, Union Street, Bath.

N.B.—The RETAIL BUSINESS, at the Crown Inn, will be continued by Mrs. MIZEN, as heretofore.

The sign for Home Brewd Beer survived, however, which is surprising, for the magistrates who renewed licences on an annual basis usually took a dim view of misleading signs being displayed. It had a close call in the early twentieth century, when they asked for it to be removed: far from it being a quaint reminder of bygone days, there were still at least 30 home-brew houses around Bath at the time, and unsuspecting customers may well have been lured into the Crown under false pretences. Thankfully it survived, and, when the brewery at the George & Dragon in Batheaston closed in 1960, bringing the history of brewing in the Bath area to an end, such questions became a thing of the past ... until, that is, home-brewed houses, after a gap of over 50 years, started opening up again. At the time of writing, there were just two – the Bath Brewhouse and the Graze Bar – but, if they start to proliferate, the sign on the Old Crown may become a bone of contention once again.

Carry on down to the junction with the High Street, and, standing on the right-hand side of the road, look across at a ghost sign between the first-floor windows of Nº 6 (**3**):

E GILLARD
NEWSAGENT
STATIONER & TOBACCONIST
CYCLE HARDWARE ETC

TOY & FANCY GOODS
DEALER
HABERDASHERY
MEDICINE
CHEMIST SUNDRIES
LENDING LIBRARY

Some of the paint has flaked away, and traces of an earlier sign can be made out underneath. Very little of this earlier sign can be read, although the few words that can be made out – STATIONERY, TOBACCONIST, MEDICINES ... SUNDRIES – suggest it was similar to the later one.

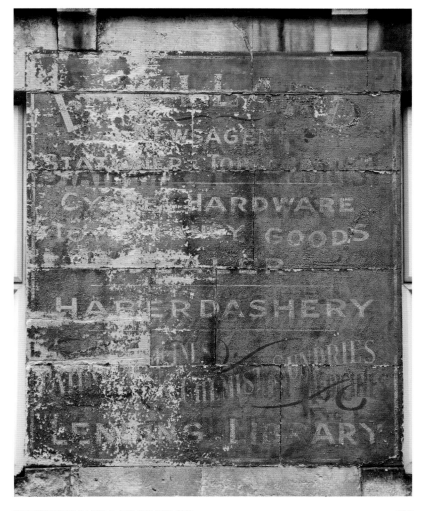

Edward Gillard was the son of a jobbing gardener from Dolemeads in Widcombe. In 1911, when he was 22, he set up in business as a newsagent and stationer at 39 High Street, Weston, next door to the King's Head. The following year, he married Annie Anstey from 79 High Street, Weston, whose father was also a jobbing gardener. By 1914, he had moved his business to 6 High Street, and probably had the first sign painted around this time. His wife died in 1915, at the age of 24, leaving him with two children, Edward, born 1913, and Violet, born 1915. The following year he was called up for military service but was granted a conditional discharge because of business and family commitments. He remarried in 1917 and continued to run the newsagents in the High Street until the 1940s, when he transferred the business to Webb's Newsagents, who expanded it into N° 5.

Walk along the High Street and, when you come to the King's Head, look across to some splendid sign-writing on the opposite corner (4). There are two signs here – a small one painted on a red background on the front wall, and a larger one on the side.

The small sign is the earlier of the two, and, although its lettering has faded almost to nothing, THE QUEEN'S HEAD can just be made out. Originally known as the Queen Victoria Inn, this opened as a beerhouse around 1842, and was renamed the Queen's Head sometime before 1861. Its licence was revoked in 1914 as part of a campaign to reduce the number of pubs in Weston. In the early 1920s, after lying empty for a time, the building was taken by JF Simmons, an insurance agent, and by 1926 his wife had opened a confectioner's. The sign on the side of the building was probably painted shortly afterwards.

It invites customers to COME HERE FOR WILLS'S GOLD FLAKE CIGARETTES (although GOLD FLAKE, presumably

Above: The old beerhouse sign, with THE QUEENS HEAD still just about visible

Opposite: The Wills's advertisement from the 1920s, with the words GOLD FLAKE all but vanished

GHOST SIGNS OF BATH

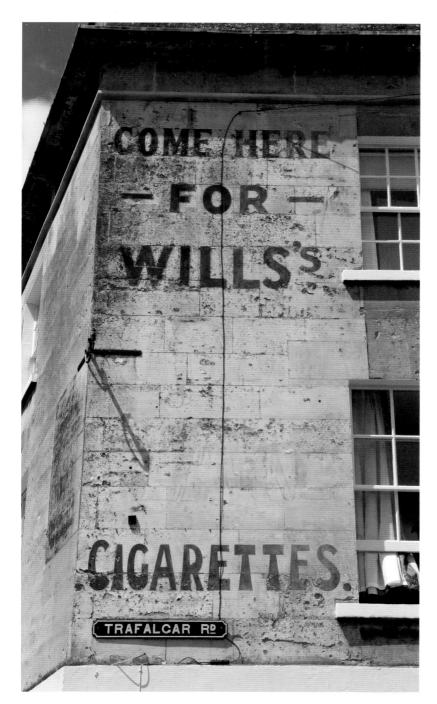

COME HERE
- FOR -
WILLS'S

CIGARETTES.

TRAFALCAR RD

WESTON VILLAGE & CHARLCOMBE

written in gold, has virtually disappeared), and is unique among Bath's ghost signs in having been signed.

Under the word CIGARETTES you will see, on the right-hand side, SELLICK BROS, Advt Contractors, BRISTOL. This firm was originally based on Oxford Road on Totterdown, and later moved to Talbot Road in Knowle.

Walk up Trafalgar Road as far as the chapel on the left, which has a sign – COUNTESS OF HUNTINGDONS CHURCH – over the entrance (5). The Countess of Huntingdon will be a name familiar to many because of the chapel she established on the Vineyards in Bath. The Countess of Huntingdon's Connexion was a breakaway Methodist sect formed in 1763.

The chapel on the Vineyards followed two years later and was the first of many more in this country and abroad. The chapel on Trafalgar Road opened around 1853; when an appeal for funds was launched that year, it was described it as 'the new chapel at Weston'.[10] Four years later, the *Bath Chronicle* reported that 'two new wings have lately been added, and a new gallery, and a bell turret placed on the front of the elevation'.[11] Although the chapel on the Vineyards closed in 1922, to be taken over by the Presbyterians and later as a museum by the Bath Preservation Trust, the chapel in Weston survived until recently, but in 2013 permission was granted for it to be converted into three houses. The sign above the door, however, survives.

Weston's final pair of ghost signs have almost faded away, and may not seem all that exciting. Researching them, however, has uncovered the fascinating story of how Weston became a brewing centre in the nineteenth century. If you look up the road a little way, you will see a building set forward, with part of its side wall painted dark red and the word BREWERY just about visible (6). If you walk up to the front of the building, you may just about make out, painted on the parapet, POINTING'S BREWERY.

This was not the only brewery in Trafalgar Road. The building opposite – now Nos 10 and 10a – was a brewery as well. There were at least two other breweries in Weston, down on the High Street. As for

The word BREWERY can still be seen on the side wall of the former Pointing's Brewery

The sign for POINTING'S BREWERY on the front of the building, however, is more difficult to make out

Henry Pointing, before he took over the brewery that still bears his name, was part owner of the one across the road and also ran one of those in the High Street. So telling his story inevitably means trying coming to grips with the almost insanely convoluted – and, at least in the early years, somewhat sketchy – story of brewing in nineteenth-century Weston.

The first reference to a brewery in Weston comes in 1827, when Samuel Bryant transferred the Weston Brewery to William Fookes.[12] In 1841, William Fookes took his nephew, Robert Fookes, into partnership with him. The brewery closed eight years later and the entire contents were auctioned off; among the lots on offer were '800 Barrels of prime sound STRONG BEER and PORTER; 28 capital Store Vats and Pieces ... 250 quarters of prime Malt, made from the best Wiltshire barleys; 50 packets of Hops; several hundred carriage Casks, all the loose utensils, 3 powerful grey Cart Geldings, handsome Pony and Harness, Drays, Waggons, Carts, and other Miscellaneous Effects, such as is usually found in an extensive and well-managed brewing establishment'.[13] We know, from the 1841 census, that the brewery was on Trafalgar Place (as Trafalgar Road was then known). What we do not know is which side of the road it was on.

By the time of the 1851 census, however, John Edgecumbe was running a brewery on Trafalgar Road and employing a man and a boy. We know this was on the east side of the road, because it was still known as the Edgecumbe Brewery when it closed 38 years later. Another Weston brewer was also listed in the 1851 census – Henry Morgan of Belton House at the west end of the High Street. His Penhill Brewery stood in front of Belton House, where modern flats now stand. He later transferred the brewery to a Mr Bird, and in 1856 it was advertised for sale along with 'a most substantial DWELLING HOUSE [and] those TWO Freehold MESSUAGES or DWELLING-HOUSES, adjoining the same, known as the GLOBE INN'.[14] There seem to have been no takers for the brewery as a going concern, but the Globe Inn, later downsized to a single house and famous as the smallest pub in Bath, survived until 1966.

Moving on to 1852, that year's *Directory* listed yet another brewer in Weston – Alexander Walker of the Weston Brewery. This was a singularly ill-starred enterprise. Just after Christmas 1852, Joseph Gilbert 'was accidentally killed ... by getting entangled in the Machinery of a Steam-Engine at Weston Brewery', and the *Bath Chronicle* carried an appeal for subscriptions to assist his widow and seven young children, who had been 'deprived of their natural support'.[15] Just over two months later, the *Chronicle* carried news of Alexander Walker's bankruptcy, and soon afterwards came the auction of his effects, including '300 Barrels of very Prime STRONG BEER ... New Copper REFRIGERATOR complete, a very Superior Iron CRANE, Four-horse power high pressure STEAM ENGINE, with Boiler, &c, complete, Capital BRUISING MILL, with Shafts and Straps, Copper PUMPS, with Gutta Percha Piping', and much more.[16] Unfortunately, we do not know where in Weston this short-lived enterprise was based, although the likelihood is that it was either opposite the Edgecumbe Brewery on Trafalgar Road or next to the King's Head on the High Street.

Three years later, Henry Pointing comes into the story for the first time. While giving evidence at a coroner's court in March 1856, after seeing a man drown in the river, he declared that, 'I am a maltster and brewer, and I live at Weston, near Bath.'[17] Henry Pointing was born at Compton

Dando, and at the time of the 1851 census, aged 22, was working in his brother's grocery store at 29 Southgate Street. By 1856, he had moved to Nelson Place in Weston and become a business partner of John Edgecumbe. In 1858, John Edgecumbe died and his widow, Elizabeth, carried on running the brewery with Henry Pointing. In the 1861 census, they were still employing six men. Later that year, however, the partnership was dissolved, and the brewery was taken over by Henry Hall Bishop, an ale and porter merchant from Stroud. On 19 September 1861, Bishop placed an advertisement in the *Bath Chronicle* to assure customers that he had secured the services of the head brewer who had worked for the previous owners.

EDGECUMBE BREWERY,
WESTON, near Bath,
September 18th, 1861.

MRS. EDGECUMBE respectfully informs her numerous Customers that the PARTNERSHIP between herself and Mr. POINTING EXPIRED on the 17th inst., and that the Business will in future be conducted by Mr. H. H. BISHOP.

Mrs. EDGECUMBE takes this opportunity of returning her sincere thanks for the very liberal patronage conferred on her late husband and herself for so many years, and respectfully solicits a continuance of the same, which will receive their best and immediate attention.

HENRY HALL BISHOP, in succeeding to the Business hitherto carried on by Messrs. EDGECUMBE and POINTING, begs to inform the numerous Customers of the late Firm that, in addition to his own practical acquaintance with the system of Brewing as practised at Burton-on-Trent, *he has secured the services of the same Brewer* who has, since Mr. Edgecumbe's decease, superintended that department of the Business, so that they may rely upon being supplied with a precisely similar article to that sold by the late Firm.

H. H. B. respectfully solicits a continuance of the favours bestowed on the late Firm, as well as the support of the Public, which shall always receive his prompt and best attention.

Above: Announcements from Mrs Edgecumbe and Henry Hall Bishop in the *Bath Chronicle* on 19 September 1861

Below: Henry Ponting announces his takeover of the brewery adjoining the King's Head on 26 September 1861

HENRY POINTING

BEGS respectfully to Thank the Customers of the Partnership lately subsisting between Mrs. ELIZABETH EDGECUMBE and himself for the Patronage received during his nine years' connection with the late Business, and to inform them that in addition to the Malthouse occupied by the late Firm, he has TAKEN the Commodious BREWERY adjoining the KING'S HEAD, WESTON, where the BUSINESS of MALTSTER and BREWER will be continued by him on his own account, and that his best efforts will be directed to the

SUPPLY of BEER, ALE, and PORTER,

Of the highest qualities, all Orders for which shall receive his immediate attention.
Weston, near Bath, 18th Sept., 1861.   [193

A few days later, Henry Pointing announced that, as well as keeping on the malthouse formerly used by the Edgecumbe Brewery, he had taken 'the commodious BREWERY adjoining the KING'S HEAD, Weston, where the BUSINESS of MALTSTER and BREWER will be continued by him on his own account'.[18] The King's Head on Weston High Street, facing the bottom of Trafalgar Road, is still open today; the brewery may have occupied the building adjoining it on the west.

While all this was going on, another brewery had opened. Around 1859, George Powney, landlord of the Bladud's Head in Ladymead and owner of the Ladymead Brewery, moved to Weston and set up the Weston Brewery on the west side of Trafalgar Place, opposite the Edgecumbe Brewery.[19] It is not clear whether this was a new enterprise, or a revival of Alexander Walker's short-lived Weston Brewery, which had closed in 1853. What is clear is that its brews soon proved extremely popular. In 1861, a series of advertisements in the *Bath Chronicle* for Hancock's Refreshment Rooms in Old Bond Street, opposite the Mineral Water Hospital, informed customers that they could 'be accommodated with a SANDWICH, and a GLASS of GEORGE POWNEY'S Celebrated WESTON ALE, GUINNESS'S EXTRA DOUBLE STOUT, or BASS'S EAST INDIA PALE ALE, all in high Perfection'.[20] This was indeed illustrious company for a small brewery in a village on the outskirts of Bath to be keeping. George Powney was still running the Weston Brewery in 1868, but by the time of the 1871 census it had been taken over by Edward and Robert Green from Exeter.

Henry Hall Bishop was still running the Edgecumbe Brewery, on the east side of Trafalgar Place, in 1864, when he placed a series of advertisements in the *Bristol Mercury*, but that is the last we hear of him – at least in connection with Weston.[21] By 1871, the Edgecumbe Brewery was being run by George Robinson of Marlborough House (which was on Davis's Lane behind the Crown & Anchor). He died the following year, and a relative called Charles Morgan (who may also have been related to Henry Morgan of the Penhill Brewery) took it on.

Edward Green left the Weston Brewery in 1877. It was taken over by Henry Pointing, who gave up the brewery next to the King's Head, and sold 'the whole of the BREWING PLANT, Steam Engine, Boiler, Copper, Store Pieces, Working-rounds, Coolers, Pumps, &c' there.[22] Pointing was at the Weston Brewery for less than six years; on the evening of 20 August 1883, he was walking along Westgate Street when he suddenly dropped dead of heart failure.[23] The business was carried on by his widow and later by his son, Henry Derham Pointing, who was only 16 at the time of his father's death.

The Edgecumbe Brewery across the road, meanwhile, passed from Charles Morgan to Edward Morgan and his cousin, George Robinson, the son of the George Robinson who had run it a few years earlier. In 1889, it was one of six breweries which amalgamated to form the Bath Brewery Company, and the Edgecumbe Brewery closed for good.

The Weston Brewery was now the only brewery in the village. Although it was being run by Henry Derham Pointing, it was owned jointly by four members of his family. In 1905 the partnership between them was dissolved and the brewery was put up for sale, along with two pubs – the Globe and the King's Head – and various other properties.[24] The whole lot was bought for £7,250 by the Bath Brewery Company, which by now had built a large brewery south of Newbridge Road in Lower Weston.

Surprisingly, that was not the end of the Weston Brewery, which continued to operate until the early 1920s, with Henry Derham Pointing as manager. Under the new regime, its name was changed from the Weston Brewery to Pointing's Brewery, presumably to avoid confusion with the Bath Brewery in Lower Weston. Although details of its operation are not known during this period, Henry Derham Pointing continued to be described in the directories as brewer and maltster; the likelihood is, however, that, while he carried on producing malt for the brewery at Lower Weston, brewing was phased out.

The Bath Brewery Company only lasted until 1923, when it was absorbed by George's of Bristol and the brewery at Lower Weston closed. It continued to produce malt, however, until it was demolished in the 1970s to make way for a trading estate.[25] Today, only the sign on Pointing's Brewery, even though it has almost faded away, survives to remind us of the time when Weston was a busy brewing centre.

Finally, we head to the Hare & Hounds pub at the top of Lansdown Road – either by walking across the fields by Primrose Hill (which involves a climb of some 150 metres), or by taking the less strenuous options of driving or catching a bus (7). The Hare & Hounds is, rather conveniently, in the parish of Charlcombe. Conveniently because it seems

always to have been the only pub in the village, which means we can date it with some confidence back to at least 1695, when Jane Wait held the licence for an alehouse in Charlcombe. Since then it has been extended many times, but the original building still survives at its heart, and if you look at the side facing the road you can see, above the old entrance – long converted to a window – the names of some of its former licensees, or at least the shadows of them. One of them – possibly the most recent – may be that of David Bardell, who was here around 1900, but there seem to be at least two others, so faded and so intermingled that it is hard to make much out.

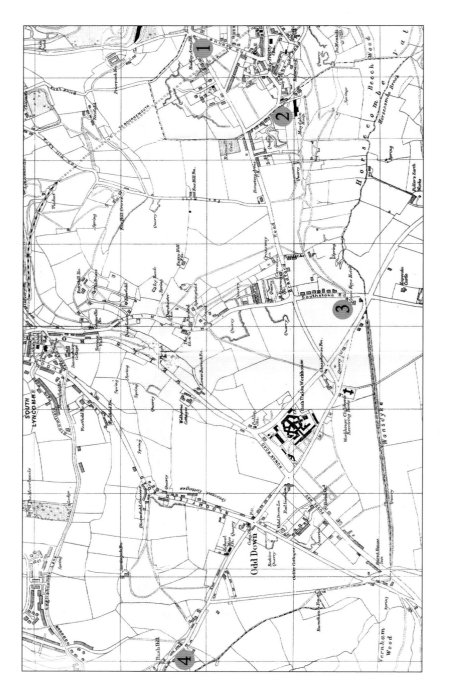

10

COMBE DOWN & RUSH HILL

There are three ghost signs to see in Combe Down, and one at Rush Hill – all of them on pubs. The first two are relatively close together, but the third is three-quarters of a mile away, while the final pub – the only one of the four no longer open – is over a mile further on.

On North Road, facing the top of Ralph Allen Drive is the Hadley Arms, built by a builder called Sam Spence from Ampleforth in Yorkshire in the 1840s (1). In the 1851 census, he was listed as its landlord, but by 1853 Frederick Garland had taken over, and the 1861 census records Sam Spence living at 11 De Montalt Place.[1] Beyond the Hadley Arms are the former Victoria Rooms, now part of the pub, but still with a ghost sign on the side wall. The first reference to the Victoria

Rooms in the *Bath Chronicle* comes in January 1888, when the Monkton Combe Conservative Association held a smoking concert there.[2] During the Second World War, an army unit stationed at Combe Down used the Victoria Rooms as barracks.

Head along The Avenue, to the left of the Hadley Arms and turn right at the end along Church Road. Carry on for 200m and, after passing a row of modern buildings on the left, you will see the King William IV, with a sign for Findlater's Stout between two of its first-floor windows (2). This has only recently been uncovered, and is a remarkable discovery. The sign was originally larger – the end of the last letter of a word (possibly an S) and a full stop can be seen above the section that has been revealed – but a small window has been inserted in part of it.

Findlater's stout was, like Guinness, brewed in Dublin, but, whereas Guinness was well known in Bath, Findlater's was virtually unknown. Indeed, the only references to it in the *Bath Chronicle* come in a series of advertisements in 1859 for FG Earle & Co of King Street in Bristol, who were, among other things, agents for 'Findlater & Co's Imperial Dublin Stout'.[3]

Findlater's Mountjoy Brewery was founded in 1852. In 1891, Billy – later Sir William – Findlater sold his interest in the brewery, which became known simply as the Mountjoy Brewery, and eventually closed in 1957. This means that the sign on the King William IV must predate 1891 – but as to why it was painted, who can say?

Follow the road round to the right and at the end turn left along Bradford Road. After 800m turn left along Southstoke Road, and at the crossroads look to the right to see the Cross Keys (3). In 1718, this was described as 'a new erected tenement or dwelling house called the Cross Keys, now a public house on Odwood Down', which means its 300th anniversary is

almost upon us.[4] Its ghost sign – above the side door facing Southstoke Road – is of more recent vintage, however, and harks back to the time when pubs still had tap rooms. In 1895, the tap room at the Cross Keys was the venue for an ill-advised jacket swap:

> Robert Newman, 46, of 35, The Pithay, St James's, Bristol, bill-poster, was charged with stealing from the tap-room of the Cross Keys, Odd Down, a man's jacket, value 7s 6d, the property of John Mitchell. Prisoner went into the tap-room of the Cross Keys on Friday morning, and seeing a coat which was in much better condition than his own lying on the table, he annexed it, leaving his own in its place. He then disappeared. The stolen coat belonged to John Mitchell, of 2 Lansdown-view, Combe Down, who was working in the house. He put the coat in the pump-house, but the landlord, thinking it was exposed there, placed it in the tap-room, as he thought, out of harm's way. PC Venn, of the County Constabulary, stationed at Norton St Philip, was informed of the occurrence as he was in the vicinity; he proceeded towards Hinton Charterhouse and captured the prisoner, who was with another man. Prisoner admitted the theft, and was fined 10s, but in default went to Horfield for seven days with hard labour.[5]

For the final ghost sign, turn right along Midford Road and left at a pair of mini-roundabouts along Frome Road. Carry on past the Sainsbury's roundabout and the Red Lion roundabout, and eventually, after passing another roundabout, the road will start to descend Rush Hill. After

another 200m you will see a row of three newly-refurbished rubble-stone cottages on the left (4). This was the Rose & Laurel, a vibrant community pub until things started to go awry around a decade ago, leading to closure in 2010. Although it no longer looks like a pub, the refurbishment has revealed the name of a former licensee above the old entrance:

FANNY E MARKS.
LICENSED TO SELL BEER, ALE, SNUFF & TOBACCO
TO BE CONSUMED ON OR OFF THE PREMISES.

Much of the lettering is fragmentary, and it is possible that, intermingled with FANNY E, is HERBERT SIDNEY or HERBERT S.

Herbert Marks became landlord of the Rose & Laurel shortly before the First World War, and when he died, suddenly, at the age of 60, in 1927, the licence was transferred to his widow, Fanny. She remained there for the next 23 years, successfully applying to have the Rose & Laurel up-graded from a beerhouse to a fully-licensed house in the 1940s, and running it until her death at the age of 83 in 1950.

The Rose & Laurel when Fanny Marks was its landlady

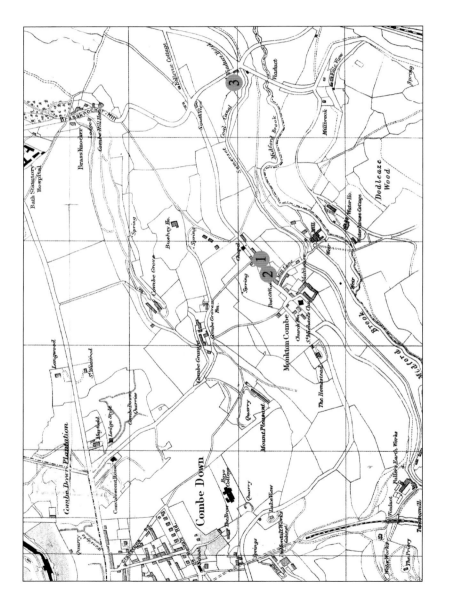

11

MONKTON COMBE

Monkton Combe has two intriguing ghost signs next door to each other, on N⁰ˢ 1 and 2 Julian Cottages. N° 1 has MONKTON COMBE written in white lettering above the entrance, while N° 2 has a superb sign, dating from the early nineteenth century, for JAMES MORGAN, LICENSED DEALER IN TEA, COFFEE, SNUFF, TOBACCO, &c (1 & 2).

The sign on N° 1 is relatively straightforward. Miss Elizabeth Orchard opened a post office here sometime between 1884 and 1891, and the name of the village is all that remains of the old sign. As for the other sign, while it is clear that a James Morgan had a shop at N° 2 in the early nineteenth century, we have been unable to find any record of him. We have, however, turned up some information on what happened to the building in the latter part of the nineteenth century which may relate back to his tenancy.

Above: The sign for MONKTON COMBE on N° 1 Julian Cottages

Below: Monkton Combe around 1904. with signs above the door of N° 1 Julian Cottages indicating it was a post office

Before the post office moved to Nº 1 it was at Nº 2, where the postmaster was George Morgan. He was born in Monkton Combe around 1802, but whereabouts in the village he lived as a boy or who his father was is not recorded. He left to join the navy, but by 1851 had returned to live in East Twerton, where he worked as a turnkey at Twerton Gaol. By the time of the 1864 *Directory*, he had moved back to Monkton Combe to work as a gardener, and the 1871 census records him as living at 2 Julian Cottages. The 1876 *Directory* still lists him as a gardener, but by the time of the 1881 census, when he was 79, he had become a postmaster. He was still a postmaster, according to the 1884 *Directory*, three years later, but that is the last we hear of him.

None of this solves the mystery of the ghost sign on Nº 2, of course, and the George Morgan who lived here for 20 years or so from around 1864 may have had nothing to do with the James Morgan who had the sign painted. But who knows – perhaps George Morgan was born in this house, perhaps his father was the James Morgan who was licensed to sell tea, coffee, snuff and tobacco, and perhaps, after sailing the seven seas and guarding the miscreants in Twerton Gaol, he returned to Monkton Combe, took the lease of his boyhood home, worked as a gardener, and, when that became too much for him, opted for the easier life of a village postmaster. Or perhaps not. One day, when information on James Morgan turns up, we may know for sure.

There is another ghost sign on the old Viaduct Inn at the bottom of Brassknocker Hill, which opened, along with the turnpike road viaduct across the valley, in the mid-1830s, and closed in 2005 (3). The range of buildings, now converted to flats, is notable for including a Victorian tower brewery. The name of the inn can also be seen – just – on the side of the building. Photographs from around 1910 show that the sign had yet to be painted, indicating that it is of twentieth century vintage.

The Viaduct Hotel in the 1950s, with a train passing on the Camerton & Limpley Stoke Railway. The pub has been closed for over a decade, but the sign, although very faded, is still visible.

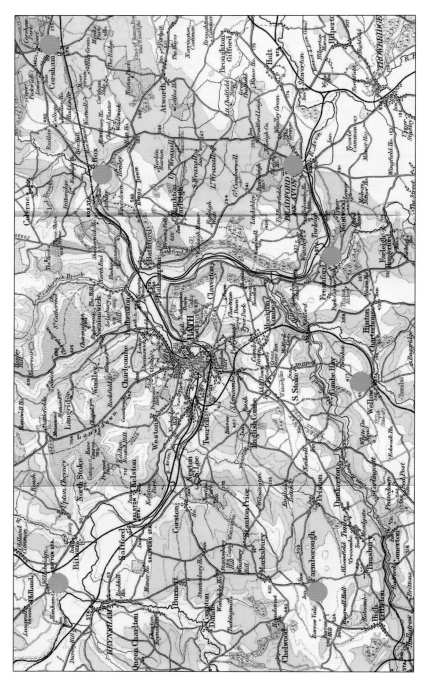

12

FRESHFORD

Freshford, where some of the scenes in *The Titfield Thunderbolt* were filmed in 1952, is one of the most delightfully unspoilt villages in Somerset. Among its many fascinating buildings are the old Freshford Brewery and, a short distance away on Brewery Lane, the former Greyhound Inn, which boasts a splendid ghost sign. The Greyhound was owned by Freshford Brewery, whose name appears on the sign, overwritten by the name of Wilkins Bros, brewers of Bradford on Avon, who took it over when Freshford Brewery closed in 1894. Wilkins was in turn taken over in 1920 by Usher's of Trowbridge, who closed the Greyhound in 1964.

There are at least three sets of lettering on the former Greyhound. The earliest – in white – reads FRESHFORD BREWERY, followed by another word, which may start with the letter E – ESTABLISHED perhaps? Then come two different versions of WILKINS BROS – the first in white, with all the letters the same size, and the second in gold, with the last three letters of BROS superscripted. The first version is followed by BRADFORD ON AVON, the second by SPARKLING ALES. It is not clear whether the FRESHFORD BREWERY sign and the first WILKINS BROS sign were smaller than the second WILKINS BROS sign, or whether they were the same size, with any other lettering obliterated.

Opposite: Map showing locations of towns and villages featured in chapters 12 to 18

Over the entrance to the former Morris's Stores on the corner of the High Street and Church Hill is a ghost sign which is so far gone as to be indecipherable. Old photographs show it quite clearly, although only part of the wording can be made out.[1] Of more interest than the sign, however, is the figure of a lion which used to be above the doorway to the left of the shopfront, but now resides across the road.

If you head west along the High Street from Morris's Stores, and carry straight on along the Tyning, you will come, after 800m, to a T junction with an archway ahead. To the right of the archway is a recently uncovered sign, in faded Old English lettering, for 'Abbotsleigh Stable'. Abbotsleigh, the large house you will just have passed on the left,

was built in the 1830s for Benjamin Edwards. Eight cottages were demolished to make way for it and its coach house and stable was built here on Rosemary Lane. Benjamin Edwards had a distinguished military career, but his father owned a plantation in Antigua. When parliament abolished slavery in the British Caribbean in 1833, the slave owners were compensated handsomely, and it seems likely that Abbotsleigh, like many large properties around this time, was built on the proceeds. The name of the house also suggests that the Edwards family came from the village of Abbot's Leigh near Bristol.[2] If so, they would have been in good company; Leigh Court, the grandest house in the village, belonged to the Miles family, one of the richest in the Bristol area. In 1833, Philip Miles received £47,403 for the 2,043 slaves he owned in Jamaica and Trinidad.

13

WELLOW

The Fox & Badger at Wellow has long been one of the most popular country pubs around Bath. It also has a ghost sign – or rather a palimpsest of ghost signs – on the porch at the side. One of them is an old licensing sign, so battered and broken up that no name can be descried; the other reads NEW INN, which was the name of the pub until it acquired its rather more colourful one in

the twentieth century. The porch is clearly much later than the rest of the building, and probably dates from 1888, when a major refurbishment was carried out – so major that a celebratory dinner was held:

> The New Inn, Wellow ... having lately come into the possession of Mr F Cole of St James's Street, St James's Square, Bath, extensive alterations and improvement have been carried out by him which have greatly increased the accommodation and comfort of the house ... The completion of the work was celebrated by a dinner to which nearly 100 guests were invited. A large proportion of these were Bathonians who left by the 4.35 train for Wellow in two saloon carriages kindly put on by the railway authorities. The dinner was served at six o'clock, an excellent spread being provided by the landlord, Mr George Steeds. Mr GW Graves officiated as chairman, while the vice-chair was filled by Mr W Cole ... The loyal toasts were heartily honoured, and the chairman gave 'Success to the New Inn' ... Mr Graves alluded to the improvements made, and expressed a hope that the owner and tenant might both profit by them ... The other toast was 'The Visitors from Bath', which was felicitously given from the chair ... During the evening a variety of songs were rendered, Mr FA Fowler accompanying on the piano. The Bathonians returned home in a special train.[1]

Would that you could still catch a train to the Fox & Badger today! This evocation of a long-lost night of revelry also gives a probable date for the first of the ghost signs, although which of them came first is difficult to say.

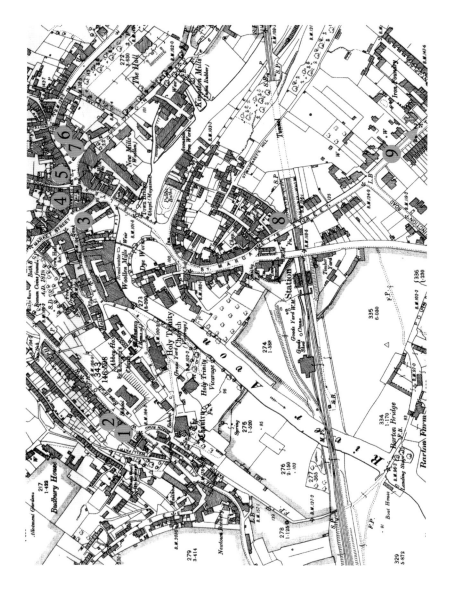

14

BRADFORD ON AVON

Bradford on Avon has a remarkable collection of ghost signs. A circular walk from the railway station, which can be reached from Bath Spa in less than 15 minutes, will not only take in these signs but also introduce you to one of the West Country's most fascinating towns.

Turn left out of the station, and, at the end of the car park, follow a path leading under the railway. After 100m, with the fifteenth-century tithe barn to your left, turn right across the medieval bridge. On the far side, where there is a choice of paths, take the one on the right. Go through a gate, cross the railway and head up another path. After this swings right, bear left up steps and right at the top. After passing the old Seven Stars Inn, you come to the archway of the Seven Stars Brewery, once owned by Wilkins Bros, whose name is on the old Greyhound at Freshford.

Bear right past the brewery along Newtown. Nº 39, on the left, was once the White Lion Inn, and still has a faded sign for HOME BREWED BEER above its first floor windows (1). The White Lion was open by 1793 but the last reference to it comes in 1863, so the sign has been slowly fading for over 150 years.[1]

Next door, at Nº 40, a painted rectangle between the two first-floor windows indicates the presence of another sign (2). Towards the top right-hand corner there are a few letters that may be the start of the word ENGINEERS or ENGINEERING, but that is about all.

Carry on along Newtown, which is a street of lost pubs. At N° 52 was the Masons Arms, closed in 2005 but still with its name on the glass in the front window and the signboard high above, while N° 62 was the Bell, closed in 1965, with a datestone of 1695 and a bracket from which a bell once hung.

Turn down a flight of steps opposite the Bell, which leads to Church Street. A right turn here will lead to Bradford on Avon's Saxon church, perhaps the most remarkable survival of all. When the Normans built a new church across the road, the old one was used as a charnel house. By the nineteenth century, hemmed in by a variety of other buildings, its nave, with an extra floor inserted, had become a school, while its chancel was a cottage, and its original function had long been forgotten. Not until 1856, when a local clergyman starting investigating the building, was its significance recognised. Today, stripped of later accretions, it stands forth in its ancient glory. One thing it does not have, however, is a ghost sign; for that you need to turn left along Church Street.

At the end, cross the zebra crossing, turn right and, on the corner of the Shambles, look over to the Swan Hotel, which has a magnificent sign, dating from the early twentieth century, on its side wall (3). The rubble-stone wall on which it is painted has also been painted or limewashed at some stage, with the lower part of the wall in a darker colour, although whether this was done before the sign was painted or afterwards, in an attempt to cover it up, is difficult to say. The effect, however, is to make the lower part of the sign more difficult to read. The right-hand edge of the sign has also been largely scoured away, although this is probably due to decades of water coursing down it from the adjacent drainpipe. What can be made out is as follows:

THE
SWAN HOTEL
FAMILY & COMMERCIAL
GOOD ACCOMMODATION
FOR CYCLISTS & MOTORISTS
COMFORTABLE COFFEE COMMERCIAL & PRIVATE SITTING
ROOMS
LUNCHEONS DINNERS [TEAS?]

... after which things get tricky. 'Posting of' can be made out, as can 'BILLIARDS', but apart from a random 'The' on the left, the only other words legible are 'HOTEL ENTRANCE' on the right, which presumably had an arrow or manicule directing customers round the corner.

A clue to what some of the illegible or barely legible words might have been comes in the form of an advertisement in Dotesio's 1902 *Directory of Bradford on Avon*. James Rose was the proprietor at the

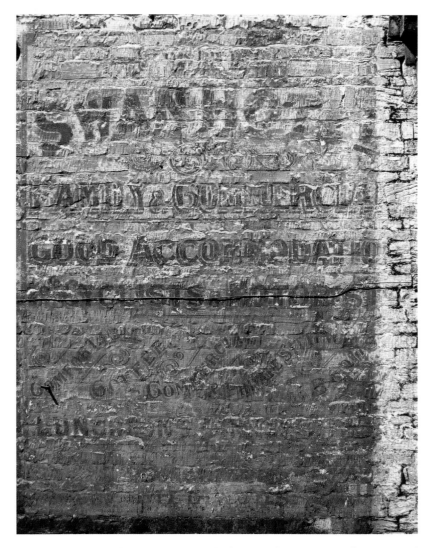

time and the advertisement includes a photograph of the hotel (unfortunately but understandably featuring the front rather than the side of the building). Among the facilities offered are 'POSTING in all its Branches, Good Accommodation for Cyclists & Motorists, BEST BRANDS OF WINES, SPIRITS AND CIGARS [and] Billiards AND Ping Pong'. The advertisement also describes the Swan as a 'FAMILY & COMMERCIAL' hotel. The similarities between the advertisement and the sign on the side of the Swan suggests that they date from around the same time and that James Rose was responsible for the sign.

Motorists were, of course, few and far between in 1901. James Rose could not have envisaged how many vehicles would one day squeeze along the narrow street beside his hotel. The pollution caused by that constant flow of traffic has had a devastating effect on the sign, and, while it is remarkable that it

has held up so well, its long-term survival must be in question. That it is one of the town's treasures has long been recognised, however, and in 2014, when the road was closed, Bradford on Avon Preservation Trust engaged Cliveden Conservation to take samples of paintwork from the sign with a view to advising them and the owner of the hotel as to how it could be restored and safeguarded.

Walk along the Shambles, and, when you come to Nᵒˢ 3-4 (currently the Grumpy Badger Café and Delicatessen), look up to see a much more recent sign for A Davis & Sons, Fish, Fruit & Potato Merchants (4). At the time of the 1911 census, a watch repairer and jeweller called Edgar Payne was at Nº 3, while Nº 4 was occupied by Thomas Coupland, a grocer and provision merchant. Albert Davis, meanwhile, was a fish-monger at 17 Market Street, with

another shop at 26 Silver Street. By 1925, one of his sons had joined him in the business, which later moved to the Shambles. It closed in 1963.

If you carry on to the end of the Shambles, you will see a large building ahead, on the corner of Coppice Hill, which until recently was the King's Arms. It had a large brewery in a yard at the back, many of the buildings of which survive, even though brewing ceased in the 1920s. If you carry on past the former King's Arms, you will see a red-brick building, part of which is now a pharmacy, with sunblinds over its windows (5). If you look underneath the blinds you will see, under the left-hand one, HARDING

& CO LTD, and, under the right-hand one, BREWERS ETC. Any lettering which may once had been painted above the next window along, where there is no blind, has gone. The lettering, and the building, can be dated precisely. In 1895, the King's Arms, along with its brewery, was taken over by William

Robert Harding, who in 1899 drew up plans to expand the brewery and build the red-brick buildings fronting Silver Street.[2] The work must soon have been completed, for the following year

> a fire occurred at Messrs WR Harding and Co's brewery at Coppice Hill, the portion affected being the copper room in the old premises adjoining the new building. PC Newman, who discovered the fire at about 3.45am, roused the fire brigade, who promptly responded, but there was no hope of saving the room, though the fire was prevented from spreading to other parts of the building.[3]

By 1903, however, William Harding had sold the business to Simeon Ruddle, whose family later owned Ruddle's Brewery in Rutland. Virtually nothing is known of William Harding, and whether his tenure was so brief because he wanted to make a handsome return on his investment, or whether he ran into financial difficulties, we have not been able to determine.[4]

A little further up Silver Street, at N° 28, is a ghost sign for a PRINTING OFFICE above the first-floor windows (6). We have managed to trace the history of this building back to 1816, when Stump & Bubb of Silver Street, Bradford on Avon were agents for Bish's lottery.[5] Pigot's 1822 *Directory of Wiltshire* reveals that Stump & Bubb were also booksellers and stationers.[6] By the time of the 1841 census, Mr Stump had gone, and John Bubb was trading by himself as a stationer. Pigot's 1842 *Directory of Wiltshire* includes John Bubb's business under the listings for booksellers, stationers and printers, although, as these three trades were not listed separately, it is by no means clear that he was engaged in all of them. The 1842 *Directory* does, however, add, in parenthesis, that John Bubb was also a silversmith, which seems an unusual sideline.

By 1851 John Bubb had retired and John Day from Box had taken over the business. That year's census describes him as a bookseller and stationer, but in Kelly's 1855 *Directory of Wiltshire* he is a 'bookseller, printer and stationer, and agent to the Globe fire and life assurance company'. This is the first positive reference to a printing office here, and the date seems consistent with the style of lettering on the sign. By the time of the 1861 census, John Day is described simply as a printer, although ten years later he is once again a 'printer, bookseller, &c'. He died in 1878, aged 62, and the business was taken over by George Farrington from Middlesex.

George Farrington was still here in 1889, but by the following year had handed over to William Charles Dotesio, son of a London wine merchant who had retired to Bradford on Avon. Dotesio was responsible for another ghost sign – less well-known than the one on the front of the building, but rather splendid none the less. You can see it if you look up at the side wall on the left of the building. This is not only a very constricted site for a sign; you also have to peer up at it as a constant stream of vehicles squeezes along the narrow street. Although some of it has been washed away, most of it can still be made out:

W DOTESIO

BOOKSELLER

STATIONER

PRINTER

BOOKBINDER

CIRCULATING LIBRARY

GOSS ...

... HERALDIC CHINA

PHOTOGRAPHIC

DEALER

DARK ROOM

Between GOSS and HERALDIC CHINA is what makes this sign special – the town's coat of arms, which appeared on Goss and other heraldic china, with the name of the town underneath.

When new, it must have looked superb, leaving anyone heading down the street in no doubt that William Dotesio was a force to be reckoned with in Bradford on Avon.[7] And, as the reference to Goss and heraldic china suggests, much of his business was with visitors to the town. Small ceramic pots and ornaments, generally inexpensive, and decorated with local coats of arms, were hugely popular souvenirs in the late nineteenth and early twentieth centuries. William Dotesio also published guide-books and directories to the town, and, from around 1904 to 1914, picture postcards were one of the mainstays of his business. The lack of any reference to postcards on the sign almost certainly indicates that it dates from before 1904.

By 1901, William Dotesio had moved the printing works to new premises further up Silver Street, on the corner of Whitehill, to increase the size of the shop at Nº 28.[8] He also opened a shop at 23 Silver Street, Trowbridge and went into partnership with his future brother-in-law, Eric Todd, who established a short-lived printing works in Lowestoft from around 1898 to 1901.

William Dotesio was a keen local historian and among the books he commissioned was a revised edition of WH Jones' historical articles on the history of Bradford on Avon. Originally published in the *Wiltshire Archaeological Magazine*, these were annotated and brought up to date by John Beddoe, a retired surgeon who lived at the Chantry in Barton Orchard. The book appeared in 1907, and in a preface William Dotesio declared it to be his 'first serious excursion into publishing'. The frontispiece is a drawing of the coat of arms which appears on Dotesio's sign, and a caption explains that it was devised by Mr Beddoe, presumably so that heraldic china could be produced for visitors. Also included is the following description of the coat of arms:

Or, a teazle between two battle axes, blades to the sinister, all proper, on a chief azure an angel flying to the sinister, proper, vested argent crined or holding on his dexter arm a cloth also argent. Crest, a gudgeon proper. The angel is taken from one of the figures in the Saxon Church. 'Crined' refers to the colour of the hair. The teazle alludes to the woollen industry. The battle axes are taken from the arms of the ancient family 'Hall', seen over the central door of the almshouses and on the badge of the almsmen. 'Proper' means of the natural colour: thus the gudgeon taken from the gilt one on the bridge chapel would be blueish on the back, white below, and with pale-red fins.

William Dotesio later took over premises at 2 Kingston Road to establish another printing works, known as the Bravon Works, as well as Eastern House, adjoining the printing works on Silver Street. In 1934, by which time the business had become Dotesio & Sons, the printing works moved to larger premises, taking over part of the former woollen factory at Greenland Mills, and the shop at 28 Silver Street was closed. The firm was still operating in the 1980s, when the sale of Greenland Mills for redevelopment prompted a move to new premises in Trowbridge, but it closed soon afterwards.

Carry on up Silver Street, passing Spencer's Ale & Porter Stores, built in 1884, on the right, and beyond it the carved heads of Silenus, Ariadne, Bacchus and Satyr. After passing Dotesio's former print works on the corner of Whitehill, turn right by the Old House (Nº 18) down Mill Lane and right again at the bottom along Kingston Road. Just before the end, you will see an archway on the right at Nº 2 which once led into Dotesio's Bravon Works (7). On a visit in the summer of 2015, this had long been blocked off, with traces of lettering – none of them substantial enough to be deciphered – over the former entrance. Plans have been submitted, however, to reopen this archway as part of a refurbishment of the building and the loss of what remains of this mysterious sign – which may have included Dotesio's name – seems likely.

Turn left and carry on across the bridge. Continue on as the road curves right and then left. At the mini-roundabout, bear left along St Margaret's Street, and after 50m look at the plat band above the ground floor of the last house on the left before the railway bridge (8). Much of the stone in the plat band looks to have been replaced relatively

recently, but on the extreme left you will see a fragment of what would once have been a sign running its entire length. Although little remains, it appears as though it might have read SIGN-WRI ... or something similar, indicating that a signwriter may once have lived here. We have been unable to track down a nineteenth-century signwriter on St Margaret's Street, but diligent trawling through local records may yet discover one.

Carry on along St Margaret's Street and continue along Trowbridge Road. After 700m, just past the petrol station, look across to N° 66 on the right, to see a newly-revealed sign. Until recently, this was Trowbridge Road Post Office, as it had been for many years. It already boasted one ghost sign of sorts, in the form of a white painted panel,

with the lettering covered up, between the windows on the first floor. After it closed, however, a new sign was revealed on the fascia board for TROWBRIDGE ROAD SUPERETTE (9). This is curious, for, although convenience stores are often known as superettes in such far-flung corners of the world as New Zealand, Newfoundland and New England, we can find no other instance of the name being used in this country, apart from here – assuming, of course, that a convenience store is what it was.

On that note, all that remains is to head back to the mini-roundabout at the end of St Margaret's Street, and head straight across to return to the railway station.

CORSHAM

15

CORSHAM

The first ghost sign in Corsham is at 55 High Street, now the Garden Veterinary Group, but once the Co-op (1). Between its first-floor windows is a ornate datestone of 1906, with a beehive flanked by garlands and

topped by a banner, on which is written INDUSTRY. Above, partly painted out, and rather overshadowed by such exuberance, is what remains of a sign for the CO-OPERATIVE STORE.

For our next ghost signs, we head west along the High Street to an inn whose age, most unusually, we know precisely (2). The Methuen Arms opened on 3 July 1816, and the following day's *Bath Chronicle* reported that

a numerous company dined at the Methuen Arms. Corsham, to celebrate the opening of that large and commodious inn; which has been built by the munificent lord of the manor, Paul Cobb Methuen, Esq, for the accommodation of families or parties visiting the picturesque park and neighbourhood; the dinner (substantial and well-drest) was admirably served by the landlord, Mr Sweatman.[1]

To find its ghost signs you need to carry on round the corner to the side door, which is flanked by two chequerboards, similar in design – although a different colour – to those on the corner of the Bladud's Head in Larkhall. The chequerboards at Larkhall have only recently been uncovered, but these at Corsham have been known about for a very long time. In *The Inns of Wiltshire*, we suggested that they may have been painted because the sign was a convenient way of informing illiterate passers-by that the building was an inn.[2] Even then, though, we felt that there might be a better reason, and subsequent discussions – and research – have now suggested what it might be.

From the start, many Masonic Lodges met at inns. In 1817, the Lodge of Rectitude met for the first time at the King's Arms in Melksham. There seem to have been issues with the accommodation, for it soon moved to the New Crown, then to the Bear, then back to the King's Arms, before moving out of Melksham to the Queen's Head at Box in 1829. Another move – to the King's Arms at Monkton Farleigh – followed in 1840, before a final move – to the Methuen Arms in Corsham – in 1859. Meetings were originally held in the skittle alley at the back of the inn – accessed through the side door – before being relocated to the more commodious dining room. The Lodge continued to use the Methuen Arms until recently, but now meets in the Masonic Hall at Pickwick.[3]

Chequerboard floors – the design believed to represent light and dark or the joys and sorrows of life – are a standard feature of Masonic Lodges, and, where marble floors are not installed, a chequered carpet is rolled out before meetings. Chequerboard patterns also occur in other Masonic contexts, and, in the days when meetings were routinely held in inns – and venues had a habit of being changed from time to time – a chequerboard sign outside the entrance would have been an ideal of ensuring that those coming to a meeting did not end up in the wrong inn. Another advantage would have been that their significance would only be apparent to the initiated; those not in the know – such as latter-day pub historians – would be left to concoct all kinds of fanciful theories to account for them.[4]

Whether that solves the riddle of the chequer-boards on the Methuen Arms, only time will tell. For now, there is another

ghost sign to see – over the window to the left of the side door, where you will see the words POST OFFICE (3). This dates from before

1841, when the post office had moved further along the High Street and was being run by a Miss Susannah Dyer. Earlier references to the post office in Corsham give no indication of where it was, so it is impossible to be more precise.

For the last ghost sign, head along Station Road, which faces the side door of the Methuen Arms (4). After 400m, just past Nursery Gardens, look to the right to see, on the redbrick wall of Nº 30,

MAYNARD
CARRIAGE BUILDER
WHEELWRIGHT

in ornate writing, with a fancy bit of scrollwork at the top. This superb reminder of forgotten trades dates from the late nineteenth century, when John William Maynard moved to Corsham from Fordingbridge in Hampshire. He was first listed as living on Station Road in the 1891 census, and was last recorded in Kelly's 1915 *Directory of Wiltshire*, by which time he would have been around 59.

16

BOX

Box has two very faded signs on either side of the High Street. The first is on a building between the Queen's Head and the old pound where stray livestock was confined. The earliest record of it dates from 1743, when a butcher called William Harding leased it from the Northey estate, although it almost certainly dates from the seventeenth

Above: The building on the High Street in 2006, before the single-storey extension at the front was demolished

Left: Traces of lettering on the main building which may include part of the word BAKER or BAKERS

century.[1] It has, however, seen many alterations and rebuildings over the years to fit it for the various uses to which it has been put. Some of the more extensive alterations were carried out by the Miller family, who acquired the property in 1918. Initially they ran a baker's and grocer's here, but gradually built up a coach and haulage business, which was based in a garage at the back. In the late 1920s, they added a single-storey extension at the front to use as a shop. This replaced the original shop, which was set further back, and was demolished to extend the garage.

The photograph opposite shows the building as it appeared in 2006, with traces of lettering above the shop, as well on the older building to the right. The shop has since been demolished, but traces of the lettering on the older building still survive. Although little can be made out, what may be part of the word BAKER or BAKERS can be seen on the right-hand side.

The other sign is across the road, opposite the Queen's Head car park, on a building that was originally the stables for the inn. The first reference to the Queen's Head comes in 1769, when catalogues for a local auction

could 'be had of Mr Lee, at the Queen's Head, at Box'.[2] The turnpike road through the village had opened eight years earlier, greatly increasing the amount of coaching traffic, and it seems likely that the inn was built to cater for this trade. Whether or not the stables date from the same time is unclear, but the sign is almost certainly no earlier than the mid-nineteenth century. Although it has all but disappeared, enough survives to indicate that it read QUEEN'S HEAD INN STABLES, and that the style of lettering is Victorian. After the stables fell out of use, they were converted to public toilets, which have now fallen victim to the nationwide cull of such facilities. In 2014, an application was submitted to convert them once again, to provide living accommodation. It was approved and the work was duly carried out, with a porch built over part of the old sign.

17

FARMBOROUGH

The first reference we have found to the Bell Inn on the main road through Farmborough is from 1799[1]. It has long ceased to be an inn, and until recently there was little, apart from a small modern sign, to indicate its former role. Recently, however, when it was repainted, the paint on the parapet was removed, revealing several layers of ghost signs, at least a couple of which look very early. BELL INN can be deciphered on one of the layers, but there is so much 'noise' from successive versions of the sign that, although there appears to be some impressive examples of the signwriter's art, little else can be made out.

Above: The Bell Inn at Farmborough in the 1940s. The tall chimney on the single-storey extension suggests that this was a brewery.

Below: The Bell today, long closed, but with newly-revealed lettering.

Opposite: Details of the lettering

18

WILLSBRIDGE

This final ghost sign is a late entry, only having been spotted in June 2016 on one of the most regrettable pub casualties in the Bath area. The Queen's Head at Willsbridge lay in the parish of Bitton, just west of Keynsham and was one of the most unspoilt pubs in the area.[1] Built in the seventeenth century, it was operating as a pub by 1719. By the 1790s, it was so busy

Willsbridge around 1910. The Queen's Head is immediately to the left of the horse and trap. It was still a free house at this time, with no painted signs on its walls.

that an extension was built at the front. It was a freehouse until 1918, when it was taken over by Bristol United Breweries. In 1956, Bristol United Breweries was taken over by Georges & Co, which became part of Courage's five years later. The Queen's Head remained a Courage pub until 1991, when it was acquired by Ushers of Trowbridge. Despite these changes, the Queen's Head remained a traditional country pub, renowned for the quality of its beer and hospitality. Even the advent of the pubco era, when it passed into the hands of the Pubfolio group, seemed initially to pose no major threat to the survival of this much-loved institution. Unfortunately, it was the sort of pub that did not fit in with the thrusting corporate ethos of the twenty-first century hospitality industry. Instead of the careful nurturing and skilled custodianship that befitted its unique status, it received a series of short-term tenants and managers, with long periods standing empty, while all the time the fabric of the building was allowed to deteriorate. In 2010, its then owners, 'The Pub Company',

These signs revealed during the refurbishment of the building date from shortly after the pub was acquired by Bristol United Breweries in 1918.

went into administration. Three years later, against the recommendations of planning and conservation officers, South Gloucestershire Council approved an application to convert to it to a private dwelling.[2]

Conversion has since got underway, and, while many heritage features have sadly disappeared, it has also become apparent how little was spent on maintaining this historically important building in recent years. Scaffolding went up around the late eighteenth-century front extension in 2016 and, as render was stripped away, old signs dating from when Bristol United Breweries took over in 1918 were revealed – along with the parlous state of the structure itself. No doubt, the building will eventually re-emerge in a better condition than it has been in for years. It seems unlikely that the signs will form part of that rebirth, but, in the somewhat forlorn hope that they will survive, they have been included here. It is just a pity that, whatever happens, one of the most defiantly traditional pubs in the area should have suffered such an inglorious end.

19

LOST GHOST SIGNS

Lost ghost signs may seem a contradiction in terms, but this final chapter celebrates those ghost signs that have disappeared. Signs disappear for a variety of reasons. Some simply fade away. Many of the signs featured in the preceding pages have all but vanished, with no more than a few fugitive fragments of lettering left. Unless their lifespan is artificially extended by some judicious (or injudicious) touching up, this is a fate which awaits them all. Others come to an untimely end – either through being scrubbed off or when the buildings they adorn are demolished.

Then there are those which are painted over or covered in render, and which may – depending on what sort of materials have been used to cover them – one day re-emerge. Some signs have been hidden for a century or more and totally forgotten about until refurbishment – and the stripping away of layers of paint – sees them reappear. In some cases, they are quickly covered up again; in others they are conserved to enhance the appearance and historic significance of the building.

Given the ubiquity of painted signs in Bath in the nineteenth and early twentieth centuries, there are hundreds, if not thousands, of signs that have been lost forever, and scores that have been covered over by paint or render. What follows, therefore, is little more than a glimpse of what has been lost or of what may one day be revealed, and, while much of the focus is on recently lost signs, we begin with some that are long gone.

Fifty years ago, when such things were little regarded, there were many more ghost signs in Bath. Most fell victim to the clean-up campaign that has left few buildings clad in the soot-blackened hue they wore for generations. On the right we see one of the casualties – a sign for the Prince of Wales at 19 Old Orchard Street, photographed in the early 1960s before work got underway to restore the building to something approaching its original appearance. The Prince of Wales was a short-lived beerhouse, open by 1861 and last recorded in 1865. The survival of its sign for over a century was little short of remarkable, but, like the soot and grime, it had to go.

Another sad loss was the collection of ghost signs on the colonnade on the north side of the Assembly Rooms. This was built to store sedan chairs while their owners were attending balls and other functions in the rooms, but by 1780 part of it had been converted to shops. When these closed in the late nineteenth century, the colonnade was painted to cover up the signs that formerly adorned it. Successive coats were added over the years, until, in 1961, all were stripped away to reveal generations of ghost signs, which, after they had been photographed, were stripped away as well.

SALT & CO.,
EAST INDIA PALE AND BURTON ALE
AND STOUT BREWERS,
BURTON-ON-TRENT,
M A R C H B R E W I N G S,
In Fine Condition, in Cask & in Bottle, now ready for delivery
Supplied by LAWSON HOWES,
WINE and SPIRIT MERCHANT,
ASSEMBLY ROOMS WINE STORES, BATH.

Only the name Davis is fully legible in the sign on the left; the only person of that name known to have occupied a shop in the colonnade was a shoemaker called J Davis, who appears in the 1800 *Directory*

There are at least two generations of lettering on display below, one of which may have belonged to Lawson Howes, a wine merchant who sold India Pale Ale – or East India Pale Ale, as he described it in the advertisement from 1880 reproduced on the left

Another sign was scrubbed away not by Bath City Council but by Avon County Council. It was a great loss, for, although the building no longer served the purpose for which it was designed, the sign was noteworthy in marking the recognition of a local hospital by a reigning monarch.

The sign was on the frieze of the Albert Wing of the Royal United Hospital in Hot Bath Street, which now forms part of the Gainsborough Hotel. The Royal United Hospital was founded in 1826 when two charities were merged. These were the Bath City Infirmary & Dispensary, run by the Bath Pauper Trust, founded in 1747 to provide care for the poor, and the Bath Casualty Hospital, founded in 1788 to deal with injuries suffered by workers in Bath's booming building industry.[1] When they merged, a 'United Hospital', designed by John Pinch the Elder, was built in Beau Street, with a façade described as 'bold in scale and severe in expression'.[2]

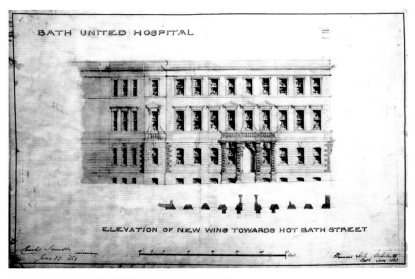

Above: One of Gill's drawings of the new wing

Left: A digitally-enhanced detail showing at least one letter drawn faintly in pencil

Right: A view of the Albert Wing in the early twentieth century

GHOST SIGNS OF BATH

In 1862, when a meeting was held to discuss the most appropriate way of honouring the memory of Prince Albert, who had died the previous year, it was agreed – although not without some dissent – that a new wing, dedicated to him, should be added to the United Hospital.[3] It was designed by John Elkington Gill, and on its frieze were painted the words ERECTED IN MEMORY OF ALBERT THE GOOD A.D. MDCCCLXIV.[4] On Gill's drawings, there is the very faint pencil suggestion of a B and possibly the whole word Albert, perhaps to give an indication of the style or suggested size of the lettering. It is also noticeable that the style of lettering on the architects' plans is precisely that used on the inscription.[5]

The foundation stone of the new wing was laid on 23 May 1864, and, in its coverage of the ceremony, the *Chronicle* noted that

> a colossal bust of HRH the late Prince Consort has been executed by an eminent sculptor, Matthew Noble, Esq, of London, which has received the high approval of Her Most Gracious Majesty, who has been pleased to approve the inscription placed on the Bust. This Bust will ornament the entrance-hall of the Albert Memorial Wing.[6]

Reports of the dedication ceremony were sent to the Queen, who was so delighted that in 1868 she 'graciously acceded' to a request that the hospital should be called the Royal United Hospital.[7]

Given its history, you would have thought that the sign would be loved and cherished. And so it was, even after the Royal United Hospital moved to Combe Park in 1932 and the building was taken over by the Municipal Technical College two years later.[8] But then, in 1973, the newly formed Avon County Council took over as the education authority. Even so, no one thought that the sign would be destroyed. Although the building was by then so black that the words had become faint, they were still distinct and the story behind them was one that visitors found charming.

In 1994, one of the authors of this book wrote a book of walks around the city called *A Window on Bath*. So confident was she that the words would remain, that she included them in the last walk, called 'So you think you know Bath?'[9] It has to be said that the inscription was being forgotten by many Bathonians – hence its inclusion in this particular walk. A year or so later, Avon County Council decided to clean the building and, to your author's horror, the words were scrubbed off. Perhaps it was thought that no one would care or even notice. A sympathetic conservation officer from Bath Council tackled Avon County Council, to be told that, when the building was washed, there was nothing there.

Today, it is clear that the cleaning was very thorough indeed – not a trace of the words remain. Perhaps, though, the new owners of the building will be inspired to replace them. After all, if saying, in one book, that they *were* there was followed quickly by their disappearance, perhaps saying they *aren't* there will prompt their reinstatement. As 2016 is the Queen's 90th birthday year, what better tribute than to revive the memory of her great-great-grandfather, Albert the Good? Who knows – she might be so delighted that she may follow in her great-great-grandmother's footsteps and 'graciously accede' to a request that the hotel be called the Royal Gainsborough Hotel.

Then there are the signs that have disappeared because the buildings they were painted on have been demolished – enough to fill another book, so a handful of examples will have to suffice. Among the buildings demolished to make way for the new South Gate mall was the old Co-op Dairy. This was built in 1913 by the Bath & District Farmers' Association, at a cost of about £6,000.[10] Two years later, it closed and, after being sold

A faded sign for BATH CO-OPERATIVE SOCIETY painted on the redbrick wall of the old dairy.

GHOST SIGNS OF BATH

A view from the old station goods yard – now the site of the Graze bar – when the dairy was owned by the Twerton Co-Operative Society, and Bath Garages occupied the single-storey extension at the front.

at auction, was acquired by the Twerton Co-operative Society, who subsequently sold the yard fronting onto Dorchester Street to the Skinner Motor Company of 6 North Parade, who built a garage there.[11] The garage was taken over by Bath Garages Ltd in 1922, the same year that the Bath and Twerton Co–operative Societies amalgamated.[12]

In 1929, the dairy was completely modernised, with new machinery for cleaning, pasteurising and bottling installed.[13] The building was badly damaged by bombing in 1942 – the *Bath Chronicle* described it as having been 'completely destroyed' – but, after being repaired, re-equipped and reopened, it continued in use until the 1960s.[14] The garage on Dorchester Street also remained open until the 1960s, after which it was taken over by Harding's, who traded there until shortly before the entire site was demolished in 2007. Thus was swept away not only a couple of ghost signs probably dating from when the dairy was refurbished in 1929, but also a building of remarkable resilience. Having survived the Bath Blitz, when buildings all around it were flattened, and the comprehensive redevelopment of the area in the 1960s, when the bus station was built behind it, it was demolished to make way for the new SouthGate.

In the photograph on the right, from around 1900, we see a painted sign on a cantilevered loading bay at Sydney Wharf that seems fast approaching dereliction. Traces of an earlier sign can also be detected, but the sign for Tucker's Hay & Corn Stores, with a head office at 52 Walcot Street, is fast fading as well. By 1910, Tucker's – now renamed Tucker & Sons – had given up the warehouse on Sydney Wharf, moved out of 52 Walcot Street, and centralised its operations at Broad Quay.

Tucker & Sons remained a major operator on Broad Quay until the redevelopment of the area in the 1960s. Below, in a view from around 1905, the warehouse on the right has the company's name painted on a projecting hoist.

The photograph below was taken during the floods of December 1963 and shows the warehouse, hardly changed and still bearing Tuckers' name, along with a Spratt's Scottie dog (last encountered on page 95). There is a larger version of the Spratt's logo on the building to the right, which, as can be seen from the sign, was also part of M Tucker & Sons' Hay & Corn Stores.[15] Carpenter House and Quay House stand roughly on the site of these buildings today.

A more recent casualty was one of the last remaining parts of Carr's Mill at Twerton. Once an imposing and historic factory complex dating back centuries, much of the site was cleared after being badly damaged by bombing in 1942. The building to the east of the main gate was set back and refaced in Bath stone, with ISAAC CARR & CO LTD WOOLLEN MANUFACTURERS painted above the second-floor windows. This company, which had owned the mill since the 1840s, went bankrupt in the 1950s, and the building was subsequently used by various businesses. The imposing gate-

way that once gave access to the site still survives, but the building was demolished in 2014 to make way for student accommodation. Thus passed a last vestige of what was once Bath's most important industry, to make way for one of the fastest growing industries in the city today.

Finally, we turn from signs that have gone and buildings that have been demolished to signs that have been painted over, and which may one day reappear. We start with some that have not been seen for decades, such as one on 21 Broad Street for GH TUCKER, PICTURE FRAME MANUFACTURER. In the photograph below, which dates from the time of Queen Victoria's Diamond Jubilee in 1897 – hence the sporting allusion on the banner – it can be seen on the left. This building retains its handsome late-Victorian shopfront and still looks much the same today. The walls, though, are painted, and, although there is no indication that any lettering lurks beneath, who knows what might re-emerge were the paint ever to be removed?

At the top of the opposite page we see New Bond Street on 19 July 1909, with the Duke and Duchess of Connaught heading for Royal Victoria Park to open the Bath Pageant. On the left, at Nº 16, can be seen a sign for the Art Needlework Depot; next to it, at Nº 17, is a sign for William Vilven, 'fruit and flower grower'. More signs can be seen further along the street, including one for JF Waddy's Antique Jewellers, but these have all been cleaned off. The walls of Nᵒˢ 16 and 17, however, are still

painted, and, while it is not clear from the postcard whether the sign for the Art Needlework Depot was painted onto the wall or onto a signboard, Vilven's sign was clearly painted onto the wall and may still be there, waiting to be revealed.

Below we see a superb array of signs on the Eastbourne Dairy on Claremont Terrace, with another on the butcher's next door, and yet another on the Rising Sun, part of which is visible on the left. All have gone and all the shopfronts have been extended forward. At first-floor level, however, there appears to have been little change, with paint still

covering whatever lies beneath – although whether or not any of the signs have survived is impossible to say. Paint also covers the parapet of the Rising Sun, where the name of the pub once appeared. The pub was recently refurbished, however, and the words POOL SKITTLES REAL ALE have been painted on the wall to the left of the entrance – another indication of the gradual revival of the signwriter's art.

The sign for Beales of Bath in 2003 ...

... and in 2011

The sign at Mile End on the London Road for Beales of Bath is a much more recent casualty, having only been painted out in 2014. Beales of Bath was established after the Second World War. When the property was taken over by Leather Chairs of Bath in 2005, permission was granted to replace Beales' sign with a new sign, but this was never done. In 2012, the company relocated to London, a property services agency moved in, and Beales' sign was painted over. Lest you should be tempted to think that its loss shatters a last link with the days of old-school motor engineers, it is gratifying to report that Beales of Bath is still going strong next to Larkhall Garage.

An even more recent casualty is a ghost sign painted on glass. This is one we discovered on the black-painted fanlight windows of 9 Abbey Church Yard. It took some time to decipher, partly because it was so indistinct, but mainly because only part of it was visible at any one time, and, if the sun was in the wrong direction, it was almost impossible to see at all. Eventually, though, the words 'SURGEON' and 'CHIROPODIST' came through and, after trawling through postal directories, we not only discovered that Joseph D'Olier, Surgeon Chiropodist to the Royal Family, had practised here, but also established that 'D'OLIER' and 'ROYAL FAMILY' were some of the words we had been puzzling over.

Joseph D'Olier set up a practice at 9 Abbey Church Yard around 1911 and by 1914 was 'professionally attending Princess Louise, Duchess of Argyll'.[16] When conscription was introduced in 1916, he appeared before the tribunal twice, before joining up on 16 September and arriving in France on 8 November. By January 1917, he was in France and had been 'promoted to corporal of horse for services rendered'.[17] By September, however, after

being 'commended for his services in carrying messages along the line during the fighting on the Somme', he was back in Bath on leave, having 'contracted bronchitis and pleurisy'.[18] He must have made a speedy recovery, for in January 1918 the *Bath Chronicle* published a letter written by him on New Year's Eve 'in the trenches, warm at heart but with cold feet'.[19] He added that he had

> come in contact with many Bath boys. They are all very merry and bright under present hardships. No one can appreciate your paper like we can. It's just a sweet touch of home to us, and carries with it the city's friendship and affection. Roll on the day when we shall all be united. Our experiences may, I think, make good citizens of us.[20]

He was discharged from the army in May 1918 'on account of ill health' and returned to Bath, where, on in November 1918, he placed an advertisement in the *Chronicle* to announce that he had 'returned to his practice as Surgeon-Chiropodist' in Abbey Church Yard 'and will be grateful for the sympathetic support of the medical profession and others'.[21]

He stayed there until 1931, when he moved to 'more commodious premises' at 10 Old Bond Street, 'opposite the Royal Mineral Water Hospital and over Leslie's Ltd Jewellers'.[22] Despite his health problems during the First World War, he lived until 1969, dying in Trowbridge at the age of 81.

The sign, painted over but still just about visible, survived until 2015, but has now disappeared – possibly covered over, possibly removed.

At 13 Broad Street, there was, until it disappeared in 2014, a ghost sign – or, rather, a palimpsest of ghost signs. The photographs below give an idea of what they looked like – and what sort of state the stonework was in after the application of so much paint. The building, which dates from around 1760, was a butcher's for most of the nineteenth century, until Mary Robinson turned it into a tobacconist's sometime before 1900. By 1903, a manufacturing confectioner called George Barrow had acquired the lease. William Gilbert Reed took over the business shortly before the First World War, and Nº 13 remained a confectioner's until the mid-twentieth century. The similarity of some of the words still decipherable on the ghost sign – before it was removed – to an advertisement Reed placed in the *Bath Chronicle* in 1924 suggests that the most legible layer of lettering dates from around this time.[23] In the 1960s the building was converted to a Chinese restaurant, any remaining Georgian features were removed, and by the beginning of the twenty-first century it was in a poor state of repair. Since then, efforts have been made to restore it to something approaching its original appearance, both internally and externally, and, in view of the continued damage being caused to the stonework by the layers of paint which had been applied to it, it was agreed that restoration – entailing removal of the ghost signs – was the only sensible course of action.

Nº 13 Broad Street in 2013, before the early twentieth-century ghost signs were removed. Beside it is a close-up of the lettering to the right of the second-storey windows. The words 'Celebrated BATH MINT BULLS EYES' and part of 'Confectioner' can be made out.

And now for something over a century older. The ghost sign on the left was revealed in the mid-1980s on a building visited earlier (see pages 100-1). Known as Ivy House, it was built on Sion Hill around 1792 for Lady Isabella King, the unmarried daughter of the Earl of Kingston, as a House of Protection for the Reception and Instruction of Young Girls. By 1822, however, the Moger family, then mainly farmers and butchers (although they later became bankers and solicitors) acquired it, and it became Moger's Dairy, with a sign above the door. When the shop changed hands, however, the sign was painted over and forgotten until the mid-1980s when the shopkeeper at the time stripped the paint away. He was very proud of this historic adornment to his premises, but, when he left about ten years later, new owners moved in, and, unimpressed by one of Bath's earliest ghost signs, painted it out in defiance of a recommendation by a planning officer. Before it disappeared, however, Graham Finch, the Bath-based architect and historical buildings consultant, cited it as a fine example of the English style of lettering also found in the incised street names of Georgian Bath.[24] Perhaps one day it will see the light of day again.

You never know what you might come across when you start stripping off paint. In May 2011, after the Fishworks restaurant in Green Street closed, work got underway to convert it to the Tasting Room. This involved removing paint from around the shop window, revealing traces of a sign which included words such as LOSSES and ASSESSORS. A financial services company, then, and, checking the postal directories, it was found that accountants and such like had been here for much of the twentieth century. The design of the sign looked to date from the 1920s, possibly slightly earlier, but it was in such poor condition that there was no question of preserving it, and it was painted over.

Next we turn to the quite extraordinary coincidence of two ghost signs, unseen for a century or more, and almost certainly advertising similar businesses, being uncovered within months of each other on the same street, before being painted over again.

In June 2015, when the façade of 28 Westgate Street was being cleaned, fragments of three painted signs were revealed, flanking the windows on the first floor. Only the sign in the middle, which read HOUSE IN BATH, gave any clue as to their provenance. To the left, only a few letters survived – what looked like an O, followed by what was probably an A (partially hidden by an iron strip attached

to the building) and then (possibly after another letter, also hidden by the strip), AINS. To the right, only faint traces of lettering, rather than complete letters, could be made out. This gave no clue as to what sort of business they had once advertised, although the style of lettering suggests they were painted in the early to mid-Victorian period, when the shop was occupied by a pawnbroker.

Sometime between 1829 and 1833, Messrs Fuller & Pile, who had already established a pawnbroker's next door at N° 29, expanded into N° 28. By 1852, Charles Thompson had taken over the business, and Thompson's pawnbroker's remained in business until the early 1920s, when, after a brief spell as a Sheffield Steel Products Store, the shop became a gentlemen's outfitters, before becoming a branch of Curry's in 1929. Given all this, it seems likely that the signs were connected with Thompson's pawnbroker's, although, given the lack of any words or fragments of words to support this theory, this must, for the moment, remain speculation. Subsequent enquiries will, however, have to rely on photographs of the signs, for in November 2015 permission was granted for flaking paintwork to be removed and the façade to be covered in limewash to improve the appearance of the building and preserve what remains of the signs.

The following month, a fragment of another ghost sign was revealed a few doors along, at 36 Westgate Street. This really was a case of 'blink and you've missed it': it emerged into the light of day around 17 December and was covered up again a week later. It was not on the front of the building, but at the side, and had been painted on the stonework

used to block up a shop window facing onto Parsonage Lane. This in itself was of interest, for, before the render was stripped off, there was nothing to suggest there had ever been a window here. Once it had been removed, however, it was clear not only that the stone was different to that in the original building, but that the courses did not match. Blocking up a shop window may seem an odd thing to do, given that most shopkeepers want to display as many of their goods as possible, but the history of the building's occupancy suggests a likely motive.

In 1819, W Rowland, draper, tailor and haberdasher was here; by 1833, Peter Williams, a cutler, had taken over. In 1838, George Kissock announced that he had opened a 'cheap linen drapery and haberdashery establishment' in the building.[25] A panorama of Westgate Street, published around 1840, shows not only Kissock's name on N° 36 but also the window on Parsonage Lane.[26] By 1850, a watch and clock maker called Meyer Fisher had taken over, but by 1856 James Lewis had opened a pork butcher's here, and he later went into partnership with his brother. It was ideally suited for such a business, as its position on a corner meant that windows could be opened on two sides, helping to create the through draught so essential for keeping temperatures down in the days before refrigeration and air-conditioning. By 1865, however, the Lewis Brothers had gone and Edwin Tucker had established a pawnbroker's here. In 1883, he was succeeded by another pawnbroker called Frederick William Reynolds. He died in 1902 and the business was taken over by John Caldicott, but it continued to be known as FW Reynolds until 1923, when it closed and history repeated itself, with Messrs Spear Bros & Clark, pork butchers, moving in.

As for the ghost sign, although very little remained, what survived not only indicated when it was painted but also confirmed the likely date for the window being blocked up. Although faint traces of paint indicated that the sign had originally covered the whole of the space where the window had been, all that was legible was part of a small section in the top left-hand corner. At the top, some way in from the left-hand border, the letters NOL were plainly visible, with a ghostly Y in front and a ghostly D behind. Below, and over to the left, painted in a slightly different style, were the letters TU, followed by what appeared to be a C.

There seemed to be the remnants of two signs here: the lower one, probably dating from the mid-1860s, bearing the name TUCKER, and the upper one, probably dating from around 1883,

bearing the name REYNOLDS. As for the blocking up of the window, this was almost certainly carried out by Edwin Tucker when he took the lease in the mid-1860s. By the nature of their trade, pawn-brokers do not need to display goods for sale in the way that other businesses do. They are also likely to have valuable – and eminently nickable – items such as jewellery on the premises. The last thing Edwin Tucker would have wanted was a large window – even one protected with shutters – in a dark alley out of sight of any policeman taking a quick look along Westgate Street in the early hours of the morning. Blocking the window up also would also have given him the opportunity to paint a large sign advertising his business – and attracting clients who might otherwise be tempted to take their goods to the pawnbroker's at N° 28.

Fortunately, the brief re-emergence of these painted fragments made it possible to uncover more about the history of the building, and to establish that there had once been a window at the side. It remains to be seen whether any future occupants will apply to reinstate the window and return the building to a semblance of its original appearance.

We now come to a truly exceptional ghost sign which was uncovered in the summer of 2011 at 25 Upper Camden Place, 200m east of Camden Crescent. This building had long been covered in render, which was in poor condition, and when some of this was removed during refurbishment, old lettering was revealed on the ground floor and between the windows on the first floor.

Only a small section of render was removed from the first floor, but this was enough to show parts of two signs. One consisted of gold lettering on a maroon background, and appeared to date from the early to mid-twentieth century. Above this were two letters – C and U – which were much older, probably dating from the 1820s or 1830s.

Much more render was removed on the ground floor, revealing lettering which also appeared to date from the early nineteenth century. Above the door and left-hand window ...DEN *PALE BEER* appeared in large letters. Between the door and the left-hand window was a rudimentary price list:

BEER

6d

5d

4d

with a chequerboard design below.[27] There was further lettering between the two windows, which it was not possible to decipher.

Until it called last orders in 1970, this was a pub called the

Rivers Arms. The photograph at the bottom of the opposite page shows it around 1910, with a fine collection of painted signs, none of which match any of those uncovered in 2011.[28] One of the signs in this photograph is for 'The Original Bath Nutritive Oatmeal Stout'. This was brewed by the Bath Brewery, indicating that they owned the pub at this time. After the Bath Brewery was taken over by George's of Bristol in 1923, the *Bath Chronicle* carried an advertisement listing the Rivers Arms as one of the local agents for 'George's Celebrated Bristol Beers and Stout'.[29] It was probably George's who painted the maroon sign with gold lettering; although very little was uncovered, the top of the first three letters of what appears to be RIVERS can be made out, while, further down, presumably below the word ARMS, is what appears to be a large C or G at the start of another word, which could be GEORGE'S. Somewhat tenuous, perhaps, but this fits in with the style of the sign.

Solving the puzzle of the earlier signs was a good deal less straightforward. Apart from the two mysterious letters – CU – above the first-floor windows, there was that ...DEN preceding PALE BEER. It was possible – although not likely – that it read GOLDEN, although, if this was so, why was it in a different style? And why list the price of beer?

The earliest reference to the Rivers Arms comes in February 1836, when William Jones was 'charged with entering the dwelling-house of Mr Culliford, of the Rivers Arms public-house, and stealing sundry wearing apparel'.[30] A few months later, on 28 September, Robert Culliford died, aged 55. His widow, Catherine, carried on running the pub for a time, but by April 1838 she had handed over to Richard Vickerage, who ran it until his death on 10 February 1862. Curiously, the 1846 *Directory* lists him as the landlord of the Camden Arms, Upper Camden Place, although in both the 1844 and 1848 *Directories* he is landlord of the Rivers Arms. Had he renamed the pub, even briefly, before reverting to the old name, and commissioned a new sign to celebrate, this could have solved the puzzle of the ...DEN – with CAMDEN being painted on one side of *GOLDEN BEER* and ARMS on the other. However, it seems more likely that the compilers of the *Directory* simply got the name of the pub wrong. Such mistakes were not uncommon; in the 1842 *Directory*, for example, it is listed as the Brewers Arms.

Further research was clearly needed – at which point we came across an earlier reference to Robert Culliford, the Rivers Arms' earliest known landlord, not as a publican but as a brewer. In June 1831, the *Bath Chronicle* advertised for sale by auction

> all that very DESIRABLE DWELLING HOUSE, Nº 1, SION-ROW, near Camden-Place; consisting of drawing and sitting rooms, kitchen, and suitable bed-rooms and offices, with walled Pleasure Garden in front. Also, a BREWERY and CELLARS adjoining, with suitable Rooms, subject to a ground rent of £4 4s, and now in the occupation of Mr Robert Culliford, on lease.[31]

When the premises had been advertised to let less than four years earlier, in December 1827, they were described as

> a most Eligible and Highly-improving PROPERTY, situate and being Nº 1 SION ROW, near Camden-Place ... together with a lately-erected and most convenient Tenement by the road side, forming an additional comfortable residence and RETAIL BREWERY, with convenient Cellerage, &c. The Premises are freehold of inheritance, subject to a yearly ground-rent of £4 4s; and, from the great increase of population in the neighbourhood, and its adaptation to the purposes of a Public-House or Retail Brewery, must prove a desirable object to a purchaser.[32]

At which point we turned to the postal directories to see if they could shed any further light, and found, in the 1826 *Directory*, a Mr MA Broom listed as a brewer at the Camden Brewery on Sion Row.

Piecing the evidence together, it seems that Mr Broom established the Camden Brewery in a new building on Sion Row, near Camden Place, sometime before 1826. He was still there in 1829, but by 1831 the brewery had been taken over by Robert Culliford, who renamed it the Rivers Arms some time before his death in 1836. The fragmentary evidence of the sign suggests that it was Culliford who had it painted, before he changed the name. The ...DEN could have formed part of CAMDEN, with BREWERY appearing after *PALE BEER*; the beer prices could have been for the information of customers buying beer to take away rather than consuming it on the premises; and the CU above the windows on the first floor could have formed part of CULLIFORD.

Which means, if our surmises are correct, that this is one of the earliest known brewery signs to have survived anywhere. The only problem is that the Rivers Arms was on Upper Camden Place and the Camden Brewery was on Sion Row ...

But where was Sion Row? To discover that we need to consult old maps, which reveal that it dated from the latter part of that frantic period of speculative building which came to an abrupt end with the economic crash of 1793, when banks failed and bankruptcies soared. As a result, most of it was never built. A map drawn by Charles Harcourt Masters in 1800 (and reproduced overleaf) shows it not as a row but as a few detached houses east of Camden Place (as Camden Crescent was then known). At the time, the road east of Camden Place did not follow the course it takes today. The map shows a road descending to meet what is now known as Gay's Hill about halfway down, with a road branching off uphill to run in front of the houses on Sion Row. The detached building shown just east of Camden Place was originally intended to be the end house of Camden Place, but the land where the houses in between were to have been built collapsed during construction. The house at the end, which was only part built, was on firmer ground and survived until July 1828, when it collapsed during a thunderstorm.

If we compare Harcourt Masters' map with one drawn by Cotterell & Spackman in the early 1850s, we can see that the road east of Camden Place was realigned to run through what should have been part of Camden Place. The line of the original road running down to meet Gay's Hill is drawn in faintly, but it has been closed off, with a new row of buildings called City View built across it. As for the detached buildings on Sion Row, these have been incorporated into a continuous row of buildings called Upper Camden Place.

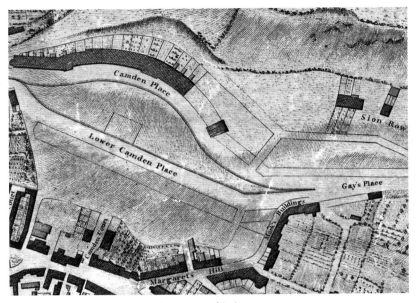

Above: Part of Harcourt Masters' 1800 map of Bath

Below: Part of one of the maps drawn by Cotterell & Spackman in the 1850s showing the same area

GHOST SIGNS OF BATH

The Camden Brewery, described as 'lately erected' in 1827, was at the far end of Sion Row. Another map drawn by Cotterell & Spackman in the 1850s shows it lying to the south of the other buildings in Upper Camden Place, the easternmost house of which is behind it. The map also shows it standing 'by the road side', as described in the advertisement of 1827.

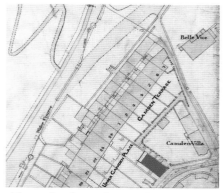

The Camden Brewery/Rivers Arms (highlighted in red) on a map drawn by Cotterell & Spackman in the early 1850s

Sadly, when the signs on the old Camden Brewery were revealed in the summer of 2011, they were soon covered up again with cement render. One of the main reasons for the refurbishment of the

The west end of Upper Camden Place, showing how the late eighteenth-century bow-fronted detached buildings of Sion Row were incoporated into an early nineteenth-century terrace

building had been to address condensation issues, and the application of inappropriate render only served to exacerbate these. In 2016, a planning application was submitted to remove the cement render and replace it with lime render, which would allow the building to breathe. We took the opportunity to draw attention to the existence and significance of the painted signs beneath the render, in the hope that a way could be found to make them a feature of the refurbished building. What nobody can know until the cement render is removed, however, is how the signs will have fared in the interim, and whether there will be anything left to reveal.

For our final lost sign, we head back to Ye Old Farm House pub, already featured on page 74. It is not the signs which can still be seen on the building that concern us here, however, but some that have long been covered up. But first, we need to look at a sign which once adorned Chandos House in Westgate Buildings.

Built by the Duke of Chandos on land leased from St John's Hospital, this was the first house designed by John Wood in Bath. By 1842. however, part of it had become a beerhouse called the Chandos Arms. In 1898, it was acquired by one of Bath's most audacious entrepreneurs, Thomas Pearce.

Thomas Albert Pearce was born, the son of a butler, at Cranmore in Somerset in 1842. His father later moved to Mells before taking over the Rose & Crown at Hinton Charterhouse. In 1865, Thomas Pearce took over the Oxford Tavern at Abingdon Buildings on Julian Road, which had its own brewery.[33] Two years later, along with five other publican-brewers from Bath and a hop merchant from Bristol, he established the Bath Malting Co Ltd. This operated from a malthouse at the back of Comfortable Place on the Upper Bristol Road until 1892, when the company was voluntarily wound up.

The 1871 census shows Thomas Pearce living, with his wife and two children, over the pub on Julian Road. Ten years later, although still running the pub, he was living at 4 City View, just along from Camden Crescent. In 1882, he acquired the Old Farm House on Lansdown Road, which still occupied the original seventeenth-century building. He also leased the Gloucester Inn in Somerset Buildings at the bottom of Hedgemead, where TR Hayes's showroom now stands.

By 1891, he had moved to the Mount at Bannerdown. The two children who were living with him 20 years earlier had left home, but he had five more, as well as a governess to look after them. The following year he set about rebuilding the Old Farm House – which he renamed Ye Old Farm House – transforming the 'quaint and ancient landmark ... with its gables and stone-tiled roof' into an imposing purpose-built pub and brewery.[34] Around the same time, he moved to York Villa at Kensington, now Norland College, which stood in two acres of gardens – now covered by a supermarket car park.

Then, 'in consequence of his having acquired an extensive business in Wales and of his leaving the city', he put his property in Bath, including York Villa, up for sale.[35] George Biggs of the Crown Brewery in New Orchard Street bought the Oxford Brewery (as the Oxford Tavern was now known) for £4,500 and Ye Old Farm House for £4,100. York Villa, however, did not find a buyer, and, although Thomas Pearce seems to have left Bath for a time, by 1898 he was back at York Villa and had established a new company – TA Pearce & Co. He took the lease of the Chandos Arms and set about transforming what he described as 'an old-fashioned sort of place into a modern public house', which he renamed the Chandos Wine & Spirit Vaults.[36] He also took the lease of the North Parade Brewery, a pub-cum-brewery at 10 Gallaway's Buildings, and in the 1901 census described himself as not only a brewer but also a wine & spirit merchant.

The Chandos Wine & Spirit Vaults around 1900

In 1902, he added the newly-rebuilt Three Crowns on London Street to his portfolio, but this was merely the prelude to a far more ambitious project.[37] Following discussions with other publicans and brewers in Bath, in December 1904 he announced the formation of a limited company known as Pearce, Reynolds, Withers & Co. Known locally as 'the Combine', this sought to achieve economies of scale by bringing 17 freehold and 16 leasehold pubs – many with their own breweries – into single ownership, and concentrating brewing at the old Avondale Brewery by the toll bridge at Batheaston, which had lain empty since the failure of the short-lived English Lager Beer Brewery Ltd in 1893. Thomas Pearce was the prime mover behind the scheme, which from the start was far less attractive a proposition than he made out. The *Investors' Review* was certainly not fooled, pointing out that 'preliminary expenses are payable by the company and appear to be unduly heavy ... The offer is far from inviting in other ways, as no mention is made of past profits earned by any of the businesses taken over, and applicants are expected to be satisfied with what seems to be an arbitrary estimate by the directors'.[38] They would have been even less enthusiastic had they known that, prior to the company being formed, WG Reynolds, one of the directors, owed over £5,000 to the bank, which held the deeds of his ten pubs. Take-up of shares was, not surprisingly, sluggish, receipts were inadequate to meet fixed interest payments or provide working capital, and the receiver was eventually called in.[39] The Bath Brewery Company took over the pubs, the brewery at Batheaston was closed, and, by the time of the 1911 census, Thomas Pearce was a 'retired brewer' living at 16 Belmont. He later moved to 23 The Paragon, where he died, aged 86, in 1928. By then, the Chandos Arms had long gone, its licence having been revoked by the magistrates in 1914 as part of a campaign to reduce the number of public houses in the city. The Oddfellows, which had used part of the building when the Chandos Arms was open, continued to meet there, and a sign for the Oddfellows Hall was painted over the name of TA Pearce & Co. In 1923, the building was acquired by the Bath Tenement Venture Trust and converted to flats. Today, it is an almshouse for St John's Hospital.

This account of Thomas Pearce's career may seem somewhat too detailed for a sign that has long disappeared, but, if it had not been for him, Ye Old Farm House, one of Bath's finest Victorian pub buildings, would probably not have been built. In the photograph of it below, dating from around 1905, the words PEARCE'S ENTIRE PURE OLD & MILD ALES are writ large below the eaves. Although long painted over, they may still be there, and may one day even re-emerge.

REFERENCES

Note: *BC* refers to the *Bath Chronicle*; *BJ* to the *Bath Journal*

INTRODUCTION

1   See, for example, an interview with Sam Roberts (http://eastldn.co.uk/2016/01/21/ghost-signs-sam-roberts-opens-the-gateway-into-our-commercial-past/)
2   In connection with this, we should acknowledge a debt to www.suncalc.net, an incredibly useful and user-friendly website that helps you determine at what time the sun will be shining on a particular building on a particular day.

WORDS ON WALLS

1   Quoted in Toulmin Smith, *English Gilds*, London, 1870, p. 405.
2   John Gay, *Trivia*, Book II, 'Of Walking the Streets by Day', London, 1716, ll. 65-69.
3   *Tatler*, 21 May 1709.
4   *New-England Courant*, 15 February 1725.
5   Quoted in James Ayres, *Art, Artisans and Apprentices: Apprentice Painters and Sculptors in the Early Modern British Tradition*, Oxford, 2014, p. 198.
6   Fawcett, Trevor, *Bath Commercialis'd: Shops, Trades and Market at the 18th-Century Spa*, Bath, 2002, pp. 95-96; the Grove was renamed the Orange Grove after an obelisk was erected commemorating the Prince of Orange's visit to Bath in 1734. The row of shops survives, but was refronted in the 1890s.
7   Fawcett, p. 96.
8   Fawcett, p. 96.
9   *BJ*, 4 June 1744.
10 Reproduced in Vanessa Brett, *Bertrand's Toyshop in Bath: Luxury Retailing, 1685-1765*, Wetherby, 2014, p. 176.
11 Ibid., p. 62.
12 *BC*, 19 March 1761.
13 *BC*, 14 October 1762.
14 *BC*, 6 December 1764; Bear Corner was near the Bear Inn in Cheap Street.

15 *BC*, 22 January 1767.
16 *BC*, 17 November 1768.
17 *BC*, 3 February 1774; *BC*, 20 October 1774; the Union Passage referred to is not the present one – which was then known as Cock Lane – but an alleyway off Stall Street.
18 *BC*, 23 January 1783.
19 *BC*, 19 March 1789.
20 *BC*, 8 December 1791.
21 *BC*, 13 December 1796.
22 Jacob Larwood & John Camden Hotten, *The History of Signboards*, London, 1866, pp. 29-30.
23 *BC*, 6 January 1774; REM Peach, in *Street-Lore of Bath*, London, 1893, p. 5, claims that 'the numbering of houses began in Bath around 1768', but unfortunately gives no examples.
24 *BC*, 21 February 1799.
25 *BC*, 31 December 1812; 11 June 1812.
26 Quoted in Ayres, p. 211.
27 A description of the exhibition can be found in Larwood & Hotten, pp. 512-26.
28 Ayres, p. 203.
29 Quoted in Larwood & Hotten, p. 26.
30 Ayres, p. 203.
31 Larwood & Hotten, p. 28.
32 Larwood & Hotten, p. 28.
33 Public Act, 2 George III, c. 21; Alison Adburgham, *Shops and Shopping, 1800-1914*, London, 1964, p. 6.
34 *BC*, 26 June 1766.
35 Rev John Penrose, *Letters from Bath: 1766-1767*, ed. Brigitte Mitchell & Hubert Penrose, Gloucester, 1983 (letter of 22 April 1767), p. 170.
36 CF Moritz, *Journeys of a German in England in 1782*, trans. & ed. by Reginald Nettel, London, 1965, p. 33.
37 Christian Augustus Gottlieb Goede, *A Foreigner's Opinion of England*, tr. Thomas Horne, 3 vols., London, 1821, I, 68.
38 Graham Finch, *Bath Shopfronts: Guidelines for Design and Conservation*, Bath, 1993, p.57.

39 Alan Bartram, *The English Lettering Tradition from 1700 to the Present Day*, London, 1986, p. 9.
40 Simon Garfield, *Just My Type: A Book About Fonts*, London, 2010, p. 43; it may seem confusing, given that slab-serif lettering is known as Egyptian, that Caslon Egyptian is a sans-serif font. However, early nineteenth-century styles of lettering were only categorised later, and terms were often interchangeable. See Bartram, pp. 9-10.

1 CITY CENTRE

1 *BC*, 6 April 1854.
2 *BC*, 25 October 1854.
3 He was recorded as a British subject in the 1851 census.
4 *Ports of the Bristol Channel: Progress, Commerce*, London, 1893, p. 254.
5 *BC*, 25 July 1942.
6 *BC*, 12 November 1896.
7 City of Bath Council & Committee Minutes, 1897, p. 19 (held in Bath Record Office).
8 Ibid, p. 22.
9 *BC*, 2 December 1944.
10 She had taken over the lease of the earlier property in 1776, when it was transferred to her on the death of her husband, Mark Lamb.
11 *BC*, 3 July 1947.
12 John Wood, *A Description of Bath*, London, 1765, p. 85.
13 Elizabeth Holland, 'Hetling Pump Room and Hetling House', in *The Survey of Bath & District: The Magazine of the Survey of Old Bath and Its Associates*, No 9, June 1998, p. 21; further information on the history of the building can be found in: George E Perrett, *Abbey Church House, Bath*, Bath, 1979; and Mike Chapman & Elizabeth Holland, *The Spa Quarter of Bath: A History in Maps*, Bath, 2006.
14 John Wood, op. cit., p. 85.
15 John Wood, op. cit., p. 85.
16 *BC*, 18 May 1775.
17 *BC*, 22 June 1780.
18 G Munro Smith, *A History of the Bristol Royal Infirmary*, Bristol, 1917, p. 189.
19 Ibid.
20 *BC*, 26 October 1780.
21 *BC*, 25 January 1781.

22 *BC*, 5 September 1782.
23 *BC*, 21 August 1783.
24 Mike Chapman & Elizabeth Holland, op. cit, p. 36.
25 Letter of 2 June 1799, in *Jane Austen's Letters*, ed. Deirdre Le Faye, Oxford, 2011, p. 43.
26 Mike Chapman & Elizabeth Holland, op. cit, p. 36.
27 *BC*, 22 October 1840.
28 *BC*, 2 November 1871.
29 For more information see Randle W Falconer, *The Baths and Mineral Waters of Bath*, Bath, 1880.
30 Jean Manco, *The Spirit of Care: The eight-hundred year story of St John's Hospital, Bath*, Bath, 1998, p. 164.
31 *BC*, 1 February 1930.
32 *BC*, 7 August 1823.
33 *BC*, 6 November 1834.
34 *BC*, 14 July 1836.
35 *BC*, 11 May 1848.
36 *BC*, 28 April 1864.
37 *BC*, 12 March 1896.
38 *BC*, 18 August 1898.
39 *BC*, 12 November 1846.
40 *BC*, 15 April 1852.
41 *BC*, 11 August 1791.
42 *BC*, 24 September 1801.
43 *BC*, 2 April 1812.
44 *BC*, 18 September 1823.
45 *BC*, 18 January 1827.
46 *BC*, 4 October 1827.
47 *BC*, 28 February 1828.
48 *BC* 4 March 1830.
49 Edward Bussey was originally at 20 New Bond Street, but transferred his business to 18 The Corridor around 1870.
50 *BC*, 15 September 1831.
51 *BC*, 15 September 1864.
52 *BC*, 15 December 1887.
53 More information on George Gregory can be found in his obituary in the *BC*, 9 August 1930.
54 *BC*, 20 February 1902.
55 *BC*, 31 May 1930.
56 *BC*, 22 February 1866.
57 *BC*, 7 January 1864.
58 *BC*, 7 January 1886.
59 *BC*, 21 September 1918.
60 *BC*, 31 March 1791; 22 November 1792; 5 December 1816; see also Andrew Swift & Kirsten Elliott, *The Lost Pubs of Bath*, Bath, 2005, pp. 327-28.

2 UPPER TOWN

1   *BC*, 22 March 1913.
2   John Wood, op. cit., p. 334.
3   Ibid, p. 332.
4   *BC*, 8 November 1827.
5   *BC*, 20 July 1865.
6   *BC*, 5 November 1927.
7   *BC*, 10 December 1875; 16 January 1890.
8   *BC*, 2 October 1920; 29 May 1920.
9   *BC*, 29 May 1920.
10 *BC*, 20 February 1890.
11 *BC*, 9 March 1899.
12 *BC*, 6 September 1838.
13 *BC*, 5 December 1850.
14 *BC*, 25 March 1869.
15 A detailed account of the company can be found in *Ports of the Bristol Channel: Progress, Commerce*, London, 1893, p. 256.
16 Kirsten Elliott & Andrew Swift, *Bath Pubs*, Bath, 2003.
17 Thomas Pearce of the Oxford Brewery in Julian Road started rebuilding Ye Old Farm House in 1892.
18 For information on Brown's Garages, see www. beath.net/browns.htm.
19 *Ports of the Bristol Channel: Progress, Commerce*, London, 1893, p. 252.
20 *BC*, 23 March 1893.
21 James Joyce, *Ulysses*, Harmondsworth, 1968, pp. 413-14.
22 Once again, we are indebted to Paul De'Ath to spotting and alerting us to the existence of this ghost sign.
23 Ingrid Tieken-Boon van Ostade, *Introduction to Late Modern English*, Edinburgh, 2009.
24 *BC*, 1 August 1771; 17 March 1774.
25 *BC*, 28 September 1775.
26 *BC*, 16 July 1778.
27 *BC*, 23 November 1780.
28 *BC*, 25 April 1782.
29 *BC*, 23 September 1784; 26 June 1794.
30 *BC*, 28 October 1773.
31 *BC*, 5 June 1777; 17 June 1777.
32 *BC*, 14 May 1778.
33 *BC*, 1 August 1782.

3 UPPER BRISTOL ROAD

1   *Bristol Mercury*, 12 February 1898.
2   *BC*, 23 October 1943.
3   Spratt's also developed logos with the company's name in the form of a cat, a canary and a fish, but it was the Scottie dog that really caught the public imagination.
4   *BC*, 28 July 1928.
5   *BC*, 17 January 1839.
6   *BC*, 7 April 1853.
7   *BC*, 28 May 1857.
8   *BC*, 9 June 1859.
9   *BC*, 11 July 1861.

4 WIDCOMBE & BATHWICK

1   *BC*, 6 April 1854.
2   A detailed description of the hotel can be found in *Ports of the Bristol Channel: Progress, Commerce*, London, 1893, p. 259.
3   *BC*, 3 September 1896.
4   *BC*, 17 December 1896.
5   *BC*, 16 September 1897.
6   *BC*, 21 October 1897.
7   *BC*, 10 July 1902; 20 November 1902.
8   *BC*, 19 March 1903.
9   *BC*, 27 February 1908.
10 *BC*, 27 February 1908.
11 A route followed – as far as possible – in the final walk in *On Foot in Bath*, published by Akeman Press in 2012.
12 *BC*, 26 October 1905.
13 A photograph of the northern end of Spring Gardens Road is on page 58.
14 *BC*, 27 August 1926.
15 *BC*, 9 October 1926.
16 Grace Parker, *Widcombe Baptist Church, Bath: The First 150 Years*, Bath, 1975, p. 35.
17 John Haddon, *Portrait of Bath*, London, 1982, p. 13.
18 Parker, op. cit., p. 35.
19 *BC*, 4 June 1896.
20 *BC*, 1 August 1833.
21 A photograph of the sign in the 1850s can be seen in Kirsten Elliott, *Queen of Waters: A Journey in Time along the Kennet & Avon Canal* , p. 115.
22 *BC*, 5 July 1832.
23 *BC*, 3 November 1836.
24 *BC*, 20 July 1843.
25 *BC*, 21 April 1898.
26 At the time he lived here, it was No 19 and there was no No 18. This was probably because Brunel demolished the top two houses of Raby Place and replaced them with a single house when he built the railway underneath. This anomaly was later corrected and the top house was renumbered.

27 Richard Kelham, *Private Owner Wagons of Somerset*, Lydney, 2014, p. 155.
28 *BC*, 22 June 1911.
29 *BC*, 22 June 1911.
30 *BC*, 26 February 1852.
31 *BC*, 31 July 1926.
32 *BC*, 27 February 1932.
33 *BC*, 25 February 1934.
34 *BC*, 19 January 1935.
35 *BC*, 17 April 1937; 9 July 1949.

5 WALCOT

1 Until renumbered in 1905, the address of this shop was 27 Cornwell Buildings.
2 *BC*, 2 April 1949.
3 *BC*, 23 May 1901.
4 *BC*, 24 September 1903.
5 *BC*, 27 June 1878.
6 *Western Gazette*, 12 April 1889.
7 *BC*, 24 March 1904.
8 *BC*, 21 September 1912.
9 *BC*, 11 January 1913.
10 *BC*, 9 March 1837.
11 *BC*, 5 October 1843.
12 *BC*, 10 October 1844.
13 *BC*, 8 May 1856; 31 October 1861.
14 See for example *BC*, 25 November 1848.
15 *BC*, 5 December 1839.
16 *BC*, 23 January 1840.
17 *BC*, 15 April 1847.
18 *BC*, 13 May 1847.
19 *BC*, 23 February 1854.
20 See Andrew Swift & Kirsten Elliott, *Literary Walks in Bath*, Bath, 2012, pp. 24-28.
21 *BC*, 25 July 1782.
22 *BC*, 16 July 1885.

6 CAMDEN & LARKHALL

1 *BC*, 8 April 1819.
2 *BC*, 22 April 1819.
3 *BC*, 24 April 1828.
4 *BC*, 24 April 1828.
5 *BC*, 22 April 1832.
6 *BC*, 29 April 1832.
7 James Britten, *Old Country and Farming Words Gleaned from Agricultural Books*, London, 1880, p. 152.
8 *BC*, 19 June 1828.
9 *BC*, 15 December 1825; Camden Mill was disposed of by the company long before it burnt down in 1879.
10 *Bristol Times & Mirror*, 25 September 1841.

11 *BC*, 7 July 1853.
12 *BC*, 29 November 1894.
13 *BC*, 20 August 1874.
14 *BC*, 9 August 1883.
15 *BC*, 23 October 1884.
16 *BC*, 29 November 1894.
17 The possible origins of the name are discussed in Andrew Swift & Kirsten Elliott, *Bath Pubs*, Bath, 2003, pp. 55-56.

7 BATHEASTON, BATHFORD & BATHAMPTON

1 Dave Pearce, *An Unsatisfactory and Disorderly Set: An Affectionate History of Bailbrook*, Batheaston, 2009, p. 43.
2 *BC*, 29 January 1857.
3 *BC*, 15 April 1858.
4 *BC*, 2 November 1865.
5 Dave Pearce, op. cit, p. 8.
6 *BC*, 17 June 1922; the story was recalled by a local resident called John Jones, then in his 96th year.
7 *BC*, 16 November 1843.
8 *BC*, 10 May 1860.
9 *BC*, 27 May 1861.
10 Information from Batheaston Historic Buildings Survey, conducted by the Batheaston Society. It can be found at https://users.bathspa.ac.uk/batheaston.
11 *BC*, 19 April 1832.
12 *BC*, 19 April 1830.
13 *BC*, 12 October 1865.
14 *BC*, 26 July 1888.
15 *BC*, 22 November 1888.
16 *BC*, 25 July 1889.
17 *BC*, 5 December 1889.
18 *BC*, 3 September 1949.
19 *BC*, 19 February 1885.
20 Harry Holloway, 'Bank Holiday at the Coopers Arms', in *Village Life, 1883-1940: Batheaston Remembers*, Batheaston, 1976, pp. 62-63.
21 *BC*, 20 April 1848.
22 *BC*, 4 November 1852.
23 Although the cottages were all freehold, the George & Dragon was leasehold, but free from ground rent and with 749 years of the lease to run.
24 *BC*, 9 February 1946; the reference to Mr Bevan is odd, given that the licence at the time was held by Miss Kate Bevan.
25 Ada Bevan, 'Around the George and Dragon', in *Village Life, 1883-1940:*

Batheaston Remembers, Batheaston, 1976, pp. 15-16.

26 The photograph is reproduced in *Bathford Past and Present* by Godfrey F Laurence (revised David A Howells), Bathford, 2010, p.53.

27 *BC*, 7 April 1934.

28 *BC*, 20 March 1823.

29 *BC*, 27 March 1873.

8 OLDFIELD PARK, TWERTON & LOWER WESTON

1 *BC*, 17 May 1821.

2 *BC*, 21 May 1840.

3 *BC*, 15 August 1862.

4 *BC*, 2 July 1868.

5 Sadly, Elizabeth died only four years after her marriage, at the age of 32.

6 *BC*, 4 June 1891.

7 *BC*, 11 June 1891.

8 *BC*, 3 December 1891.

9 *BC*, 9 April 1896.

10 *BC*, 9 April 1896.

11 The Twerton Co-operative Society also acquired a fleet of coal wagons with their name painted on the side, one of which appears in a photograph in Kelham, op. cit., p. 122.

12 John Owen, *Life on the Railway*, Bath, 1989, p120.

13 RA Cooke, *Track Layout Diagrams of the GWR and BR (WR): Section 21, Bath and Westbury*, Harwell, 1988, p.5.

14 If it is still there. An application to redevelop the site was rejected in 2007, but, given the rate at which student accommodation is spreading along the Lower Bristol Road, a further application seems inevitable. It would be nice to think that this façade, with its ghost sign, could be incorporated into any such development – nice, but probably fanciful.

15 *BC*, 27 November 1927.

16 *BC*, 18 May 1899.

17 *BC*, 24 June 1909.

18 The Royal Oak on Dafford Street, later renamed the Brains Surgery, closed in 2009 and is now student accommodation.

19 *BC*, 14 August 1890.

20 The 1891 census return erroneously records him as 37 years old rather than 47. However, as his wife and children are as recorded ten years earlier – with ten years added to their age – there can be no doubt that it is the same man.

21 *BC*, 19 November 1891.

22 *BC*, 22 December 1892.

23 *BC*, 23 November 1893.

9 WESTON VILLAGE & CHARLCOMBE

1 Although the distance is hard to make out, an OS map of 1886 confirms that it was a mile and a half away.

2 *BC*, 25 May 1837.

3 *BC*, 15 October 1840.

4 *BC*, 13 October 1842; 26 March 1846.

5 The earliest reference to him occurs in *BC*, 20 May 1858.

6 *BC*, 22 January 1874.

7 *BC*, 20 November 1902.

8 *BC*, 7 February 1942.

9 *BC*, 30 October 1862.

10 *BC*, 15 December 1853.

11 *BC*, 23 April 1857.

12 *BC*, 5 April 1827.

13 *BC*, 17 May 1849.

14 *BC*, 11 September 1856.

15 *BC*, 27 January 1853.

16 *BC*, 7 April 1853; 28 April 1853.

17 *BC*, 27 March 1856.

18 *BC*, 26 September 1861.

19 The Bladud's Head & Ladymead Brewery were at 90 Walcot Street.

20 See, for example, *BC*, 7 March 1861.

21 He went on to be involved with several more enterprises, including the Redcliff Mead Brewery, which later became part of Bristol United Breweries.

22 *BC*, 15 November 1877.

23 *BC*, 23 August 1883.

24 *BC*, 23 February 1905.

25 In 2015, a new microbrewery, Electric Bear (www.electricbearbrewing.com) opened on the trading estate, bringing brewing back to Weston for the first time in almost a century.

10 COMBE DOWN

1 *BC*, 12 May 1853.

2 *BC*, 26 January 1888.

3 See, for example, *BC*, 17 November 1859.

4 John Canvin, *Southstoke History*, n.d., p. 52.

5 *BC*, 4 July 1895.

12 FRESHFORD

1 See Alan Dodge, *Freshford: The History of a Somerset Village*, Freshford, 2000, p. 216.
2 Ibid, pp. 149-50.

13 WELLOW

1 *BC*, 23 February 1888.

14 BRADFORD ON AVON

1 Jack Mock, *Bradford on Avon's Pubs and Breweries*, Bradford on Avon, 2012, pp. 91-92.
2 The plans are held in the Wiltshire & Swindon History Centre (G13/760/17).
3 *Western Daily Press*, 22 October 1900.
4 More information on the King's Arms and its brewery can be found in Mock, op. cit., pp. 39-44.
5 *BC*, 22 August 1816.
6 Pigot's 1822 *Directory of Wiltshire* gives the address not as Silver Street but as the Market Place. Other directories and censuses from the mid-nineteenth century also give the address of this building as the Market Place or the Old Market Place, indicating that there was a lack of consensus as to where it was. An added complication is that in the early 1900s, when there had long been unanimity on it being in Silver Street, the street was renumbered, and it went from being No 15 to No 28.
7 A detailed account of William Dotesio's business can be found in *Ports of the Bristol Channel: Progress, Commerce*, London, 1893, p. 264.
8 A photograph from around 1930 shows a large painted sign – WM DOTESIO, PRINTER, BOOKBINDER & ACCOUNT B ...' above the first-floor windows of this building. It is now occupied by Moxhams Antiques and the first and second floors have been painted over – perhaps with the sign still lurking beneath.

15 CORSHAM

1 *BC*, 3 July 1816.
2 Andrew Swift & Kirsten Elliott, *The Inns of Wiltshire in old photographs*, Bath, 2010, p. 100; see also Kirsten Elliott & Andrew Swift, *Bath Pubs*, Bath, 2003, pp. 55-56.
3 <http://www.pglwilts.org.uk/lodges/central-wiltshire/lodge-of-rectitude/. Site accessed 29 March 2016.
4 Pamela M Slocombe, in *Wiltshire Town Houses: 1400-1900* (Bradford on Avon, 2001), p. 32, also draws attention to 'chequer wall painting in the upstairs chamber of the George Inn at Trowbridge', which lends support to the theory that such signs were connected with meetings held in inns.

16 BOX

1 The deed is held in the Wiltshire & Swindon History Centre (212B/450).
2 B*C*, 23 March 1769.

17 FARMBOROUGH

1 *BC*, 9 May 1799.

18 WILLSBRIDGE

1 For a full history of the pub, see Lydia Wells, *Time-Honoured Cheer: A History of the Queen's Head*. Willsbridge, 2nd ed., Willsbridge, 1995; see also www.flickr.com/photos/brizzlebornandbred/2095759892.
2 Ray Holmes, 'Queen's Head Failed by South Gloucestershire Councillors', in *Pints West: Multi-Award-Winning Magazine of the Bristol & District Branch of CAMRA*, 101, Spring, 2014.

19 LOST GHOST SIGNS

1 From A Potted History of the RUH on www.ruh.nhs.uk/about/history.asp?menu_id=1, with additional information from Kate Clarke.
2 Robert Bennet, 'The Last of the Georgian Architects of Bath: The Work and Times of John Pinch', *Bath History*, IX (2002), 87-103, p. 99.
3 *BC*, 20 February 1862; 27 February 1862.
4 The drawings bear the names of Manners and Gill, but it is clear from newspaper reports that Gill was the architect; the soubriquet 'Albert the Good' comes from the dedication to a revised edition of Tennyson's *Idylls of the King*. Princess Alice had asked

Tennyson to 'idealize' her father, and as the Prince himself had told Tennyson that he admired the *Idylls*, the poet included lines to his memory in the new edition. These were quoted in full in *BC*, 6 February 1862.

5   A report about the intended building in *BC*, 26 May 1864 makes it clear that the words were intended to be cut; escalating costs probably resulted in their being painted to look three-dimensional.

6   *BC*, 26 May 1864.

7   *BC*, 9 June 1864; 7 May 1868.

8   *BC*, 17 December 1932; the Bath Municipal Technical College had previously been in the Guildhall – hence the carvings on its northern wing. *BC*, 20 January 1934 includes report of the last prize-giving at the Guildhall, when the chairman of the governors announced that work to convert the old hospital would begin immediately and the college would be in its new home by the end of the year.

9   Kirsten Elliott, *A Window on Bath*, Bath, 1994, pp. 124-25.

10 *BC*, 4 January 1913; 15 June 1929.

11 *BC*, 29 May 1915; 11 October 1919.

12 *BC*, 21 January 1922.

13 *BC*, 15 June 1929.

14 *BC*, 6 March 1943.

15 Tucker & Son became Tucker & Sons around 1940.

16 *BC*, 16 May 1914.

17 *BC*, 20 January 1917.

18 *BC*, 29 September 1917.

19 *BC*, 5 January 1918.

20 *BC*, 5 January 1918.

21 *BC*, 2 November 1918.

22 *BC*, 2 May 1931.

23 *BC*, 13 December 1924.

24 Graham Finch, *Bath Shopfronts: Guidelines for Design and Conservation*, Bath, 1993, p.57.

25 *BC*, 10 May 1838.

26 Reproduced in James Lees-Milne & David Ford, *Images of Bath* (Richmond, 1982), illustration 891.

27 The possible significance of this chequerboard design is discussed on pp. 166-67 and 241-42.

28 See also *Kegs & Ale: Bath and the Public House*, Bath, 1991, pp. 92-93.

29 *BC*, 11 August 1923.

30 *BC*, 11 February 1836.

31 *BC*, 9 June 1831.

32 *BC*, 27 December 1827.

33 The Oxford Brewery was demolished shortly after being damaged by bombing in 1942.

34 *BC*, 1 September 1892.

35 *BC*, 20 June 1895.

36 *BC*, 22 September 1898.

37 The Three Crowns now forms part of TR Hayes's furniture store.

38 *Investors' Review*, XV, 381, 22 April 1905, p. 491.

39 A detailed account of the company's brief history can be found in Mike Bone, 'The Rise and Fall of Bath's Breweries: 1736-1960', in *Bath History*, VIII, 2000, pp. 106-33.

BIBLIOGRAPHY

The following sources were used extensively:

Census returns for 1841, 1851, 1861, 1871, 1881, 1891, 1901 and 1911, accessed through www.ancestry.co.uk.

Newspapers, in particular the *Bath Chronicle*, first published in 1760 (and now available online via the British Newspaper Archive: www.britishnewspaperarchive.co.uk), and the *Bath Journal*, first published in 1744. Other regional newspapers, accessed mainly via the British Newspaper Archive, were also used.

Directories consulted for Bath included the following: Gye's *New Bath Directory* (1792), Robbin's *Bath Directory* (1800), Brown's *New Bath Directory* (1809), Wood & Cunningham's *New Bath Directory* (1812), Gye's *Bath Directory* (1819), Keene's *Bath Directory* (1824, 1826 & 1829), Silverthorne's *Bath Directory* (1833, 1837, 1841 & 1846), Hunt's *Bath Directory* (1848), Clarke's *Bath Directory* (1849), Erith's *Bath Directory* (1850), Vivian's *Bath Directory* (1852 & 1854), Robinson's *Bath Directory* (1856), Lewis's *Post Office Bath Directory* (published biannually from 1858 to 1892, and annually from 1894 to 1927; thereafter in 1932, 1933, 1938, 1939 & 1940), Kelly's *Directory of Bath & Neighbourhood* (published in 1929, 1930, 1931, 1934, 1935, 1936, 1937, 1947, 1950, 1952, 1955, 1957, 1959, 1961, 1963, 1965, 1967, 1968, 1969, 1970, 1971 & 1972).

Other directories consulted included Pigot's *Directory of Wiltshire* (1822 & 1844), Kelly's *Directory of Wiltshire* (1855 & 1915) and Dotesio's *Directory of Bradford on Avon* (1902).

Comprehensive collections of Bath directories are held in Bath Record Office and Bath Reference Library. The following can also be consulted online at the University of Leicester Special Collections website (http://specialcollections.le.ac.uk/): Bath directories for 1846, 1852, 1864, 1876, 1884, 1895, 1902 & 1911; Wiltshire directories for 1822, 1842, 1855 & 1915.

For more information on Bath newspapers and directories, see *Bath Guides, Directories and Newspapers*, published by Bath Municipal Libraries, 2nd ed., 1973.

Also consulted was the Bath BMD website, which gives summary information on births, marriages and deaths in the city (www.bathbmd.org.uk).

Other works consulted:

Batheaston Historic Buildings Survey, Batheaston Society, 2001-2002 (Available online at https://users.bathspa.ac.uk/batheaston).

Kegs & Ale: Bath and the Public House, Bath, 1991.

Ports of the Bristol Channel: Progress, Commerce, London, 1893.

Village Life, 1883-1940: Batheaston Remembers, Batheaston, 1976.

Adburgham, Alison, *Shops and Shopping, 1800-1914*, London, 1964.

Ayres, James, *Art, Artisans and Apprentices: Apprentice Painters and Sculptors in the Early Modern British Tradition*, Oxford, 2014.

Bartram, Alan, *The English Lettering Tradition from 1700 to the Present Day*, London, 1986.

Bennet, Robert, 'The Last of the Georgian Architects of Bath: The Work and Times of John Pinch', *Bath History*, IX (2002), 87-103.

Bone, Mike, 'The Rise and Fall of Bath's Breweries: 1736-1960', in *Bath History*, VIII, 2000, 106-33.

Brett, Vanessa, *Bertrand's Toyshop in Bath: Luxury Retailing, 1685-1765*, Wetherby, 2014.

Canvin, John, *Southstoke History*, n.d.

Chapman, Mike & Elizabeth Holland, *The Spa Quarter of Bath: A History in Maps*, Bath, 2006.

Dodge, Alan, *Freshford: The History of a Somerset Village*, Freshford, 2000.

Elliott, Kirsten, *A Window on Bath*, Bath, 1994.

Elliott, Kirsten, *Queen of Waters: A Journey in Time along the Kennet & Avon Canal*, Bath, 2010.

Falconer, Randle, *The Baths and Mineral Waters of Bath*, Bath, 1880.

Fawcett, Trevor, *Bath Commercialis'd: Shops, Trades and Market at the 18th-Century Spa*, Bath, 2002.

Fawcett, Trevor, *Georgian Imprints: Printing & Publishing at Bath, 1729-1815*, Bath, 2008.

Finch, Graham, *Bath Shopfronts: Guidelines for Design and Conservation*, Bath, 1993.

Fisher, Colin, *Pieroni's Fountain*, Bath, 2014.

Garfield, Simon, *Just My Type: A Book About Fonts*, London, 2010.

Goede, Christian Augustus Gottlieb, *A Foreigner's Opinion of England*, tr. Thomas Horne, 3 vols., London, 1821.

Haddon, John, *Portrait of Bath*, London, 1982.

Holland, Elizabeth, 'Hetling Pump Room and Hetling House', in *The Survey of Bath & District: The Magazine of the Survey of Old Bath and Its Associates*, No 9, June 1998.

Kelham, Richard, *Private Owner Wagons of Somerset*, Lydney, 2014.

Larwood, Jacob & John Camden Hotten, *The History of Signboards*, London, 1866.

Laurence, Godfrey F, *Bathford Past and Present*, rev. David A Howells, Bathford, 2010.

Lees-Milne, James & David Ford, *Images of Bath*, Richmond, 1982.

Lewery, AJ, *Signwritten Art*, Newton Abbot, 1989.

Manco, Jean, *The Spirit of Care: The eight-hundred year story of St John's Hospital, Bath*, Bath, 1998.

Mock, Jack, *Bradford on Avon's Pubs and Breweries*, Bradford on Avon, 2012.

Moritz, CF, *Journeys of a German in England in 1782*, trans. & ed. by Reginald Nettel, London, 1965.

Owen, John, *Life on the Railway*, Bath, 1989.

Parker, Grace, *Widcombe Baptist Church, Bath: The First 150 Years*, Bath, 1975.

Pearce, Dave, *An Unsatisfactory and Disorderly Set: An Affectionate History of Bailbrook*, Batheaston, 2009.

Penrose, Rev John, *Letters from Bath: 1766-1767*, ed. Brigitte Mitchell & Hubert Penrose, Gloucester, 1983.

Perrett, George E, *Abbey Church House, Bath*, Bath, 1979

Slocombe, Pamela M, *Wiltshire Town Houses: 1400-1900*, Bradford on Avon, 2001.

Smith, Toulmin, *English Gilds*, London, 1870.

Swift, Andrew & Kirsten Elliott, *Bath Pubs*, Bath, 2003.

Swift, Andrew & Kirsten Elliott, *Literary Walks in Bath*, Bath, 2012.

Swift, Andrew & Kirsten Elliott, *The Lost Pubs of Bath*, Bath, 2005.

Wood, John, *A Description of Bath*, London, 1765.

ARCHIVE MAPS USED IN THE TEXT

Chapters 1-6: *Post Office Directory Map of Bath*, published by William Lewis & Son, Bath, n.d. (This map was published shortly before the construction of the Empire Hotel and shows a proposed new road, drawn in red, running from the bottom of Bridge Street to Pierrepont Street. This was never built, although another road, called Grand Parade, was built to link Newmarket Row with the Orange Grove. The map can thus be dated to around 1900.)

Chapter 7: 1903 1:2500 Ordnance Survey map of Batheaston (with 1967 city boundary drawn in); 1904 1:2500 Ordnance Survey map of Bathford; 1904 1:2500 Ordnance Survey map of Bathampton.

Chapters 8-11: Bacon's *Large Scale Plan of Bath*, published by William Lewis & Son Ltd, Bath, n.d. (c. 1905)

Summary map for chapters 12-18: From MJB Baddeley, *Bath and Bristol and Forty Miles Round (Thorough Guide Series)*, London, 1902.

Chapter 14: 1901 1:2500 Ordnance Survey map of Bradford on Avon.

Chapter 15: 1921 1:2500 Ordnance Survey map of Corsham.

ACKNOWLEDGEMENTS

Thanks must first of all go to everyone who has pointed us in the direction of ghost signs we would not otherwise have discovered, and in particular to Paul De'Ath, whose indefatigable forays into Bath's past have identified some of the most fugitive and fascinating signs in the city.

Thanks also to Sam Roberts for writing the foreword, Tobias Newbigin for designing the titles, and Nick Cudworth for permission to feature his wonderfully atmospheric painting of Cleveland Terrace on the cover.

As so often in the past, special thanks are also due to Colin Johnston and the staff of the Bath Record Office for their help in tracking down archive material.

Finally, very many thanks to all those listed below who have allowed us to use their photographs and illustrations in the book.

PICTURE CREDITS

Bath Record Office, 11, 12, 13 (all), 25, 37 (both), 76, 106, 163 (top), 250, 251 (top & bottom), 252 (both), 255, 272 (both), 273 (top); Bruce Crofts, 57; Paul De'Ath, 24, 264, 268 (top & middle), 269; Colin Hamilton, 44, 140 (bottom), 143; Geoff Hiscocks, 257 (top); Steve Lord, 173 (top); Museum of Bath at Work, 268 (bottom); Museum of Bath at Work/Robbie Hale-Monro Archive, 221; Museum of Bath at Work/Mike Williams Archive, 275; Steve Plumridge, 180, 247 (top); Ron Toop, 225

The following are from the Akeman Press Archive: 5, 8, 10, 17, 19, 20, 21, 22, 26, 27, 28, 29, 30, 31, 33, 34, 35, 36, 38, 39, 40 (top), 41 (bottom), 42, 45, 46, 47, 48 (bottom), 49, 50 (top), 51, 52, 53, 55 (top & bottom), 56, 58, 59, 60, 61, 63, 64, 65, 67, 68, 69, 71, 72, 73, 74, 75, 76 (bottom), 77, 78, 79, 80, 81, 82, 83, 84, 85, 87, 88, 89, 93, 94, 95, 96, 97, 98, 99, 100, 101 (top), 103, 104, 105, 108, 109, 110, 111, 112, 113, 114, 115, 116, 118, 119, 120, 122, 123, 124 (top), 125, 127, 128, 131, 133, 134, 135 (top), 136, 137, 139, 140, 141, 142, 144, 145, 146, 148, 149, 150, 151, 152, 153, 157, 158, 159, 160, 161, 162, 163 (bottom), 165, 166, 167, 169, 171, 172, 173 (bottom), 174, 176, 177, 178, 179, 181, 184 (top), 185, 187, 189, 192, 193, 194, 195, 196, 197, 198, 200, 201, 202, 203, 207 (top & bottom), 209, 210, 211, 212, 213, 217, 219, 220, 221 (top), 223, 224, 227, 228, 229, 231, 233, 234 (bottom), 235, 237, 238 (bottom), 239, 241, 242, 243, 244, 245, 246, 247 (bottom), 248, 249, 253, 254, 256, 257 (bottom), 258, 259, 260, 261, 262, 263, 264, 265, 266, 267, 273 (bottom), 276.

INDEX

Andrew Swift & Kirsten Elliott founded Akeman Press in 2003. As well as publishing books by several local authors, they have written, either individually or jointly, several books on Bath, as well as on subjects including pubs, canals and railways. Recent titles have included books of town and country walks. More walk books, along with new pub history books are planned. Kirsten also plans to publish a long-awaited book on Bath's 101 Best Buildings in the not too distant future. To check out the Akeman Press back catalogue and keep up to date with new publications, go to www.akemanpress.com.

Sam Roberts (who wrote the foreword) is the founder of Ghostsigns, a research and publishing initiative dedicated to fading painted signs. His projects have included curating the History of Advertising Ghostsigns Archive, researching and leading walking tours in London, and regularly speaking to academic and professional audiences. Sam has written numerous articles and book contributions about ghost signs, and is a contributing editor to the first academic volume dedicated to the topic. He also runs Better Letters, promoting contemporary signwriting, and providing opportunities to learn the craft. (www.ghostsigns.co.uk; www.betterletters.co)

Tobias Newbigin (who designed the titles) specialises in the art of traditional signwriting, letter cutting and decorative arts. After studying at Camberwell College of Arts and being apprenticed with Nick Garrett of NGS London, he set up Newbigin Signs and continues to travel the country, working alongisde other traditional signwriters and sharing his knowledge and passion for the craft. (newbiginsigns.co.uk)

Nick Cudworth (who painted the picture of Cleveland Terrace on the cover) owns the Nick Cudworth Gallery in Bath, which can be found where Walcot Street joins London Street. Here, alongside a large collection of cityscapes and landscapes in paintings, drawings and prints, you are also likely to meet Chuck Berry, Franz Kafka, Gustav Mahler, Tommy Cooper and Thelonious Monk. At the rear of the gallery, Nick Cudworth has his accessible studio where all these works are made. Born in 1947, he has been a professional artist for 38 years with works in countless public and private collections throughout the world. He designed the Commonwealth Games Stamps in 1986 and his portrait of Ken Loach is owned by the National Portrait Gallery. A book of his Bath City Paintings, which includes works from 1996 to 2014, is available from Akeman Press. (www.nickcudworth.co.uk)